MIRACLE AT FENWAY

ALSO BY SAUL WISNIA

Fenway Park: The Centennial

For the Love of the Boston Red Sox

Chicago Cubs: Yesterday and Today

The Jimmy Fund of Dana-Farber Cancer Institute

Baseball's Prime Time Stars

Wit and Wisdom of Baseball

MIRACLE AT

FENWAY

THE INSIDE STORY OF THE BOSTON RED SOX 2004 CHAMPIONSHIP SEASON

SAUL WISNIA

FOREWORD BY DAVE ROBERTS

ST. MARTIN'S PRESS ✪ NEW YORK

MIRACLE AT FENWAY. Copyright © 2014 by Saul Wisnia. Foreword copyright © 2014 by Dave Roberts. All rights reserved. Printed in the United States of America. For information, address St. Martin's Press, 175 Fifth Avenue, New York, N.Y. 10010.

www.stmartins.com

"'Twas the Night Before Ownership," courtesy of Rick Swanson.

Designed by Steven Seighman

Library of Congress Cataloging-in-Publication Data

Wisnia, Saul.
    Miracle at Fenway : the inside story of the Boston Red Sox 2004 championship season / Saul Wisnia; foreword by Dave Roberts.
        p. cm.
    ISBN 978-1-250-03163-1 (hardcover)
    ISBN 978-1-250-03164-8 (e-book)
    1. Boston Red Sox (Baseball team)—History—21st century.
I. Title.
    GV875.B62W59 2014
    796.357'640974461090511—dc23

                                          2014008191

St. Martin's Press books may be purchased for educational, business, or promotional use. For information on bulk purchases, please contact Macmillan Corporate and Premium Sales Department at 1-800-221-7945, extension 5442, or write special-markets@macmillan.com.

First Edition: July 2014

10 9 8 7 6 5 4 3 2 1

To my own Miracle team—Michelle, Jason, and Rachel

CONTENTS

ACKNOWLEDGMENTS

Everybody seems to have a 2004 Red Sox story. I've got a couple.

The first is really an '03 story. I was watching Game 7 of the ALCS at home with my wife, my Pedro Martinez bobble-head and other talismans atop the television, when my friend Scott came strolling through the front door. It was the top of the seventh inning and the Red Sox were beating the Yankees, 4–1.

"Can you believe this? We're going to the World Series!" Scott yelled. He and I had been attending Sox games together since high school, and had been taunted into submission by Mets fans as Syracuse classmates in 1986, so he was looking forward to a chance at redemption. "Shut up, you idiot," I yelled, but of course it was too late. Just like I did when I asked my girlfriend Wendy to take a photo of me and the TV screen when Calvin Schiraldi got the final out of the '86 World Series, Scott had chosen his words poorly.

The second story is from August 16, 2004. Astute fans will recognize that as the day the Red Sox began one of the hottest stretches in team history—20 wins in 22 games that helped propel them into the playoffs with the confidence needed to go all the way. I was on Brookline Avenue that night, but not at Fenway Park. I was a few blocks away, at Beth Israel Hospital, with my wife, Michelle, for the birth of our daughter, Rachel.

As the Red Sox started winning—and winning, and winning—I began to wonder if perhaps my little baby girl was some sort of living, breathing talisman. Maybe the tiny Red Sox hat I put in her bed at the hospital had given her some power to produce victories. I took to calling the turnaround of the team the "Rachel Effect" and I still believe it had something to do with what transpired that October. You better believe Rachel was up and watching every out of the World Series, along with our son, Jason. Back then, Red Sox fans looked for luck wherever we could find it.

Scott, however, was barred from the premises.

That's the thing about 2004. Everybody has a story (or two). It was also the challenge for this book. There were so many stories, and only so much room and time to tell them in. I tried to choose the best, from Red Sox players, fans, front office staff, and everybody else I could find. Some stories didn't make it in, and for that I apologize. I could fill another entire book with the ones that didn't make it, but will have to settle for sharing them on my blog, *Fenway Reflections*. Look for them at saulwisnia.blogspot.com.

I relied on many primary and secondary sources as well, books and articles by friends and colleagues and fans. All quotes from interviews I conducted myself are attributed in the present tense (i.e., "says" or "recalls"), while quotes from other sources have past tense attribution (i.e., "said"). Online resources were also invaluable, as was video footage on You-

Tube and other sources. I'll list what I can remember using here, but again apologize for any omissions.

Who to thank? At the Red Sox, it starts with Pam (Ganley) Kenn and Dr. Charles Steinberg, both of whom devoted much of their time to making sure I had the best stories and the best people to tell them to me. They were fantastic sources of support and I hope this book does justice to their efforts. Other Yawkey Way folks, including Sarah McKenna, Dick Bresciani, Debbie Matson, Sarah Coffin, Jackie Dempsey, Fay Scheer, Dan Rea, Leah Tobin, Abby DeCiccio, Jon Shestakofsky, Brenna Peterson, Frank Resnek, and of course Larry Lucchino, were all gracious with their time and assistance.

Thank you to Marc Resnick at St. Martin's Press for believing in this project and me after the success of our first collaboration, *Fenway Park: The Centennial,* and thanks for seeing this one through to the end. Jake Elwell of Harold Ober Associates is an outstanding agent and a better friend and I know we have more great things ahead of us together.

My parents, Madelyn Bell and Jeff and Judy Wisnia, have always been a source of great support, love, and confidence, and siblings Adam, Ben, and Julie Wisnia keep me grounded. My bosses Steve Singer and Michael Buller and colleagues in the Communications Department at Dana-Farber Cancer Institute have long supported my "other work" and for that I am forever appreciative. Richard Johnson remains a wise mentor who is there for me wherever needed. Debra Bennett of Core Harmony is a terrific life coach who helped me find time for everything when it didn't seem possible and always brought me coffee. The Boston SABR group is a wonderful network of passionate baseball folks. Jack McElduff was an enthusiastic, industrious intern and has a great writing future ahead of him. Friends who supported me through it all are too many to mention but you know who you are. Wally the Coolest Cat continues to be a great fact checker and lap warmer.

The only problem with taking on projects like this is the time it takes you away from the people you love the most. I can never give back that time to my wife, Michelle, son, Jason, and daughter, Rachel, nor can I take back any angst I've put them through, but I promise they will always be the people I want to come home to when the work is done. I look forward to many more wonderful days with them at Fenway Park and everywhere else life takes us.

As for everybody else, here it goes: Mike Andrews, Rob Barry, Uri Berenguer, Steve Buckley, Ellis Burks, Kirk Carapezza, Joe Castiglione, Herb Crehan, Christian Elias, Peter Farrelly, Nancy Wall Farrington, Jessamy Finet, Keith Foulke, Ronni Gordon, Joanne Hulbert, Jeff Idelson, Ilana Ivan and Effective Transcriptions, Patrick Languzzi, Dave Laurila, Ken, Shelley, and Jordan Leandre, Walter Martin, Kevin McCarthy, Ryan McCarthy, Kris Meyer, Kevin Millar, Joe Morgan, Nancy Morrisoe, Erin Nanstad, Bill Nowlin, Steve O'Neill, Scott Paisner, Ken Powtak, Dave Roberts, Roger Rubin, Eric and Debra Ruder, Mike Shalin, Darryl Houston Smith, Lynne Smith, Ted Spencer, Rick Swanson, Trudy Tocci and Tony Signore of Trutony's Deli, Elizabeth Traynor, Kevin Vahey, Joe and Donna Varitek, Tim Wakefield, and anybody else I may have unintentionally forgotten.

Okay, okay, here's one more story. Nancy Morrisoe and Nancy Wall Farrington, aka "The Women of Section 30," have become two of my favorite Fenway companions. Both are constant sources of fun stories but somehow didn't make it into the manuscript. But this story from Nancy M. is too good not to include, so here it is, in her words. It's about her daughter, Isabel, who like my Rachel was born during the 2004 season:

"Isabel was born in May and slept for probably 20 minutes every six hours the first few months. Seriously. By October I was delirious. She was starting to sleep for longer periods but would wake up multiple times throughout the night for extended periods of time. After the 19–8 beat-down I was asking myself why am I staying up any longer. I need my sleep, they're not going to win. Get your rest.

"In Game 4 Isabel woke up in the ninth inning and I ran upstairs to grab her and take her to a different television on the top floor to see Mo get the final out. Instead he walked Millar and I said to this little night owl, 'Wow, Isabel, he never does that. Something is going to happen here, just you wait.' She just sat on my lap staring at me like what on earth are you talking about lady!

"The World Series? Surreal. Surreal. Sheer joy. Tears of pure joy. Two things I thought I'd never see in my lifetime— being a parent and a Sox World Series. In 2004 I was blessed with my beloved Isabel shortly before my 42nd birthday and I got to share a World Series with my elderly parents who really thought they'd never see the day."

See, Nancy—I told you I'd fit you in!

FOREWORD

One day in early September of 2004, about a month after I joined the Red Sox, I was out in Kenmore Square near Fenway Park with my wife and young son. This older gentleman—probably in his sixties—approached us. He looked me up and down, paused, and then said, "You guys got my grandfather. You got my father. Now you guys are coming after me."

It was kind of funny, but also very genuine. When you put on that Red Sox uniform in 2004, you felt a sense of responsibility to live up to the expectations of a fan base that had been hurt so many times over eighty-six years since the team had last won the World Series. The fans were passionate and supportive, but you also got a sense that deep down they were all like that guy in Kenmore Square—just waiting to see how we were going to let them down and blow it again.

I was traded to the Red Sox from the Dodgers on July 31, 2004. A lot of people think I was part of the big Nomar trade that happened the same day, but I wasn't. Still, it was a very emotional time to be joining the team. Nomar had been the star there for so long, and now here I was, dressing in his old locker right next to Bill Mueller. Bill made a joke once about how I had really big shoes to fill, but I knew I was no Nomar Garciaparra. I just wanted to fit in and help the team win baseball games with my speed, my defense, and maybe once in a while with my bat.

From the moment I first walked into the visitor's clubhouse at Tropicana Field after the trade, I knew this was a special group of guys. Everybody was so welcoming, and there was a feeling in the clubhouse like, "Okay, this is it for the moves. We've got our guys now—let's try and make a run at this." We felt like we had something important to do, and a lot of people were counting on us.

Every single day it continued picking up momentum, and I became more aware of how vital the Red Sox are to New England culture. A lot of times, as big league ballplayers, you're playing for the fans, and you're also playing for each other to win games and win a World Series. But when you play for the Red Sox, you're playing for *generations*— generations of people who have waited to see the team finally do it.

I think to a man we all felt that responsibility. And after we made the big comeback against the Yankees and ultimately *did* win the World Series, we felt it even more when we came back for the Rolling Rally. It was raining and cold, but we had 3.2 million people out there. It seemed like all of New England wanted to share that moment with us, and all that winter people were coming up to me saying things like, "My father never had a chance to see the Red Sox win the World Series, and after you guys won it he passed away a couple days later— his life complete because he got to see the Red Sox lift up that World Series trophy."

It's amazing. I went on to play for a couple other teams,

and now I'm on the coaching staff of the San Diego Padres, but the bond that I made with ownership, staff, and players on that 2004 team has not changed. A couple years ago, the Red Sox put me up in a Kenmore Square apartment for a month while I was undergoing radiation treatment at Dana-Farber Cancer Institute for Hodgkin's lymphoma. There was nothing made public; they just did it for me and my family. That makes me so grateful to be a part of the Red Sox.

When the Sox honored us during the 2013 World Series, I talked to David Ortiz—the last guy left on the '13 roster from 2004—about how the two teams paralleled one another. Both were comprised of unselfish guys who played for each other and the fans, and the city really wrapped its arms around both ballclubs. I'm still getting fan mail every day, the same thanks and gratitude from all these people who are part of Red Sox Nation.

There is no other place where it could have sustained this momentum and energy, and no place I would have rather been.

—Dave Roberts

MIRACLE AT FENWAY

1. RUNNING MAN

THE FIRST THING HE THOUGHT ABOUT WAS MAURY Wills.

In this, the biggest moment of his baseball life, Dave Roberts was trying to focus on the topic at hand. It was the ninth inning of Game 4 of the American League Championship Series, the Red Sox trailed, 4–3, and Roberts stood on first base representing the tying run. If the Sox lost, their season was over; the Yankees led the best-of-seven series three games to none, and were set to celebrate on the Fenway Park grass after just three more outs. They had the right man on the mound to get those outs in Mariano Rivera, the greatest closer of his or any generation.

The home fans were abuzz, urging on a Boston rally, but Roberts could not hear them. Inserted into the game moments earlier as a pinch runner for Kevin Millar, whose lead-off walk against Rivera had raised the masses to their feet, Roberts knew it was *his* feet that everybody in the ballpark and millions of TV viewers were now watching. He was a reserve outfielder who had not played in a week, and he had been put in here for one reason: to steal second base and give the Red Sox a chance to tie the game on a single. The crowd knew it, the TV and radio analysts were pontificating on it, and the cameras were bracing for it—zoomed in and ready to capture the moment.

Roberts could feel the sense of urgency, could anticipate the eyes upon him. Still, poised on the grandest of stages, he had the clarity to think back 10 months to moments in a near-empty ballpark 3,000 miles away. Moments spent with Maury Wills.

Wills was a baserunning instructor for the Los Angeles Dodgers, for whom he had once set the major league record with 104 stolen bases in a single season.* Now in his 70s, slower afoot but richer in experience, he had worked with Roberts at Dodger Stadium over the previous winter on the art of the perfect steal.

There will come a time, Wills had imparted, when you will be called upon to swipe a bag without the art of surprise in your arsenal. A quartet of defenders will be poised to stop you. The pitcher, sure you'll be running, will be keeping you close. The catcher will be ready to take the pitch and whip it to second. The shortstop will be moving to second with the pitch, ready to receive the throw from the catcher and apply the tag. And the first baseman will be tight on the bag, in case you stray too far and there is a chance for the pitcher to gun the ball over and pick you off.

---

*Wills was named NL MVP in 1962 when he set his record of 104 steals and scored 130 runs for the World Series champion Dodgers. His record stood until 1974, when Lou Brock broke it with 118 steals. Rickey Henderson now holds the single-season (130) and career (1,406) stolen base records, but it is Wills who helped revive the steal as a key offensive weapon.

In such a situation, Wills told his protégé, you'll need to first get a big lead, and then rely on everything you've learned about the pitcher's tendencies: his windup, his release point, and any moves he might make to warn you he's ready to spin and make a pickoff throw. Roberts followed the advice. He watched video of all the Yankee pitchers, studied many of them live, and in the case of Rivera and New York catcher Jorge Posada already had some firsthand success to build on. A few weeks before, in the waning days of the regular season, Roberts had stolen second against this All-Star battery and scored the tying run in an eventual Red Sox win.

The big difference, of course, was that this was the playoffs, and an elimination game at that. If Posada gunned Roberts down here, or, worse yet, if Roberts guessed wrong on his initial jump toward second and was picked off, it could mean Boston's season. Roberts felt his anxiety level rising, but then he remembered something else Wills had told him: *You can't be afraid to steal that base.*

I might not be afraid, Roberts remembers thinking to himself, but I am most definitely nervous.

"The game felt like it was going very fast; my mind was racing," Roberts recalls nearly a decade later. "I've got a big lead, but to just go out there and steal, it's pretty tough. I know what Mariano is going to do; I've got the information. I'm getting as loose as I possibly can, but this is October, and it's cold."

The next batter, Bill Mueller, stepped into the box. Rivera set, and then, just before starting his windup, quickly spun and threw over to first baseman Tony Clark in a pickoff attempt. Roberts dove back to the bag just before Clark slapped him with his glove. In that moment, and those that quickly followed it, the base runner felt a change come over him.

"I think you can actually see it in the footage," says Roberts. "He throws over one time, and my nerves start to calm. The game starts to slow down. Then he throws over a *second* time, and he almost gets me, which is great because for me it slows the game down even more. My focus started to get even better—at that point it felt like I was a part of the game."

Roberts thought of something else as he dusted himself off a second time: maybe the pitcher was as nervous as him. Rivera possessed outstanding control; he almost never walked anyone, let alone the leadoff man in an inning. His ability to calmly put games to bed for the Yankees had earned him the nickname "Sandman" around the league, and while Rivera's cool exterior did not hint at it, Roberts hoped that Millar's base on balls might have rattled the unflappable pitcher just a bit.

There was also recent history to consider. In addition to the September victory in which Roberts had a key steal, the Red Sox had beaten Rivera in July as well on a walkoff home run at Fenway by the same man now at the plate—Bill Mueller. Roberts hoped all these things were on Rivera's mind; if they were, it might give him a bit more of an edge were he to try for second.

The only thing Roberts knew for sure was this: eventually Rivera was going to have to deliver a pitch to Mueller. The question was when. Throughout Fenway Park, and beyond, fans watching the game on NBC or listening to the play-by-play of Red Sox broadcasters Joe Castiglione and Jerry Trupiano wondered as well. Joe Morgan, the former Red Sox manager who had lived and died with the team for his entire 74 years, leaned forward in his basement sofa and stared at the TV—trying like Roberts to read Rivera's mind. So did Fenway vendor Rob Barry, a former Northeastern University pitcher who had achieved his own bit of glory as the ballpark's premier peanut-bag tosser. From his current spot in the box seats just behind Boston's dugout, Barry had a perfect view of both Roberts in profile and the broad back of the right-handed Rivera—with its familiar black 42 first made famous by fellow legend Jackie Robinson.

A moment later, the number blurred as Rivera spun once more and threw to first. Again Roberts lunged back, and as he got to his feet a third time he felt confidence surging through him.

"Now it felt like I had played all nine innings," Roberts remembers with a smile. "My legs felt like they were ready to go, and I could fire to get a great jump. If he wanted to go to the plate, I had him. I knew I had him. If he had just thrown to the plate without throwing over, I don't know if I could have felt [capable of getting] a great jump. But then, just from all the diving back, I felt like, 'I've got you now.'"

Just wait him out, Roberts said to himself. A moment later, as Rivera finally began his full windup—indicating he was going to throw home to Mueller—Roberts took off, head down and arms pumping, for second base.

The pitch was a fastball away, considered ideal for a catcher in terms of nabbing would-be base stealers. Mueller didn't swing, and as the ball slammed into Posada's glove he was already leaping up to unleash his throw toward second. It was near-perfect, and a slightly crouching Derek Jeter grabbed it just to the left of the bag and then in a fluid motion swept down his left arm into Roberts's left shoulder as he dove in headfirst.

It was so close a play that for an instant nobody could tell whether Roberts had made it. Posada ripped off his mask and stared out at second base umpire Joe West, and Jeter and Roberts lifted their heads to do the same. Rob Barry, Joe Morgan, and everybody else watching live, in bars, or at home held their collective breaths—knowing that if Roberts was called out, the Red Sox would be all but out as well.

Then West spread his hands in the familiar motion known by every Little Leaguer.

Safe.

2. KINGS OF PAIN

WHEN DID THE MIRACLE START? IT DEPENDS WHO you ask.

Most Red Sox fans watching or listening as Dave Roberts made his dash for second base would have been hard-pressed to believe it was a true turning point at the time. There was so much of a mountain left to climb, and Roberts had only gone 90 feet. Whether you were at Fenway, in your living room, or on an Army base in Iraq, the thinking was the same—if the Sox were involved in a close postseason game, which was often the case, they were likely to lose it. Late-breaking frustration was a fact of life for Boston rooters; great comebacks were not.

Rick Swanson knew this as well as anyone. The UPS-driver-turned-teacher had been on hand for some of the most exciting moments in Boston baseball history, a litany of primarily near-misses that hardened his soul as well as his resolve. "My first game was in 1957; I was seven, and my dad took me to Fenway," the New Britain, Connecticut, native recalls more than a half-century later. "Ted Williams homered in the bottom of the ninth against the Yankees . . . and the Red Sox lost, 8–5, in 10 innings."

It was Swanson's first lesson in Sox watching: however promising the situation, be ever ready for disappointment.

Undeterred, he had rooted on. Like many New Englanders, Swanson grew up with baseball as an integral part of both his day-to-day life and his history lessons—cheering in the present as he learned about the past. Taught at the feet of parents and grandparents, he and other young fans became well versed in the team's backstory, including the glorious early years that left no hint of the heartache to follow.

Charter members of the American League in 1901, the Red Sox had beaten the Pittsburgh Pirates in the first modern World Series two years later and added four more world championships in 1912, 1915, 1916, and 1918 for a then-perfect Fall Classic mark of 5–0. Tris Speaker, Smoky Joe Wood, and the rest of this stellar club made their home at beautiful, red-bricked Fenway Park, which opened in the heart of Boston's growing Kenmore Square neighborhood on April 20, 1912— just in time to host the franchise's decade of dominance. Jokes comparing the fates of the Red Sox to those of the *Titanic*, which sank five days before Fenway's debut, were not yet applicable.

The team's most ardent fans during this period were a group of primarily first-generation Irish immigrants who called themselves the "Royal Rooters." These die-hards brought their own brass band to Fenway to serenade their heroes, and shared postgame beers with Red Sox players at the nearby Third Base Saloon (billed as the last place you stopped on the way home). The Rooters even traveled by train and boat to road games in New York, Baltimore, and other AL venues where they made their presence proudly heard. The song "Tessie," which has gained immense popularity in recent years as a Fenway celebratory anthem, was first sung by the Royal Rooters to praise the Sox at home and away.

"Boston was the baseball capital of the world," says Richard Johnson, curator of the Sports Museum in Boston and coauthor with Glenn Stout of the acclaimed team history, *Red Sox Century.* "In the years from 1871 through the 1918 season, you had five major league teams including the Red Sox and the Boston (now Atlanta) Braves representing the city. All five won championships during this period, and in the teens the Red Sox were acknowledged as the class of the American League—the best team with the most passionate fans."

Of all the diamond stars Bostonians cheered for in the teens, few could match the magnetism of a stellar young Red Sox pitcher who emerged just before World War I: George Herman "Babe" Ruth. A left-hander from the rough streets of Baltimore, Ruth was a two-time 20-game winner by age 22 and yet was so strong a hitter that Boston manager Ed Barrow took the unorthodox step of playing him regularly in the outfield between pitching starts. The move paid immediate dividends; in addition to tossing 29 and a third straight shutout innings over three World Series appearances, Ruth led the American League with 11 homers in 1918 and a record 29 the next year—more than 13 of 16 *teams* in the majors hit that same summer.*

The Red Sox slumped to sixth place in 1919, however, and owner Harry Frazee—whose real passion and talent was in

---

*Although Ruth set dozens of records as a hitter, he always said he was most proud of his mark for consecutive shutout innings in World Series play—a record not broken until 1962 (by Whitey Ford of the Yankees).

theater production, not baseball—felt Ruth's lascivious late-night appetites were overshadowing his contributions and poisoning the club. Rather than give his star the outrageous $20,000 salary he was seeking for 1920, Frazee sold baseball's most electric performer to the New York Yankees. The move was abhorred by the Royal Rooters, who soon disbanded as additional dismal trades by Frazee sent the Sox crashing to the American League cellar. Attendance at Fenway plummeted while Ruth was winning 10 more home run titles in the Bronx—including a record 60 blasts in 1927.

Most of the worst swaps Boston made during the '20s happened to also involve New York, and the players who went south helped to spark a dynasty that would pass from Ruth to Lou Gehrig to Joe DiMaggio to Mickey Mantle. In the 44 seasons between 1921 and 1964, the Yankees won 29 American League pennants and 20 World Series championships, while the Red Sox reached the postseason just once over the same lengthy span—a seven-game World Series loss to the St. Louis Cardinals in 1946.

Everybody loved a winner, even Bostonians desperate for a return to glory.

"Hatred of the Yankees is a fairly modern phenomenon," says Richard Johnson. "In the 1920s most every kid, even those in Boston, wanted to be Babe Ruth or Lou Gehrig. The Red Sox lost close to 100 games every year, and Ruth was Santa Claus in pinstripes. When the Yankees of Ruth, Gehrig, and later DiMaggio came in, it was like the circus was in town. Attendance could rise from 4,000 to 28,000 at Fenway in one day."

After Frazee's dismantling of the club in the early part of the decade, the Red Sox owners who followed him were constantly struggling to pay their bills—a condition that prompted even more one-sided trades in the late '20s and early '30s as strong players were swapped for cash and second-rate performers rather than comparable replacements. Then, in 1933, came a dramatic and literal reversal in fortune; Thomas Austin Yawkey, a Detroit native and Yale graduate who had just inherited his family's vast lumber and mining reserves on his 30th birthday, purchased the Boston club and vowed to turn it around.

Money was no object. After rebuilding Fenway Park during his first winter in town, Yawkey went about filling it with fans by buying and paying top salaries to stars like Joe Cronin, Jimmie Foxx, Ted Williams, Bobby Doerr, and Dom DiMaggio in a championship quest. Other than that lone '46 pennant, however, Yawkey came up short, and his ball clubs developed a reputation as fat cats who couldn't win big games. The Yankees, of course, usually *did* win them, and over time this sparked in Boston fans a resentment of the New York club— and an accompanying inferiority complex—that would extend into the first years of the 21st century.

Although Yawkey was still atop the Red Sox letterhead when Rick Swanson made his initial pilgrimage to Fenway in 1957, the losing was getting too much for the tycoon to handle. He began spending much of the season away from the ballpark, letting dubious characters like third-baseman-turned-manager Mike "Pinky" Higgins preside over years of dismal finishes and withering attendance. The Red Sox always seemed to lack the pitching, defense, and depth to contend, too often filling their lineup with one-dimensional sluggers tailored to fit Fenway's cozy dimensions.

Even more disturbing was that under narrow-minded leaders like Higgins, who somehow gained a promotion to general manager in the late '50s despite his lack of success as manager, the club seemed stuck in the past. During the years immediately before and after the Major League Baseball color line was broken in 1947, the Red Sox passed on chances to sign Jackie Robinson, Willie Mays, and other great African American players, who went on to help other teams to World Series glory.

Robinson and Sam Jethroe,[†] both future Rookie of the Year honorees, were actually given a tryout at Fenway in 1945 along with fellow Negro League standout Marvin Williams. The move was made by Red Sox management to pacify a local politician, however, not out of any noble intent; after the trio was told "don't call us, we'll call you," their phones never rang. Brooklyn Dodgers president Branch Rickey did call Robinson a few months later, and instead of being first to knock down the game's racial barriers, Yawkey would keep his team lily white until mid-1959—thus making the Sox the *last* big-league franchise to integrate.

"You can't help where you're from and where you were brought up," says Johnson. "By all accounts Tom Yawkey was a good guy who treated people well, but he—like many individuals of his time and station—was not particularly progressive, to put it mildly, on the racial issue. He also hired bad people, and he paid a real price for it."

That price became increasingly evident once the brilliant Ted Williams retired in 1960 after 19 seasons and 521 home runs. Despite the presence in the early and mid-'60s of young stars

---

[†] Jethroe, like Jackie Robinson, would be signed by the Dodgers, but while still in the minors was traded to the Red Sox's cross-town rival Boston Braves. It was with the Braves that Jethroe broke the Boston baseball color line in 1950, when he was named National League Rookie of the Year after hitting 18 homers and leading the majors with 35 stolen bases.

like Carl Yastrzemski and Boston native Tony Conigliaro on their roster, the Red Sox became known throughout the majors as a "country club" where well-paid players felt no pressure to win. Johnson jokingly refers to this as the "Crony Island" period in team history, when Higgins and other Yawkey drinking buddies almost ran the team into the ground—or, as the owner considered mounting financial losses, out of town.

Then came 1967.

This was the year when Swanson, Johnson, and many other New England baby boomers truly came of age as baseball fans. Yawkey had finally grown sick of all the losing, and fired Higgins as general manager in 1965 during the waning days of a 62–100 season. Dick O'Connell, who had worked for the Red Sox in various capacities after serving in naval intelligence during World War II, was given the GM post and set about rebuilding the franchise. O'Connell never played the game professionally, but he had grown up rooting for the Sox in nearby Winthrop, Massachusetts, and abhorred the backward racial views of Higgins and the good ole Southern boys who had held the reins too long.

The changes came quickly. O'Connell began signing and developing young black ballplayers like George Scott, Reggie Smith, and Joy Foy, and for 1967 also hired a new manager in Dick Williams, whose playing career had ended as a reserve with the Country Club Sox just a few years before. Williams brought a crew-cut, working-class attitude to the job and employed a style of play not seen in Boston in many years: stealing, hit-and-runs, and general all-out hustle.

Williams's tough-guy approach irritated his players—until they saw the results.

After finishing ninth in the 10-team American League in 1966, with a 72–90 record, the Red Sox of '67 responded to

Williams's discipline and found themselves in a real pennant race for the first time in a generation. While the Beatles led a Summer of Love on the music scene, teenagers like 17-year-old Swanson fell in love with the youngest and most surprising team in baseball. Yastrzemski was reaching his full potential as a power hitter and left field successor to Williams, handsome Stanford man Jim Lonborg was electrifying the pitching staff, and Yawkey, who had been threatening to move the team if Boston would not fund construction of a new ballpark to replace aging Fenway, began showing up again in his familiar rooftop box. He was not the only fan emerging from years of hibernation; attendance soared as the summer progressed.

"It's amazing, there are still 10 to 12 games from that season which I can remember in every detail, every at-bat," says Swanson, who entered his senior year of high school as the 1967 campaign was reaching its climax. "It was just so special a team—everybody contributed in some way to win, and they needed every win they got."

In July Swanson and his father attended a doubleheader at Fenway between Boston and the Minnesota Twins, two of five teams then battling for the American League lead. "Let's buy tickets for the last game of the year; it might mean something," his father said on the spur of the moment, and it proved smart thinking. The finale on October 1 was also against Minnesota, and the two teams entered the contest tied atop the AL standings at 91–70.

Swanson's dad made him wear a white shirt and red tie to the game, an outfit befitting a coronation. Lonborg delivered a 5–3, complete game victory, and after the last out was recorded fans jumped the walls and stormed the mound in true Royal Rooter tradition—carrying the winning pitcher off on their shoulders. "It seemed like there were 5,000 people on the field, but my dad wouldn't let me go," Swanson says with a laugh. "He told me there were still more games to be played, and he didn't want us harming a single blade of grass."

These being the days when the winner of each 10-team league went directly to the World Series, Swanson was given the okay from his parents to skip school if he and his dad could secure tickets for the Fall Classic (as in 1946, against St. Louis). Lacking insider connections, they were left to haggle with the scalpers outside Fenway Park. "We paid $10 each for the first game, and $12 each for Game 6," recalls Swanson. "Game 7 was on Columbus Day, so there were more people looking for tickets. We were out there at 12:55 P.M., close to game time, when a guy came up to my father and said, 'I've got two bleacher seats for $50.' My father said, 'I'll give you $40.' That was still a lot of money for him, but we were in."

Cardinals great Bob Gibson bested a weary Lonborg (pitching on two days' rest) that afternoon for the world championship, but the "Impossible Dream" Red Sox had rejuvenated Boston baseball and saved Fenway from the wrecking ball. Yawkey stopped his talk of moving, the old ballpark was now routinely filled, and Swanson had caught the big-game bug.

The Sox made it back to the World Series in 1975 behind elder statesman Yastrzemski and red-hot rookies Jim Rice and Fred Lynn, and Rick's dad stood in line outside Fenway starting at 4 A.M. after standing-room tickets went on sale. At Game 6 Rick worked his way down to box seats, squeezed himself in next to a Pittsburgh Pirates executive, and had a perfect view as Carlton Fisk's 12th inning, game-winning home run bounced off the foul pole and into history. For once the good guys had won the big one.

Even after Fisk and his teammates lost Game 7 the next

night, blowing a 3–0 lead at Fenway, Swanson never lost hope. The Yankees spoiled Boston's plans the next two years, but the 1978 "Super Sox" looked unbeatable with an All-Star lineup featuring Rice, Yastrzemski, Fisk (all future Hall of Famers), Lynn, Dwight Evans, and Rick Burleson backed by strong starting pitching from Luis Tiant, Dennis Eckersley, Mike Torrez, and Bill Lee. Boston built a seemingly impenetrable American League East lead by mid-season, and then promptly lost it all due to injuries, lack of bench depth, and a surge by those same damn Yankees.

This was the period—from 1976 to 1979—when the Red Sox–Yankees rivalry reached and surpassed anything experienced before. It started with two hard-nosed All-Star catchers, Thurman Munson of New York and New Hampshire–bred Carlton Fisk of Boston, who seethed with a mutual passion for the game and a mutual loathing for each other. This extended through the rosters; there was no chummy chatter between the two teams during batting practice, and their epic in-game brawls included one in which Boston pitcher Bill Lee suffered a separated shoulder and missed three months of action.

The tension even extended to the Fenway bleachers, where fans in Yankee gear found themselves regularly goaded into fistfights in defense of their club. Things got so bad that in addition to a regular police presence at games, the Red Sox hired a group of burly Boston College students—many of them football players—to roam the stands and break things up. While the two teams would eventually square off three times in six years between 1999 and 2004 for the American League Championship, postseason matchups that drew huge media coverage and fan scrutiny, the roots of those made-for-TV battles took hold in the gritty Sox-Yanks atmosphere of the late '70s.

Never was the pre-'99 era between baseball's Athens and Sparta more dramatic than in 1978. After New York erased its 14-and-a-half-game deficit in the standings and pulled ahead of Boston by as many as three and a half games, they were caught by the Red Sox—who went 14–1 in the final two weeks—on the season's final day. The two combatants finished with identical 99–63 records, necessitating a one-game, winner-take-all playoff at Fenway.

Swanson, of course, had to be there. Continuing his tradition of never purchasing tickets beforehand, he made the trip with his dad and five buddies and undertook the necessary negotiations with scalpers ($20 per bleacher seat) to get inside. There they saw Torrez outduel Yankees ace Ron Guidry in the early going, and the Red Sox hold a 2–0 lead with two outs in the seventh as light-hitting Yankee shortstop Bucky Dent stepped to the plate.

After all these years, it's still hard for Swanson and other Boston fans to fathom how a team as stacked as the '78 Sox could fail to make the postseason. It's even harder to comprehend how a club pitching with a 5–3 lead, nobody on base, and one strike away from a world championship could fail to seal the deal. Swanson saw both calamities up close.

He was there at Fenway on October 2, 1978, to see Dent's dinky fly ball reach the left field screen for a game-changing three-run homer off Torrez, as the Yankees rallied for a 5–4 win and the American League East title. Eight years later, Swanson was at Shea Stadium in New York on October 25, 1986—courtesy of a friend who called that morning with an extra ticket—to see the chain of unfathomable events unfold in Game 6 of the World Series. After Mookie Wilson's ground ball rolled through the legs of Red Sox first baseman Bill Buckner, and the winning run scored for the Mets, it didn't really matter that there was a Game 7 left to play. Swanson and other numbed Boston fans sensed what was coming, and naturally the Sox blew a 3–0, sixth-inning lead in the finale to make it four straight seven-game setbacks in the World Series.

Damaged but still not defeated, Swanson named his first son "Ted" after the iconic Williams and his second "Casey" after the fictional slugger in poet Ernest Thayer's tale of the doomed Mudville Nine. The Red Sox continued to provide thrills; there were 25 straight home wins and an AL East title in the summer of 1988, and another division crown two years later. Joe Morgan, manager of both those clubs, was a working-class leader in the Dick Williams mold who grew up 20 miles from Fenway, but even a local guy with the Midas touch and "Morgan's Magic" on his side couldn't get the Sox over the hump. Boston had the game's best pitcher in Roger Clemens and hitters like Evans, Wade Boggs, and young outfield stars Ellis Burks and Mike Greenwell, but was swept four straight in both the '88 and '90 American League Championship Series by a superior Oakland A's club.

Things took a big step in the right direction on several fronts a few years later. Charismatic first baseman Mo Vaughn, a New England native, led the Red Sox to a 1995 AL East title with 39 homers, a league-leading 126 RBI, and a penchant for hitting in the clutch. He received ample support in the lineup from shortstop and former Seton Hall teammate John Valentin, along with big-bicepted slugger Jose Canseco—a favorite villain from the Oakland A's who had ousted the Sox in the playoffs a few years before. Helping anchor the pitching staff along with veteran ace Clemens was a young knuckle-baller who emerged from the minor league scrap heap to win 14 of his first 15 decisions with Boston that summer—Tim Wakefield.

But despite the emergence of these new heroes, a trend was developing; instead of waiting until the World Series to break the hearts of Swanson and other fans, the Red Sox were now getting knocked out in earlier playoff rounds.

After the two ALCS losses to Oakland in 1988 and '90, Boston was swept by the Cleveland Indians in the 1995 AL Division Series, a third playoff round added when the American and National Leagues expanded to three divisions the previous year. This made it 13 straight postseason losses for the Red Sox since Game 6 of '86, a stretch of futility made more frustrating by the fact that by the mid-1990s the Yankees were reemerging as a dynastic club under manager Joe Torre. The Yanks won the World Series in 1996 with great young homegrown talent—rookie Derek Jeter at shortstop, Bernie Williams in center field, starting pitcher Andy Pettitte, and reliever Mariano Rivera—and with Jorge Posada added at catcher two years later fashioned an incredible 114–48 record.

Boston finished 22 games behind this juggernaut in the AL East, but got their own ticket to the '98 postseason thanks to a new innovation: the Wild Card. In addition to the three divisional winners in each league, a fourth team—the one with the best record *not* to take a divisional crown—would now make the playoffs as the Wild Card entrant. This change rankled many traditionalists who argued against the logic of rewarding a team for finishing second, but Red Sox fans would soon come to accept and even embrace it.

Another welcome transformation was the growing diversity

of the team. The 1998 club featured four African Americans in the starting lineup: Vaughn, center fielder Darren Lewis, left fielder Troy O'Leary, and designated hitter Reggie Jefferson. Vaughn, with his Paul Bunyonesque physique, engaging smile, soft spot for kids, and affinity for charitable work, was one the most popular athletes in Boston and the unequivocal leader of the team. He handled the toughest questions from the city's demanding press corps, and was more outspoken than black players had felt comfortable being on past Red Sox clubs. Like Rivera on the Yankees, he wore Jackie Robinson's number 42 with pride and had a clear understanding of his place in helping change Boston's baseball culture.

Additional credit for this shift, and for many of the great organizational decisions that helped form the core of the franchise for years to come, could be attributed in large part to another young New Englander who joined the team during this period. Dan Duquette, a native of Dalton, Massachusetts, and a lifelong Red Sox fan, was named general manager of the club for the 1994 season. Just 35 years old, he was similar to Dick O'Connell in the 1960s and '70s—a guy who had not played professional baseball but was an excellent judge of talent and not afraid to take risks. On his watch, winning seasons quickly became the norm.

Since the Yankees were now entrenched atop the East, where they would eventually win nine straight division titles, the Wild Card gave the Red Sox—second-place finishers *eight* years in a row—another chance to reach the playoffs. They didn't make much of the opportunity in '98, losing to the Indians again in the Division Series while New York won another world title, but in 1999 appeared poised to give the Yanks a strong fight in the East. Having lost Clemens and Vaughn to free agency, Duquette replaced them with two more superstar talents in pitcher Pedro Martinez and short-stop Nomar Garciaparra. Martinez, one of the influx of great young Latin players to emerge in the '90s, was rail-thin but locomotive fast and had gone 19–7 during his first season with Boston in '98. Garciaparra, a dynamic hitter and fielder who drew comparisons to Ted Williams at the plate, was coming off back-to-back seasons for Boston in which he was Rookie of the Year and MVP runner-up. Wisely, Duquette signed both to long-term contracts at what would prove excellent value.

This pair did their thing again in 1999, and with catcher Jason Varitek and Vaughn's successor Brian Daubach at first base also emerging, Boston was right on New York's heels in the East by mid-season. The All-Star Game that July was scheduled for Fenway Park, and it proved a memorable one. Martinez, already 15–3 on the season, started for the American League and struck out five of the six batters he faced to get the AL started on its way to victory. All-Star Week also included the naming of baseball's "All-Century Team," an epic home run derby featuring Ken Griffey, Sammy Sosa, and Mark McGwire, and the last visit of Ted Williams to his old home ballpark, so Swanson and many others on hand for some or all of the festivities counted the experience among their greatest Fenway thrills—even though the game itself meant nothing.

Meaningful contests, however, were soon to come.

The '99 Sox finished four games back in the East, but as Wild Card playoff entrants finally got past Cleveland in the divisional round. This set up a Yankees–Red Sox postseason series, the first ever between the two bitter rivals after nearly a century in the same division or league. Although the Yanks, playing at home, took the first two games of the best-of-seven matchup, Game 3 at Boston was hyped as a classic well before the first pitch. Martinez, 23–4 on the season, faced an aging but still brilliant Clemens, his predecessor as Red Sox ace and a free agent signee by the Yankees that year. Tickets for the "Cy Young vs. Cy Old" contest went for $1,500 and more, and after Martinez get the best of Clemens in a 13–1 laugher, Sox fans had hope that this could finally be "The Year."

It wasn't. The Yanks broke Boston's momentum with a 9–2 win the next day, and finished out the series in five games. Watching Torre's pinstriped crew celebrate an American League pennant on the Fenway grass was the ultimate indignity for Red Sox rooters.

It had now been 13 years since the Sox had played in the World Series and—famously—81 years since they had last won the Fall Classic in 1918. *Boston Globe* sports columnist Dan Shaughnessy had authored a 1990 book entitled *The Curse of the Bambino* that traced—and, in tongue-and-cheek fashion, blamed—the bad fortunes and near-misses of the Red Sox since World War I on the team's sale of Babe Ruth shortly thereafter. Poor management, cronyism, racism, a lack of pitching depth, and decades of slow-footed, slugger-heavy lineups tailored to fit Fenway Park's cozy dimensions were the real culprits, but "The Curse" became a popular catchphrase.

According to Red Sox management, there was another factor taking on increased significance in the team's long World Series title drought: Fenway Park. The oldest and smallest ballpark in the majors had served as the perfect backdrop for the All-Century Team ceremonies, when superstars of yesteryear like Henry Aaron, Willie Mays, and Stan Musial were honored along with Red Sox legends Williams and Yastrzemski. Like these icons, however, Fenway was getting long in the tooth—at least in the opinion of some connected with the team.

Foremost among the anti-Fenway set was Red Sox president John Harrington. A Boston native who had risen from a humble background to a successful accounting career, he was named team treasurer by Tom Yawkey in 1972 and over time became a surrogate son of sorts to his widow, Jean Yawkey—who had no children of her own. Jean made Harrington a trustee of the Jean R. Yawkey Trust, which owned a portion of the Red Sox as well as Fenway Park, and after the trust became the majority partner in 1987 she named him president in charge of all baseball decisions. Upon Jean Yawkey's death in 1992, the will stipulated that Harrington be made head of the JRY Corporation. Seen by many as simply a front man for Mrs. Yawkey, a paper tiger who was acting in the interests of his elders even after they had left the scene, Harrington was never very popular among Boston fans.

He was, however, not afraid to speak his mind when it came to the ballpark the Yawkeys had loved so dearly. Although he had the means to assemble a (usually) very competitive team in the mid- to late 1990s, Harrington claimed that Fenway Park put the Red Sox at a distinct financial disadvantage. Unlike other professional sports leagues, in which the total budget for team salaries is capped so that no franchise has an unfair edge, the Major League Baseball Players Association voted consistently to keep a salary cap out of MLB.

This stance was good for player salaries, of course, but also assured that big-market teams with larger stadiums and lucrative broadcasting deals such as the Yankees would have the most money with which to pursue and purchase talent—

and would not have to share it with smaller-market clubs. Harrington was convinced that in a changing financial landscape, where long-term, multimillion-dollar free agent signings were becoming the norm, the Red Sox simply could not compete with the likes of New York if they continued playing in their current home.

In addition to having less than 35,000 seats, far fewer than the nearly 56,000 at Yankee Stadium, Fenway also had fewer of the luxury boxes that were becoming increasingly popular and lucrative viewing areas within ballparks. After finishing first or second in the AL in attendance each year from 1967 to 1978, the Red Sox were now annually in the middle of the pack. New Englanders still appreciated Fenway as a connection to their childhoods, and the setting for iconic moments like Carlton Fisk's World Series homer and Lonborg's last-day win, but the ballpark where heroes dating back to Babe Ruth had roamed was no longer above reproach. In fact, as Fenway approached its 90th year of operation, fans were grumbling more than ever about its obstructed views (caused by steel reinforcement beams dating from the 1930s), cramped seats (built for the much shorter fans of the early 20th century), and a lack of adequate parking, restrooms, and refreshment stands.

Aesthetically, Fenway was also losing its luster. A shining, red-bricked diamond in comparison to the mammoth concrete "cookie-cutter" stadiums built in the 1960s and '70s, it looked more tired and dated once retro ballparks like Orioles Park at Camden Yards in Baltimore and Jacobs Field in Cleveland began sprouting up in the mid-1990s. These venues, of which Camden Yards was the first to open, in 1992, combined the old-time feel of Fenway while adding modern fan and corporate amenities. Unlike the cookie-cutters, uninspiring ovals that in many cases were also home to pro football teams, the retro ballparks were baseball-only venues that had unique dimensions and architectural features that made each distinctive and memorable.

There was, under Harrington's watch, nothing very distinctive or memorable being done to Fenway. He had made some cosmetic improvements over the years, including adding elevators and restaurants, but his biggest architectural change—the first extensive remodeling to the park since 1934—had fallen flat: construction of the "600 Club," a swanky, oft-ridiculed restaurant/bar with stadium club seating that replaced the old press box behind home plate. Here fans watched games through bulletproof-glass-thick windows that could not be opened even on the loveliest summer's day, meaning sounds of the ballpark had to be piped in by speaker. Seats in the 600 Club were often left empty as negative reviews of the climate-controlled area spread, and when Boston home run totals dropped it became popular to blame them on wind currents cut down by the club's 1988–89 construction. "I always envisioned a little boy going into the 600 Club with his well-heeled dad," *Boston Herald* sports columnist Steve Buckley jokes today, "and the boy saying 'Daddy, can we go outside and watch the baseball game for a while?'"

Even the name of this restricted area was out-of-touch with fans, as most people didn't know that the "600" referred to the approximate number of seats (610) in the club. In addition, reporters and broadcasters were understandably miffed by having their TV/radio booths and seats on press row forced much higher above home plate (literally atop the 600 Club) by the change—severely impacting their up-close view of the action. In years to come, when Fenway underwent extensive renovations that improved the ballpark experience for so many people on so many levels, the 600 Club would stand as a symbol of why well-thought-out change was needed on Yawkey Way.

Could Fenway be fixed rather than razed?

"It would be easier to straighten the Leaning Tower of Pisa," Harrington stated early in the 1999 season. "It just doesn't make economic sense. And even after spending a lot of money, we'd end up with something that doesn't provide what the fans and the team need at this point."

In May 1999, just a few months before Boston played host to baseball's All-Star Game, Harrington made his big public relations push. Calling a press conference, he unveiled an architectural model of "New Fenway Park" for media and MLB commissioner Bud Selig. Harrington said architects and building experts had told him Fenway could not be safely refurbished given its current infrastructure of crumbling pillars and pipes, most of which dated from either the original 1912 construction or the 1934 Yawkey renovations. A new ballpark, he explained, could be built directly next to the existing Fenway, some of which (including the former diamond) would be kept intact as a public meeting spot and museum. Approximately 10,000 additional seats, more luxury boxes, and enlarged, open concourses were also featured in Harrington's proposal, which had the same on-field dimensions as the original Fenway and retained the Green Monster wall. The price tag varied between $545 million to $629 million, about half of which Harrington hoped would be publicly funded.

To further plug the potential project, the Red Sox unveiled an interactive Web site with colorful architectural renderings of the new Fenway, as well as printed brochures featuring the same drawings that were inserted into local newspapers and splashed across team calendars. All this focus on the proposed venue coincided with less attention paid to the existing one—which was in desperate need of, among other things, a new paint job, new seats, and a drainage system to stop the dugout flooding that had become commonplace with each rainstorm.

Far from everyone wanted a new Fenway. Local politicians, many of whom had grown up attending and in some cases working at the ballpark, railed against the prospect of the state having to foot so much of a very expensive bill. Traditionalists, many of whom admitted to having not seen Camden Yards and other retro ballparks, could not get their heads around the idea of tearing down such a significant part of Boston history—or the fact that an attractive new venue could be built that gave deference to the old. The most ardent protesters, in true activist fashion, formed a group called Save Fenway Park! and set up tables right in the shade of the Green Monster on Lansdowne Street where they handed out bumper stickers, pamphlets, and opinions. Boston architect Charles Hagenah, their flyers touted, said that Fenway could be safely renovated with an upper deck and 73 luxury suites added that would increase attendance to 43,500—and make cramped seats and obstructed-view pillars a thing of the past.

Harrington took to the op-ed pages of *The Boston Globe* to defend his position.

"Our engineers, Walsh Brothers, have renovated historic landmarks, including [in Boston] the Wang Center and the Custom House Tower, and are experts on historic preservation," Harrington wrote. "Our architects, HOK Sport, have both renovated facilities and built the best new ballparks of this generation in Baltimore, Cleveland, and Denver. These professionals have exhaustively studied a renovation of Fenway Park and concluded that it is impractical from virtually every perspective. Their key finding is that in order to 'renovate' Fenway, we would have to destroy it. And we would destroy much of Red Sox baseball while trying to get it done."

As the future of the ballpark remained up in the air, the fortunes of the team that played there were becoming stagnant. Although Boston led the AL East early in 2000, and Martinez and Garciaparra remained among the game's elite, a horrible midsummer slump doomed the Red Sox—celebrating their 100th birthday—to second place and out of the Wild Card running. The Yankees won their fourth World Series in five years that October, as dictatorial and deep-pocketed New York owner George Steinbrenner continued supplementing his "Core Four" of Jeter, Pettitte, Posada, and Rivera with the best teammates money could buy. Steinbrenner had a formula for success that was in many ways the modern equivalent of Tom Yawkey's team, but Steinbrenner's bucks bought and brought glory rather than near-misses.

Jeter and Co. were in the playoffs, on the way to title number four, when John Harrington briefly took the postseason spotlight away from New York with an October 6, 2000, announcement: the JRY Corporation was set to sell its 53 percent majority interest in the Red Sox and Fenway Park, and would be accepting bids from interested parties.

Harrington, who told reporters he had a drawerful of letters from people who had expressed interest over the years in buying the team, said he hoped that the new owner would be "a diehard Red Sox fan from New England" and forge ahead with plans to build a new Fenway Park. Plenty of potential local suitors were suggested or declared interest in the days and weeks that followed, from entertainment industry billionaire Sumner Redstone to bestselling author Stephen King. Even a group led by team legend Ted Williams was brought up as a possibility by Williams's publicity-seeking son, John Henry.

It was Harrington's public hope that the team and ball-park trade hands by the start of the 2001 baseball season. This being Boston—where the line between sports and politics often blurs, and the Red Sox are revered as a sacred trust—it would take much longer.

3. ARCHITECTS OF REVIVAL

AFTER 37 DAYS UNDER HOSPITAL QUARANTINE, Larry Lucchino had finally been cleared to spend some time outside.

His care team at Dana-Farber Cancer Institute, led by Drs. Tom Frei and Lee Nadler, warned Lucchino that he should stay away from crowds. A bone marrow transplant and other procedures necessary to treat his non-Hodgkin lymphoma, a cancer of the white blood cells, had severely weakened his immune system and left it dangerously susceptible to infection. On this Saturday afternoon, however, the only place in Boston Lucchino really wanted to go was where 30,000 people and their germs would be packed tightly together amidst cigar smoke and beer.

Fenway Park.

Lucchino, a hard-nosed lawyer used to doing whatever it took to succeed in court and life, had the necessary connections to make such an outing medically feasible. In his position as vice president and general counsel of the Baltimore Orioles, he approached Red Sox president John Harrington for help, and Harrington secured a private box at the ballpark where Lucchino could watch that day's game while safely separated from the multitudes. Although he can't quite remember Boston's opponent—he thinks it was the Oakland A's—Lucchino knows the visit took place in June 1986, when the Red Sox were in the midst of a drive to the American League pennant.

"My good friend Edward Bennett Williams, the owner of the Orioles, was also treated at Dana-Farber, and Jay Emmett, who was on the team's board of directors, donated a satellite dish and had it installed on the roof of Dana-Farber so I could follow the Orioles while in the hospital," recalls Lucchino, now a two-time cancer survivor. "It was great, but I missed going to the ballpark. I appealed to John [Harrington] as a fellow baseball executive who had never been to Fenway. It was a chance to check something off on my baseball bucket list."

What Lucchino saw that day made an immediate impact. Growing up a working-class kid in Pittsburgh, he had spent many afternoons in the early 1960s watching shortstop Dick Groat and his beloved Pirates at Forbes Field—like this, one of the classic ballparks built in the second decade of the 20th century. A middle-infielder like Groat with his own big-league aspirations,* Lucchino loved how close fans at Forbes were to the field. He felt the same sense of intimacy here at

---

*Lucchino was an All-City second baseman and basketball guard for the Taylor Allderdice High School Dragons in Pittsburgh, and was drawn to Groat because he had excelled in the same two sports at Duke University. Lucchino's baseball career ended in high school, but he did play three years on the Princeton University varsity basketball team—including for two Ivy League championship squads.

Fenway, where the venue, with all of its quirky angles and the great Green Monster wall in left field, was as much a part of the experience as the game itself.

"I was impressed—very impressed," says Lucchino of that first visit. "Little did I know that I would be back there in a couple of different ways."

His first major reconnection to Fenway would come just a few years later. After the death of his boss and longtime mentor Williams to cancer in August 1988, Lucchino was part of a group that purchased the Orioles prior to the 1989 season. Baltimore was coming off a year in which it had started a record-setting 0–21 en route to a last-place finish, so there was plenty of work to do. Along with rebuilding the roster, the incoming owners were committed to constructing a baseball-only ballpark for the franchise, which had shared cavernous, all-purpose Memorial Stadium with the Baltimore Colts football team since the 1950s.

By this point president and CEO of the Orioles, Lucchino headed up the project. He brought in an expert in urban planning and architecture, Janet Marie Smith, and made her vice president for design and development of the new ballpark (later, he called her hiring "our best off-season move of 1988–89"). During the next four years, while also overseeing operations of the ball club with general manager Roland Hemond, Lucchino worked alongside Smith to create and bring to life a blueprint that would transform the way modern baseball venues were designed and built—taking them away from the cookie-cutter, multiplex, stark behemoths of recent vintage and back to the days when each team's identity was formed largely by an instantly recognizable home.

"We proposed it in the documents as a 'traditional old-fashioned ballpark with modern amenities,'" says Lucchino.

"It was to be irregular, quirky, asymmetrical for sure, with intimate seats as close to the action as possible."

They used as their models three classic locales: Forbes Field, naturally, due to Lucchino's personal connections to it; Ebbets Field, the beloved home of the Brooklyn Dodgers, which despite double-decks was perhaps the "coziest" of all the old parks prior to its 1960 demolition; and the scene of his aforementioned outing, Fenway Park.

Lucchino was fond of telling how when he was a teenager everything he needed was in a close, walkable radius 10 minutes from his house: the Carnegie Library where, as son of a bar owner turned court bailiff, he charted his course to college; the YMHA basketball courts where he perfected the game that would earn him a spot on the varsity at Princeton University; the pizza parlor where he satisfied his appetite for food and friendships; and Forbes Field, where he and his big brother Frank watched Groat, Roberto Clemente, and the rest of their idols do battle.

Now, with Smith's help, he wanted to bring that same neighborhood feel to Orioles fans.

"When it comes to baseball I had one good original idea in my life, and that was it," Lucchino jokes today. "It just seemed to me to make perfect sense. Why did a new ballpark have to look new? I mean, baseball is such a game of history, with memories for everyone that accumulate over time. Why couldn't the ballpark do that as well?"

As work on the project got under way, Lucchino insisted that everybody in the Oriole organization buy into the concept. Nobody was to think of the new facility going up as a stadium—it was a *ballpark*. "You had to always keep that in mind," explains Lucchino. "If people used the 'S Word' they were fined five dollars. This was not to be something massive and concrete and multipurposed and distant. That's a stadium, and you can play a lot of things in a stadium. This was to be small and cozy and intimate and irregular—a ballpark. You play baseball in a ballpark."

Constructed beside Baltimore's Inner Harbor district, and built to conform to the classic late-19th-century architecture surrounding it, Oriole Park at Camden Yards was a revelation from the moment it was unveiled on Opening Day 1992. A short walk from the waterfront and its many shops and restaurants, the redbrick and black steel ballpark featured natural grass, an asymmetrical playing field 16 feet below street level, wrought iron gates and seat backs detailed with the original Orioles insignia, and old-fashioned bleachers in right-center that seated just 2,000 fans. Even modern necessities like luxury suites and a high-tech scoreboard were given an antique feel.

Accessibility was another key to the ballpark's charm. For a very cheap ticket, fans could stroll along wide, game-accessible walkways that surrounded the playing field, look in, and even catch the occasional home run. The outside concourse featured souvenir stands, activities for kids, and dining options including Boog's Barbeque—where sausages and ribs were often served up by former All-Star first baseman Boog Powell himself. Even the Orioles' offices had a retro feel, as they were located in the mammoth B&O Warehouse that loomed just beyond the outfield walls and further made the brand-new ballpark feel like it had sat on the same spot for a century or more.

Camden Yards was a game-changer. The Orioles packed the house for nearly every game no matter their record, and the look and feel of the place delighted younger fans while reminding their parents and grandparents of their own childhoods. Baltimore's great shortstop Cal Ripken, a "throwback" player who never missed a day of work, was the perfect Camden Yards hero; when he passed Lou Gehrig's record for consecutive games played during the park's fourth season, in 1995, the final days of the chase were counted down in low-tech but powerful fashion through huge numerals placed in windows of the warehouse—capped by a 2-1-3-1 unveiled for the new standard in September. An MLB strike that started the previous August had wiped out both the 1994 World Series and the first month of the '95 season, and many credit a ballpark revival spurred by Lucchino and Smith's handiwork for helping bring disillusioned fans back to the game. Beautiful new venues sprouted in Cleveland, Denver, Atlanta, and elsewhere—nine in all between 1994 and 2000—and a Camden Yards influence was apparent in them all.

By this point, however, Lucchino had moved on to a new challenge. After Orioles majority owner Eli Jacobs declared bankruptcy and sold the team in 1993, Lucchino was encouraged by new owner Peter Angelos to stay on as president, but says "it became clear to me that Angelos didn't need a copilot." Looking around for other opportunities, Lucchino began negotiations to join a group aiming to buy his hometown Pirates. Then, before that deal could be finalized, he received an offer to help a group interested in purchasing yet another big-league team: the San Diego Padres.

"John Moores was trying to acquire the Padres from Tom Werner, so I helped them along the way, with the understanding that I was soon going to buy my hometown team," says Lucchino. "But then Moores got the Padres deal before the

Pirates deal could be finalized. He came to me and said, 'I won't buy this team unless you agree to take a piece of it and be the president and CEO.' It was a tough decision, but a bird in the hand is worth more than two in the bush. There was no guarantee things would work out in Pittsburgh, so I went out to San Diego."

There Lucchino faced a challenge arguably harder than taking over the last-place Orioles—who had a rich legacy of winning and loyal fans to get them through tough times. The Padres, in contrast, were a struggling team whose history dated only to 1969 and included few high points. Although the Los Angeles Dodgers had proven big-league baseball could thrive in Southern California, the area 100 miles south around San Diego had not been as quick to embrace it; the Padres had the worst revenue and attendance figures in the National League and were coming off a 61–101 season.

As he showed in hiring Janet Marie Smith, however, Lucchino had a knack for finding the right people to partner with him on his goals. In this case, he didn't even have to go outside his previous organization. He encouraged Orioles public relations director Charles Steinberg to join him on the journey west, knowing that Steinberg was the perfect man to complement his legal, business, and baseball acumen. Before Camden Yards made sellouts a common practice, Steinberg had been the creative juice behind numerous promotions and events geared to help raise Orioles attendance at old Memorial Stadium. While Lucchino certainly had a creative side, his was more a quiet, behind-the-scenes style. Steinberg was the choreographer to his director.

Baltimore born-and-bred, Steinberg had rooted for the Orioles since childhood. He was seven when the Birds swept the Dodgers to win the 1966 World Series, and fondly recalls his mother driving him and his sister downtown to watch the bedlam unfold firsthand after the final out at Memorial.

"We parked the car, and there was this explosion of horns blowing, streamers flying, people hugging," says Steinberg. "My mom bought me a flannel pennant that said, 'World Champions,' and then this big kid came up to me, pointed to a man getting into a taxi cab, and said 'Get his autograph.' So I did—my first autograph. It was Harry Walker, a former big-league batting champ who I think was scouting for someone.

"That was the day I fell in love with baseball, seeing the response of a city to its team."[†]

Steinberg's interest in both the Orioles and his favorite player, iconic third baseman Brooks Robinson, had been sealed from that point on. His father was a dentist who also played first violin for various Baltimore community orchestras, and his mother was an artist, so young Charles grew up in a home filled with music, books, artwork, and baseball on the radio.

In terms of playing the game, Steinberg learned much earlier than Lucchino that a career in baseball was not attainable on the field. "In two years of Little League I had exactly two

---

[†] Later, on hearing Steinberg recount this story, Cal Ripken told him that "it was the same day for me." The future Hall of Famer had been sitting in the upper deck at Memorial Stadium for the '66 World Series clincher as a six-year-old, and when Frank Robinson homered for the only run of the game, Ripken said to himself, "That's what I want to do—play baseball." As Steinberg puts it, "he fell in love with the action, and I fell in love with the reaction."

hits, and both came in my second season," Steinberg says with a laugh. "When I told that to Ted Williams, he said at least I showed improvement. And while I did letter in baseball on our JV team, it was as the statistician and equipment manager."

Like with Lucchino, Steinberg's first visit to Fenway Park made a deep impression—and added a touch of irony to his later association with the venue. Charles was a freshman at the University of Maryland in 1977 when he attended the National Collegiate Honors Council's annual conference in Boston, and as an avid fan wanted to check out the summer home of Yaz, Fisk, and Rice close-up. The Red Sox were on the road, however, and when Steinberg and some buddies took the trolley over to Fenway, they found the ballpark locked up like a fortress.

"It was raining, and we were content to touch the redbrick and peer through tiny apertures and see green," he recalls. "They had not created Fenway Park tours at that point, so we did what we could do."

By this point Steinberg had already gotten his first taste of working for his hometown team, interning with the Orioles as a 17-year-old senior at nearby Gilman School. He continued his Memorial Stadium apprenticeship while at Maryland, serving as a statistician for Orioles manager Earl Weaver. Weaver, a future Hall of Famer, was ahead of his time when it came to statistical analysis. One of the first managers to delve into deep number-crunching such as how certain hitters fared against certain pitchers, he wanted the ability to call upon these figures at any point in a game. Laptop computers were still a few years away, so index cards were Earl's preferred method of dugout stat-keeping—and Steinberg his preferred statistician.

In 1979, during the first game of the American League

Championship Series, the Orioles were locked in a tight contest when the visiting California Angels brought in a relief pitcher named John Montague. He had been traded to the Angels a month after the Orioles last faced California during the regular season, so Steinberg had not moved Montague's stats card into Weaver's Angels notebook. When the manager couldn't find Montague's numbers, a call went out through the ballpark to find Steinberg. He dug up the stats, updated the card, and got it to Earl in time for the manager to send up pinch hitter John Lowenstein—3-for-4 lifetime with two homers against Montague—to face the pitcher in the bottom of the 10th inning. Lowenstein promptly homered to win the game.

"Even after he hit it, I still thought I had lost my job," recalls Steinberg, who was 20 at the time. "I went down into the clubhouse, walked through to Earl's office, and when I opened the door all the writers were crowded around his desk. I said, 'Mr. Weaver, I'm so sorry,' and he said, 'Charles Steinberg! Come sit down! Have a beer—you won us the game!'"

Even with an ego boost like this, Steinberg's devotion to his parents matched his love of baseball. He followed in his father's professional footsteps by attending Maryland's dental school while continuing as Weaver's statistician, and after getting his Doctor of Dental Surgery (DDS) degree in 1984 took on a unique dual role with the Orioles working in the front office and as team dentist. He was also a founding and charter member of the Academy of Sports Dentistry, a forum for dentists, physicians, trainers, coaches, and others at all levels of athletics to exchange ideas about the dental needs of athletes at risk to sports injuries.

Steinberg began devoting more and more time to ballpark operations as the years passed. He created the Orioles' first video production department, its first customer service department, and as head of public relations for the team used his love of history, theater, and music to orchestrate three memorable events: the final weekend at Memorial Stadium in 1991, the opening of Camden Yards in '92, and the All-Star Game in 1993. By now he and Lucchino had become close, and their partnership was dynamite in generating support for the team. During their 16 years working together with the Orioles, the organization's fan base grew from two million to six million and its season ticket base from 1,600 to 28,000 (plus a 13,000-person waiting list).

When they made the move cross-country to San Diego in 1995, both men worked in overdrive to effect similar change for the Padres. As president and CEO, Lucchino put together a roster that reached the playoffs two years later and the World Series by 1998; Steinberg, still his key choreographer, focused on bringing out the fans—more than doubling attendance from the moribund depths of 16,700 per game to a franchise-record 35,500 a contest by building loyalty step by step.

"We decided to make Saturday night baseball night in San Diego, with all kinds of promotions to boost attendance," says Steinberg. "Once you show people that this is where San Diego goes on a Saturday night, you can build onto that with Firework Fridays. Now you've got two big nights and you're cooking, so you make Sundays free for children and seniors, at which point you're drawing maybe 40,000 on Friday, 50,000 on Saturday, and 30,000 on Sunday. Then you start working backward from Thursday."

In Steinberg's opinion, there are three necessities to building a strong team following that he learned in Baltimore and has used ever since: a winning ball club, a great fan experience, and a welcoming, memorable ballpark. By the late 1990s the Padres had two of the three, and Steinberg and Lucchino were determined to put the third in place. Qualcomm Stadium, the home the Padres shared with the NFL's San Diego Chargers just outside the city, was one of the all-purpose arenas that both men abhorred, and they pushed the city to help finance construction of a new ballpark in the heart of the city's business and entertainment district. Aiding them in this effort was Sarah McKenna, a Springfield, Massachusetts, native who had moved west years before and was hired by the Padres to gain grassroots support for the project from local citizens and politicians.

"Construction of the ballpark was to be a public-private partnership, with the public portion paid through tourist tax dollars," says McKenna. "Visitors to the city who stayed at San Diego hotels would pay a little extra in taxes depending on how long they stayed, and the debt would get paid off in city bonds. San Diego residents themselves wouldn't have to pay higher taxes; getting them to understand this was the key to the ballpark proposal passing."

The Padres reached the World Series in October 1998, helping generate enthusiasm for the proposal, and two weeks later voters overwhelmingly approved Proposition C—allowing for construction of a new downtown park at a cost of $411 million. Much of this total, approximately $225 million, would be funded through the hotel tax, with $115 million more guaranteed by the team through private investors. Upon getting this green light, Lucchino worked with designers as he had in Baltimore to create a structure that fit in perfectly with the city surrounding it.

"We built a ballpark that looked and felt and smelled and reflected San Diego, the same way Camden Yards did in Baltimore, but they are two different looks and smells and reflections," says Lucchino. "Petco Park is contemporary, with traditional baseball values built into it, while Camden Yards is an old-fashioned baseball park through-and-through." Made of white steel, a sandstone facade, and shaded by palm and jacaranda trees, Petco Park is as much Southern Californian as the redbrick-and-black-steel Camden Yards is industrial Baltimore. Similarly, as Camden Yards did with the Inner Harbor district in Baltimore, Petco helped revitalize the neighborhoods surrounding it.

There were some hurdles along the way, resulting in the project taking two years longer than anticipated, but 42,000-seat Petco Park opened in 2004 to rave reviews. Lucchino, however, was not in San Diego to enjoy the fruits of his latest labors firsthand. He says now of his time with the Padres that "I had seven years there, six that were wonderful and a seventh in which the principal owner, John Moores, and I were not on the same page."

What happened, Lucchino explains, was that in 2000, Moores—who had brought him west back in '95—was undergoing a grand jury investigation into his potential undue influence over a city councilwoman involving negotiation of the lease for the new ballpark. As a result, says Lucchino, "he wanted to kick me upstairs as a vice chairman and have me step down as CEO so I could focus primarily on getting the ballpark done. I wasn't interested."

During this same period, Red Sox president John Harrington announced he was putting the team up for sale. Tom Werner, who had sold the Padres to Moores but was still a limited partner in San Diego, decided to throw his hat into the ring for the Red Sox franchise.

A New York City native who had grown up playing stickball

in the streets and dreaming of being the next Mickey Mantle, Werner had wound up succeeding in another form of entertainment. He was a television visionary, who along with his partner, Marcy Carsey, had created groundbreaking sitcoms including *The Cosby Show, Third Rock from the Sun*, and *Grace Under Fire*. Werner also had fond memories of his college days in Boston, which had begun as a Harvard freshman in September 1967—the very month the Red Sox completed their "Impossible Dream" march to the American League pennant. Fenway Park made such a big impression on Werner that he wound up producing a documentary about the ballpark while at Harvard.

"Tom said to me, 'I'm trying to buy the Red Sox. If you're not going to be able to stay CEO with the Padres for 2001, 2002, and beyond, I would like nothing better than for you to come and join us in Boston,'" says Lucchino.

The offer—which, if Werner got the team, would result in Lucchino becoming president and CEO of the Red Sox—would take some doing to become a reality even if Larry were interested.

In addition to Werner's group, there were five others that emerged from the dozens of initial inquirers and submitted bids to Harrington and the minority owners in November 2001. Several were led by Boston-area business leaders: Frank McCourt, a land developer with intentions to build a new ballpark on his waterfront property in South Boston; Charles Dolan, chairman of Cablevision Systems Corp.; Jeremy Jacobs, owner of the Boston Bruins hockey club; and the partnership of Boston Concessions owner Joe O'Donnell and mall developer Steve Karp. Werner did have Maine ski mogul Les Otten on his team, but as the leader of the group was still considered one of the two "outside" bids from beyond the New England region, along with New York attorney/financier Miles Prentice.

The pending sale of the club was one of two major Red Sox stories dominating Boston's newspapers and airwaves during the waning days of the 2001 season. Harrington had hoped for a competitive and relatively trouble-free final year for the Yawkey Trust, but he got nothing but headaches. Major injuries to Pedro Martinez, Nomar Garciaparra, and Jason Varitek[‡] kept the team from fulfilling its offensive potential, and overshadowed another excellent signing by Dan Duquette for the lame-duck owners: outfielder Manny Ramirez.

One of the best pure hitters in the game, Ramirez had helped the Cleveland Indians to a pair of World Series berths and in 1999 drove in 165 runs—the most in the major leagues since Jimmie Foxx 61 years before. Duquette likened Ramirez to a modern-day Foxx, the Hall of Fame slugger who hit .321 for the Red Sox from 1936 to 1941 while averaging 36 home runs and 129 RBI. Throughout most of the 2001 season Ramirez lived up to this billing, but with the major injuries to Garciaparra and Varitek, Manny's efforts as another big bat in the order to complement them could not be fully utilized.

Frustrated and no doubt worrying about his job security with the pending ownership shift, Duquette took an unorthodox step. Although the Red Sox were just five games behind the Yankees on August 15, the GM fired manager

---

[‡] Garciaparra underwent wrist surgery for a split tendon in spring training, and only played 21 games all year. Varitek fractured his elbow while diving for a foul pop-up on June 7, and was out the rest of the season. Martinez, who developed shoulder tendinitis in mid-season, made just 18 starts.

Jimy Williams and replaced him with pitching coach Joe Kerrigan, who had been coaching professionally for 18 years but had never managed at any level. Duquette hoped the switch would light a fire under his listless club, but Kerrigan appeared to be in over his head from the start. Boston limped to a 17–26 record the rest of the way and finished a very distant second to New York at 82–79.

Squabbles and infighting became commonplace in the waning days of September, and several players begged out of the lineup or left the team altogether after it was eliminated from the Wild Card race. The negative commentary and production spewed forth by underachieving malcontent center fielder Carl Everett further turned fans against the ball club, and Duquette was roundly booed when he appeared on the field during a tribute to retiring Orioles great Cal Ripken Jr. before the season's final home game. "No one wants to [expletive] play here," Garciaparra was quoted as saying.

Still, these were the *Red Sox*, and each of the groups striving to take over ownership of the club surely felt they could come in and turn things around. When the Sox are going well, they all knew, there is no better place to be in New England than Fenway Park. Despite all its problems, the 2001 team still set a home attendance record of 2,625,333—an average of close to a full house each game. In considering Werner's offer to help his bidding group, Larry Lucchino remembered both the way he had felt on his own first visit to Fenway as well as what his mentor, Edward Bennett Williams, had told him 20 years before:

If you ever get a chance to run a baseball team in Boston, don't pass it up.

There is nobody, before or since, for whom Lucchino holds more reverence. As founder of a high-powered boutique litigation law firm in Washington, D.C., the self-made Williams was an outstanding trial attorney and passionate sports fan who saw in young Lucchino a kindred soul—a kid from modest means who was trying to rise up. A kid who gutted it out for three years coming off the bench for the Princeton basketball team and earned a Final Four watch with the Bill Bradley–led Tigers of 1965. A kid who went straight from Yale Law School to Capitol Hill, fighting the good fight against Richard Nixon—and alongside law school classmate Hillary Rodham—on the Senate Watergate impeachment committee. Williams had fought the good fight too, including, while an attorney for football's Washington Redskins, successfully pushing team owner George Preston Marshall to integrate the NFL's last all-white franchise back in 1962.

"The first day I was with Williams's law firm, he came in and sat in my office and we talked for two hours," Lucchino recalls. "I had been saying to myself, 'This is the big leagues of litigation; do I really belong here?' He just made me comfortable. We got along extremely well right from the get-go. Some of it probably had to do with my being from the same socioeconomic ascendancy he had experienced a generation before; he opened all the doors for me."

Williams was like a father to Lucchino, grooming him for a career in sports—first as a litigator with the Redskins (of which by this point Williams was president) and then as an executive with the Orioles.§ Before he died of cancer in 1988,

---

§ Lucchino helped Williams acquire the Orioles in a transaction that was finalized in August 1979. Two months later the Orioles played Lucchino's hometown Pirates in the World Series, and Larry says he got a hard time from his family about his swift shift in loyalty. The Pirates won the series in seven games.

at age 68, Williams arranged for his protégé to take over the Orioles, and since then the same photo of Williams cheering at a Redskins game had adorned a wall in each of Lucchino's offices. Now there might be an opportunity for it to do so at Fenway Park, where the Redskins had actually played as a Boston-based team during the Great Depression.

"At one point in the early 1980s, when Williams owned a piece of the Redskins and 100 percent of the Orioles, he and I were at a football game in Boston, along with one of his friends, Joe DiMaggio," Lucchino recalls. "This was pretty heavy stuff for a kid from Pittsburgh. Anyway, we're talking about Boston things, and at one point Williams says to me, 'I'd give up my interest in the Redskins *and* the Orioles to own the Red Sox. There is something special about the Red Sox.'"‖

Lucchino knew it himself after all his years in the game; Baltimore and San Diego were fun places to make a mark, and each proved a challenge in its own way, but Boston was a baseball Mecca.

"I was out in San Diego, helping revive baseball out there, but this would be like coming from New America back to Old America," Lucchino remembers thinking about being part of a Red Sox ownership team. "I once saw an article that defined New America as cities [like San Diego] that didn't have major league baseball teams before World War II, and Old America as cities with older teams and Italian restaurants where the waiters are named Vinnie. In New America, the waiters are named Dwayne."

Anxious to dine with Vinnie, Lucchino recalls "jumping

‖ Williams had grown up in Hartford, Connecticut, in the 1920s and '30s, and Lucchino says he was a Red Sox fan—which is impressive considering the post–Babe Ruth, pre–Ted Williams Sox were mostly miserable.

into the project with vigor" during late 2001 by helping pull together additional people interested in joining a Werner-Otten group. Around this same time, however, another party entered the picture.

John Henry, a billionaire commodities trader, had recently gotten into baseball by purchasing the Florida Marlins for $150 million in 1998. He and Lucchino had become friendly at MLB meetings, and now Henry, frustrated by an apathetic fan base and political roadblocks in trying to win approval for a new stadium in South Florida, was considering a proposal to buy the Anaheim Angels. He sought help from Lucchino, who he knew had extensive knowledge of the West Coast market, and like Werner offered him a shot to be president and CEO if Henry got the team. Lucchino turned him down.

"I told him I was already trying to buy the Red Sox with Tom, and it was just too much to also be involved with him," Lucchino recalls. "I couldn't ride two horses, plus I still felt a connection to the Padres [a competitor with the Angels for fans]. I had to focus my efforts on getting the Red Sox deal done."

A week or so later, on November 3, Lucchino was at a Yale football game when Henry called him and posed a single question: "Do you think there is room for me in Boston?"

Henry's negotiations with the Disney Company, which owned the Angels, were not going well. He had grown up listening to radio broadcasts of St. Louis Cardinals games on powerful KMOX from his family farms in Illinois and Arkansas, and was called "St. Louis" by friends because he always wore a Cardinals cap. The chance to be at the helm of another of baseball's most storied and successful franchises was becoming more and more appealing.

For Lucchino, the interest from Henry was a godsend.

Almost a year after John Harrington had put the Red Sox up for sale, and with the final decision on a new owner looming in just a few months, press and public sentiment was still very much with the prospective buying group led by a pair of Boston-area businessmen—mall developer Steve Karp and Boston Concessions owner Joe O'Donnell. In terms of purchase power, there was nobody in the fight with more cash than Charles Dolan, chairman of Cablevision. Along with a few other groups, Werner and Otten were still considered long shots at best.

"Room for you?" he told Henry. "You'd be perfect. You've got baseball experience. Tom and I have baseball experience. You've been approved before [with the Marlins], and you can provide the financial stability we need. Come on and join us.'"

Werner and Henry had never met, but Lucchino was convinced that they would hit it off. He arranged for Henry to fly out to California for a weekend so the pair could get to know one another without him around. "They got along famously," Lucchino says, "and we gradually incorporated John into our group."

Because the Red Sox were considered one of New England's most beloved and scrutinized treasures, fans and reporters expressed almost universal hope that one of the local groups get the nod. Bob Ryan of *The Boston Globe* filled an entire column with a Red Sox quiz that he believed any prospective buyer should have to pass, much like that a devoted Baltimore Colts fan put his bride-to-be through in the movie *Diner.* Karp and O'Donnell were the clear favorites among the media and political allies they had gathered in Boston through the years.

When the six groups submitted their bids to Harrington on November 29, however, Dolan's was by far the highest. He came in at around $405 million, versus $300–$370 million from the others, and was set to go even higher when his advisers leaked to reporters that he was also prepared to buy out the limited partners—who had previously expressed no interest in selling their combined 47 percent stake. Surprised by this development, Harrington gave the other five groups a chance to make similar 100 percent offers. This meant each would have to come up with an additional $350 million or so, something Lucchino says the Otten-Werner group would have been hard pressed to do without Henry's involvement.

As Christmas neared, rumors about who would get the votes of Harrington and Boston's minority owners intensified. The day before the announcement of the winning bid, superfan Rick Swanson took to the Internet as "something like a baseball Saint Nick" to express his feelings about both the pending sale and John Harrington's departure from the scene. Swanson's entire life as a Boston baseball fan had been defined by the Yawkeys and their associates; it was all he and anybody under 70 knew. Now there would finally be a changing of the guard, and Swanson recrafted Clement Clarke Moore's classic 1822 Christmas poem to express his feelings of anticipation.

T'was the night before ownership and all through the park
Not a limited partner was sleeping, not even Aramark
The buyers were nestled all snug in their estates
While visions of Nomar and Pedro could be their new mates
John in the owner's box, and Dan in the 600 club sat
Had just settled their brains to fill their pockets fat

When out on the green wall there arose such a clatter
They both got up to see what was the matter
And there on the screen was a miniature limo
With bidders inside that he called out by name
On Dolan, on Werner, or Prentice, on Karp,
On Henry, on O'Donnell, on Jacobs, on McCourt

From on the green monster to the top of the wall
More cash my way, cash away, bid higher all
And soon in a moment they reached 700 million
With hopes it will rise to be a one whole billion

And then in a moment he slid down the flag pole
He went straight to the mound to fit in his role
He was dressed all in red from his cap to his sox
And began unloading hurlers to fill out the rotation
To please all the fans that are part of Red Sox Nation

But now it is time to choose the new owner
And John can go back to be a complete loner
I heard him exclaim as he rode out of Boston
The new owner will be one we'll call a real lucker
And by fate we found out, his name is Bill Buckner

A final decision on a new Red Sox owner was due by the MLB owners' meetings in January. Dolan was now willing to pay up to $695 million, which many speculated was too rich for the O'Connell-Karp team to match. For some period there was discussion of the O'Connell-Karp and Otten-Werner-Henry groups merging—a move that would satisfy public fervor for local owners and Commissioner

Bud Selig's wish that proven baseball people be involved. It would also result in an offer that could at least come close to Dolan's.

In the end, one major reason this über-partnership did not materialize was a fundamental difference about where the Red Sox would spend their long-term future. O'Connell and Karp, like Dolan, wanted to build a new ballpark elsewhere in the city. Henry's group planned to stay put.

"Tom Werner and Les Otten were the two founding fathers of our partnership, and the premise of that group was always to renovate Fenway Park," says Lucchino. "When we did our projections, they were all predicated on renovating and improving the ballpark. We didn't declare at the beginning that we would be here forever, because we had to see if we could do some things [to the current facility] that would be successful. But of the six groups, we were the only one that talked about staying in Fenway."

On Friday, December 21, after John Harrington and the limited partners met to discuss the five remaining bids—Karp and O'Donnell having dropped out after the failed merger with Henry—Harrington made the statement that all but ended nearly 70 years of Yawkey ownership: "I am delighted to announce that the Boston Red Sox partners have voted unanimously this evening to sell 100 percent of the team's interests to the group led by John Henry, subject to approval by Major League Baseball." The final group also included additional partners, among them former Senate majority leader George Mitchell and the New York Times Company (parent to the lead newspaper covering the Sox, *The Boston Globe*). The final price was $660 million, and included the ball club, Fenway Park, and the team's 80 percent stake in the New England

Sports Network (NESN), a powerful cable enterprise that was the primary broadcast partner of Red Sox games.

It is ironic that in the end, Harrington—the man behind the initial fervor to rebuild Fenway in the mid-1990s—wound up selling the team to men focused on saving the ballpark. However he might have felt about Fenway's viability, it was clear to him and the partners that the Henry group was not only financially stable, but also had the baseball experience and subsequent blessing of Commissioner Selig that would make MLB approval likely.¶

Not unexpectedly, the decision led to some initially loud cries of a "bag job" from newspaper reporters and sports talk radio hosts who claimed Selig had handpicked the winners due to his friendships with Werner and Henry. Sportswriters also questioned if the newcomers had an appropriate grasp of Red Sox history to warrant their purchase, just as the *Globe*'s Bob Ryan had done with his quiz of the previous December. There was an investigation by Massachusetts attorney general Tom Reilly into the sale, because of his role as overseer of the state's charities—due to benefit greatly from money coming in to the nonprofit Yawkey Trust. Dolan even submitted a new bid for $700 million in hope Harrington could be swayed to change his mind.

"I wish I felt good about this and I hope I'm wrong," wrote *Globe* columnist and *Curse of the Bambino* author Dan Shaughnessy. "I wish I could get on the bandwagon and believe good things will come of this. Maybe John Henry and Tom Wer-

---

¶There was also concern with a potential conflict of interest surrounding the Dolan group. Charles Dolan's brother, Larry, owned the Cleveland Indians, a purchase he had financed in part with money from family trusts overseen by Charles.

ner will be the best Boston sports owners since [Celtics owner] Walter Brown. Maybe they will build a new jewel of a ballpark in South Boston and reward us with a string of championship teams in the next decade.** But forgive me if I don't trust these guys."

Nothing came of any of the mudslinging, and MLB owners voted unanimously on January 16 to approve the sale. A decade later it's tough to question the decision. Concerns that outsiders would come into Boston for a few years and then take off into the night—leaving behind a wrecked franchise— have proven unfounded, and a new group of limited partners with strong local ties was quickly brought on board. As the public faces of the Red Sox, Henry, Werner, and Lucchino have shown the type of passion New England fans demand, and have worked to make the Red Sox and Fenway Park a team and ballpark of the people. Whereas most fans could never have imagined setting foot on the Fenway grass during the three generations of Yawkey rule, there would soon be numerous opportunities to do so each year from picnics to Father's Day Catches.

Hints at bigger changes to come became apparent as Lucchino and the team's new senior management group began moving into the Fenway offices at 4 Yawkey Way. Along with Steinberg, who was made executive vice president of public affairs, other staffers who had worked with Team Lucchino in San Diego and/or Baltimore headed to Boston in advance of the '02 season. Sarah McKenna, who had helped secure the funding for Petco Park, was coming home to Massachusetts

---

** Shaughnessy would not be far off in this tongue-in-cheek prediction; it took the new owners just 12 years to win three World Series championships.

as director of fan services; Janet Marie Smith, the architectural mastermind behind Camden Yards, would now be tasked with modernizing and expanding Fenway Park.

On the baseball operations side, those heading east included a young man who had grown up just a mile from Fenway in Brookline, Massachusetts, and risen from a summer internship under Steinberg in Baltimore to become the Padres director of baseball operations by age 26. Lucchino liked this kid's Ivy League education and law degree, his sense of the game, and his workaholic nature—which no doubt reminded him of his own. Theo Epstein's first job with the Red Sox would be as assistant general manager, but he wouldn't have it long.

Awaiting this crew in Boston were holdovers from the Harrington regime, some folks just a few years out of college and others—like vice president of public relations Dick Bresciani—with tenure dating back to the 1970s and Tom Yawkey himself. Pam Ganley was one of the newer staff, a Burlington, Massachusetts, native and 2001 graduate of the University of Massachusetts at Amherst who had been helping Bresciani with everything from press briefings to assembling newspaper clippings over the previous two years. She had even occasionally taken the seat long occupied by one of the legendary figures of Fenway, switchboard operator Helen Robinson. Answering virtually every incoming call to the ballpark between 1941 and 2001, Robinson had fiercely protected the privacy of ballplayers from Ted Williams to Nomar Garciaparra. When she passed away at age 85 on October 2, 2001, Ganley was one of three young women who rotated filling the slot until a permanent replacement could be found.

"We used to just answer the phone 'Red Sox,' with no 'Hello,' because that was the way Helen had always answered the phone," says Ganley, now Kenn and senior director of public affairs. "I was 22, so I didn't question anything."

Then, one day shortly after the sale of the team was made official, the phone rang. Ganley answered it.

"Red Sox."

"Hello, this is Charles Steinberg."

Ganley had yet to meet Steinberg, who was still closing up the San Diego offices, but she knew he was part of the incoming leadership.

"It would be great," he told her, "if from now on when you answered the phone you could say, 'Hello, thank you for calling the Boston Red Sox.'"

Ganley said sure, and hung up.

A few seconds later, the phone rang again.

"Hello, thank you for calling the Boston Red Sox."

"Hello, this is Charles. Thank you."

It would be two years before the miracle at Fenway would be complete, but a new day was dawning at the old ballpark. The incoming owners might not initially be able to answer questions from Bob Ryan like "What Red Sox pitcher routinely smoked a cigar while relaxing in the whirlpool?" or "What Red Sox player owned a bowling alley on Soldier's Field Road?" but they had every intention of writing their own piece of Boston baseball history—and of preserving its central repository. "I know that even the best baseball teams cannot win every night," said Henry, "but I want to make sure our fans win every night, that they enjoy as many aspects of our

game, our tradition, and the Fenway experience as they can."
It was a hint of what was to come.

Change was certainly the order of the day when Lucchino,
Henry, and Werner arrived at their first Red Sox spring training at City of Palms Park in Fort Myers, Florida, in February
2002. They held their first press conference on lawn chairs
set out on the field, and while some reporters poked fun in
print at Henry's big Panama hat, it was dramatic to see him
walking and talking so comfortably amongst the fans—
something few could remember ever seeing Harrington or
Mrs. Yawkey do. Henry joked about how he had set a record
for most strikeouts at a Chicago White Sox boys camp, and
was "so sidearmed" as a pitcher that he scared kids who stepped
in against him.

Fans were still skeptical. One asked Henry to autograph a
book about Pope John Paul II, explaining that "I'm going to
pray for your team." But the new bosses worked quickly, and
much of the dissension that had wracked the club the previous September was dramatically dealt with right off the bat.
On February 28, just 18 hours after taking legal ownership of
the club, the newcomers fired general manager Duquette and
awarded his job (with an interim label) to assistant GM Mike
Port.[††] Then, a few days later, they ended the short, disastrous
managerial reign of Joe Kerrigan and gave his position to
Grady Little, a bench coach for the Sox under Jimy Williams

[††] Duquette, who had believed he might keep his job right up until
the end, deserved a better fate. He had made many strong moves in his
eight years at the helm of his hometown team, several of which would
have a major impact on the makeup and accomplishments of the 2004
champions.

from 1997 to 1999 and a veteran of nearly 2,000 games as a minor league manager.‡‡

Little was a familiar face to many Red Sox players, and his hiring was met with great enthusiasm among their ranks. The team gave him a rousing ovation when he first entered the clubhouse after the announcement, and players shared their excitement about the change.

"I loved the guy when he was here [as a coach]," Sox pitcher Derek Lowe said. "I think that's the consensus of all the guys who have ever played with him. He's easy to get along with, a good baseball man, and he has managed before." Garciaparra praised his affable nature: "He's easygoing, easy to get along with. When times are down, he'll probably make a joke and make fun of you. Instead of getting all fired up, you have a tendency to laugh. He's a good-natured person and now we have to go out there and play for him."

Asked if it mattered that Little was known as a "player's manager" more than a drill sergeant–type, Lowe said, "I don't think this team needs a tough manager. With the new guys we have, I think we'll be able to police ourselves no matter who we have."

When it came to self-policing, ridding the team of players like miserable Carl Everett didn't hurt, nor did bringing in guys like his replacement in center field—free agent signee Johnny Damon. A great base stealer and productive bat at the top of the order, he was also immediately popular among teammates and fans as a fun but hard-nosed athlete willing to play hurt. Those players who had been with the Sox for

‡‡An interesting twist on the firings of Duquette and Kerrigan so close together was that Duquette, then GM of the Montreal Expos, had given Kerrigan his first major league coaching job in 1992.

several years like pitcher Tim Wakefield could already feel a big difference around the club with the new owners and manager.

"This group of guys came in and did a complete 180 degree turn," Wakefield says, looking back. "They wanted to change things—and change them in the right direction with what was best for the players. We had roundtables where we could discuss things; they were interested in what our needs were, so it was a more direct line of communication with the ownership group versus the way it was before."

The roundtables were one of Lucchino's ideas, something he had tried successfully in Baltimore and San Diego. He felt it was important for players to have the chance to air their concerns and grievances with ownership, and that it was a win-win situation; the players felt empowered and better able to do their job for the team and each other, while the owners had a better handle on what their employees did and didn't like.

"From a player's standpoint, there was definitely a different aura, a different chemistry," Wakefield says. "We felt as players that maybe we were turning the corner here."

One thing the owners vowed not to change was the special relationship the Red Sox enjoyed with the Jimmy Fund. The affiliation between the team and the charity, which supports cancer research and care for pediatric and adult patients at Boston's world-renowned Dana-Farber Cancer Institute, had existed since 1953 and was the most unique team-charity partnership of its kind in all of North American sports. Beginning with Ted Williams, Red Sox players had for a half-century visited patients at Dana-Farber, located less than a mile up the road from Fenway, and helped raise millions for the cause through personal appearances, public address announcements, and events. A Jimmy Fund billboard above the right field grandstands was for several decades the only advertising Tom Yawkey allowed in Fenway Park, and the Jimmy Fund's longtime chairman was former Red Sox second baseman Mike Andrews of the '67 Impossible Dream team.§§

Given Lucchino's history as a cancer survivor and former Dana-Farber patient, it was only natural that the partnership between the two organizations continue. In another move that showed their interest in expanding the horizons of the team, the owners announced the establishment of the Red Sox Foundation to focus on philanthropy in the areas of health, education, athletics, and urban social issues. In a classy gesture, the foundation's first public action was a $150,000 donation during spring training to the Joey Fund, which fights cystic fibrosis in the memory of Joey O'Donnell—who died of the congenital lung disease at age 12 and was the son of their former bidding rival Joe O'Donnell.

Getting the post-Yawkey era at Fenway off to a memorable start was another priority, and here a team approach came into play. Sam Kennedy, a former baseball teammate of Theo

---

§§ The Jimmy Fund was originally the official charity of Boston's "other" major league team—the National League's Boston Braves. Started in 1948 with the help of Braves players, who visited a 12-year-old cancer patient of Dana-Farber founder Dr. Sidney Farber as a nationwide radio audience listened in (the boy was dubbed "Jimmy" to protect his privacy), the Jimmy Fund over the years would become known as "New England's favorite charity." When the Braves announced their move to Milwaukee in 1953, Braves owner Lou Perini appealed to his Red Sox counterpart Tom Yawkey to take on the Jimmy Fund—and Yawkey complied. Today both the Perini family and Yawkey Foundation are still staunch supporters of the charity and cancer center.

Epstein's at Brookline High who had worked alongside his childhood friend for Lucchino in San Diego, was another of the California-to-Boston transplants taking a new position with the Red Sox—in his case, as vice president of corporate partnerships. Kennedy thought that creating a huge American flag as big as the left field wall, and then unfurling it on the Green Monster during pregame ceremonies on Patriots' Day, would wow the fans. Charles Steinberg agreed, but with one exception: the flag would also make a Green Monster appearance on Opening Day.

The problem, of course, was finding someone to make a flag approximately 37 feet high and 220 feet long in two months. Amazingly, Sarah McKenna found a company just six blocks from Fenway that could meet the request, and the super-duper Stars & Stripes was ready for the opener. Once it came down, and a short chant of "USA! USA!" passed through the crowd, the drama continued as Boston native Steven Tyler of the rock band Aerosmith crooned the first National Anthem of the year, and 25 members of the New England Patriots—just coming off their first Super Bowl championship—emerged from behind the flag clad in jeans and uniform jerseys.

Led by quarterback Tom Brady, who wore a big smile and a glove like a little kid in sports heaven, the Patriots walked across the field to throw out 25 simultaneous first pitches to their Red Sox counterparts. Pats safety Lawyer Milloy thrust up the Lombardi Trophy earned with the NFL championship, and the crowd exploded in sustained cheers. Fans were encouraged to lead a countdown to the throws—"3–2–1!"—and immediately after they were completed, the loudspeakers began blasting out U2's "Beautiful Day" as football and baseball players embraced. The Pats tossed balls into the crowd before descending into the Red Sox dugout, the starters for the Sox ran out to their positions, and everybody from John Henry to the guy in the last row of the bleachers took a moment to savor the sheer joy of it all.

Four hours later, after the Red Sox had blown a three-run lead in the late innings of a 12–11 loss to Toronto, the question remained for Henry and his compatriots Werner and Lucchino to ponder:

How long would it be before they were celebrating a *baseball* championship at Fenway?

4. SHAPE OF THINGS TO COME

IF THE FIRST STEPS TOWARD A NEW RED SOX ownership group and front office team were taken when Larry Lucchino visited Fenway Park in 1986, it was a move made a little over a decade later that proved the springboard to the revamped roster that would give Lucchino and his colleagues the opportunity to make history.

Back in the summer of '97, then Boston general manager Dan Duquette was presiding over an underachieving ball club. Just two years removed from an AL East Championship, the Red Sox were scuffling along under .500 and far closer to last place than first. Other than sensational rookie shortstop Nomar Garciaparra and power-hitting first baseman Mo Vaughn, Boston fans had little to be excited about. The pitching staff was in especially sorry shape; the departure of free agent Roger Clemens to Toronto the previous winter had left the starting rotation without an ace, and when Boston did manage to build a late-game

lead, it was often in jeopardy due to closer Heathcliff Slocumb's wildness.*

Besides these on-field problems, the Red Sox endured
challenges away from the diamond. Vaughn was in the last
year of his contract, and negotiations between the front office
and its top slugger were not going well. Vaughn's normally
gregarious mood turned sour as he and Duquette began
clashing in the newspapers, but this negative press was nothing compared to that garnered by Boston outfielder Wil Cor-
dero. Expected to be a strong contributor to the offense, he
was arrested for allegedly assaulting his wife in June and
played only sporadically the rest of the year before being released.

It was clear by mid-season that this troubled team had no
realistic shot at the postseason, so Duquette took the logical
step of trying to build for the future. The first major opportunity to do so was the July 31 trade deadline, when contending
teams traditionally look to trade young but still raw players for
veterans that might make a difference down the stretch. The
last thing a sub-.500 team needs in August and September is
a closer, so when Slocumb got hot just as the deadline neared,
it offered Duquette the perfect opportunity to move him.

The Seattle Mariners, then battling for first place in the
AL West, seemed to present a perfect trade partner for Bos-

---

*Perhaps no single game was more emblematic of the team's frustrating
1997 season than that of July 12, when Clemens—whom Duquette had
stated was "in the "twilight of his career" and not worth his salary
demands—pitched at Fenway for the first time as an opposing player and
struck out 16 in a 3–1 Toronto win. Clemens, who glared up at Duquette's
box as he left the mound, would go on to win 21 games and pitching's
Triple Crown for Toronto.

ton. Loaded with elite talent like Ken Griffey Jr., Alex Rodriguez, Edgar Martinez, and Randy Johnson, the Mariners
lacked the type of lights-out reliever considered crucial for a
deep playoff run. Slocumb, back on pace for his third straight
30-save season and still in possession of a strong slider and
fastball, could fit the bill.

This was the logic Duquette employed with Mariners GM
Woody Williams, and Woody went for it—even after Slocumb blew a ball game at Kansas City late on the night of
July 31. Before Williams had much time to reconsider, the
Red Sox sent the disappointing right-hander to Seattle,
where he resumed struggling and eventually finished the year
0–9 with a 5.16 ERA and a new legion of miserable fans. In
return, Boston got a pair of promising minor leaguers—a lefty
pitcher and a switch-hitting catcher—whose value would become clearer a bit down the road.

That night the phone rang in the Florida home of Donna
and Ed Varitek, a few miles outside Orlando. It was their
son, Jason, telling them that he and Derek Lowe—his teammate and batterymate on the Triple-A Tacoma Rainiers—
had just been told to get off the team bus rather than head to
another Pacific Coast League outpost. "They told us to wait
for future orders, because we were no longer property of the
Mariners, we were now property of the Red Sox," Ed remembers his son telling him. Was Jason upset? "Not at all,"
says Ed Varitek. "He said this might be the best move for
him, because Boston was a great organization."

The deal, father and son both knew, also offered the
younger Varitek a better chance at a starting job in the majors. Jason wasn't slated to be a regular anytime soon with
Seattle, since the Mariners already had an established catcher
in Dan Wilson, who was still in his prime. The Red Sox,

however, had no clear incumbent at the position, and by the very next year Varitek was splitting duties in Boston with Scott Hatteberg. One year after that, in 1999, he was an everyday star—slamming 20 homers and 39 doubles for a playoff team while suiting up alongside his old Georgia Tech and Olympic teammate Garciaparra.

Varitek's success was not totally unexpected—he had, after all, earned the Golden Spikes Award as the nation's top amateur baseball player in 1994—but his talent had never come easily. Born in Detroit, he was a grade school hockey goalie about to join his first travel team when his father got a new job that sent the family to Florida. Here baseball was king, and Jason and his three brothers traded in their skates for cleats. Soon his parents began waking up each morning to the thumping sound of Jason throwing a ball against the side of the house and practicing the quick, tricky bounces he'd get as a catcher. Not a natural at the position, he worked doggedly to make himself proficient behind the plate, since he loved being part of the action on every play. This was the case in football too, where he was an option-running quarterback and even kicked for Lake Brantley High School.

The traits that would make Varitek a great leader and pitcher's confidant with the Red Sox—his tremendous work ethic, durability, and dedication to focusing on each day's opponent—were already becoming apparent. As a high school senior he turned down a college football recruiting trip to West Point, a guaranteed fun weekend for any teenage athlete, because he had a feeling he was going to be concentrating on baseball the next year and didn't want to waste the school's time. His diamond skills were strong enough to secure Varitek an offer from the Houston Astros, but he opted for college when his parents showed him with the help of an income tax form just how fast Uncle Sam, new car payments, rent, and the lack of an undergraduate degree could eat up a $100,000 bonus.

Varitek was expected to back up at Georgia Tech as a freshman, but when the catcher ahead of him didn't make grades Jason seized the opportunity and started 61 of 68 games. In leading their team to the 1994 College World Series, .400 hitters Garciaparra and Varitek batted first and third respectively in the Yellow Jacket lineup, with another future Red Sox—outfielder Jay Payton—holding down the cleanup spot. By the time Varitek signed a pro contract in 1994, he was a three-time All-American worthy of Seattle's number one draft pick. It is a measure of the respect he holds in school history that Varitek's No. 33 remains the only number retired by Georgia Tech.

Even after turning pro, Varitek remained a student. A few credits shy of graduating, he returned to Tech after his first summer in the minors to finish off his management degree. Once that was complete, his parents would still notice him bringing home piles of papers to study, only now it was scouting reports on pitchers and hitters his team would soon be facing. He was always looking for an edge, another quality that ingratiated him to coaches and teammates—especially his own club's pitching staff. The hard work paid off, and just a few months after his trade to Boston, the Detroit native made his major league debut for Boston at his "first" hometown park of Tiger Stadium and delivered a pinch single as his family looked on.

By 2000, with Varitek firmly entrenched as Boston's starting catcher and Heathcliff Slocumb out of the majors, the other participant in that trade had also emerged as a stand-out performer. Derek Lowe, after initially serving as a middle reliever and spot starter for the Red Sox, became an All-Star closer who led the American League with 42 saves that summer. Not a prototypical bullpen ace who simply blew the ball past batters, he employed a terrific sinkerball that messed with batters' timing and induced grounder after grounder.

Many of Lowe's saves that year came at the end of games started by a pitcher considered to be baseball's best—another pickup by Duquette that was paying off big-time. Pedro Martinez had earned the National League Cy Young Award in 1997 for the Montreal Expos, just a few years after Dodgers officials predicted the 5-foot-11, 170-pound kid brother of their ace Ramon Martinez was "too skinny" to make it as a starter. Having long since proven them wrong, the proud hurler from the Dominican Republic had a year left on his contract and at age 26 was just entering his prime. Duquette knew small-market Montreal was in no position to meet Martinez's likely asking price, so he pounced, swapping the Expos minor league hurlers Carl Pavano and Tony Armas Jr. for Martinez and then signing the young ace to a six-year contract extension worth $75 million.

He would be worth every penny. Martinez had three "out" pitches—a fastball that topped out at 98 miles per hour, a devastating curve, and a deceptive change-up—that along with pinpoint control made him impossible for batters to outthink. He also had intelligence that shone through his slow, controlled English, and intense charisma on the mound that endeared him to Boston fans. He pumped his fist after strike-outs and looked and pointed skyward after completing a big outing, not simply to show up the batters (although he certainly enjoyed that), but also because he truly loved what he was doing. So did the crowds, who packed Fenway to the bursting point from his very first home start, a 12-strikeout, complete game win against Seattle in April 1998.

By that summer, even if someone arrived at Fenway having no idea who was starting that day's game, he or she could deduce the hurler merely by looking at the stands filling up with Dominican flags, horns, and K cards that fans would wave after each Pedro punch-out. Many of these revelers were themselves Dominican, mostly young men who had not spent time at Fenway before, but were now coming up regularly from Latino neighborhoods in Massachusetts, Rhode Island, and beyond to see their hero in action. It was a more diverse crowd than the old ballpark had ever experienced for baseball, and the type of electric connection between demonstrative fans and an emotional player that was reminiscent of the bond shared by Fenway patrons with beloved Cuban pitcher Luis Tiant in the 1970s.

After warming up to the harder-hitting American League with a 19–7 campaign in 1998, Martinez put together back-to-back seasons that defied description because there was simply nothing with which to accurately compare them. Even the deified name of Sandy Koufax was inadequate, for while Martinez's statistics in 1999–2000 were Koufaxian on the surface—a combined record of 41–10, 597 strikeouts in 430 innings, an earned run average well below 2.00—they were even more impressive when lined up against his contemporaries. Koufax outpitched Hall of Fame rivals like Bob Gibson and Juan Marichal in the 1960s, but Martinez simply *annihilated* the field. In 2000, his 1.74 ERA was so far ahead of the runner-up (old pal Roger Clemens, at 3.70), it was like

Pedro was pitching in his own stratosphere.[†] Like Yogi Berra once joked about Koufax, the question wasn't how Martinez won 18 games that year, it was how he managed to lose six.

If Martinez was Boston's answer to Sandy Koufax, Tim Wakefield was its 21st century Phil Niekro.

Like Niekro, who carved out a 318-win, Hall of Fame career throwing primarily knuckleballs, Wakefield used this gravity-defying pitch to confound American League batters and serve as the yin to Pedro's yang. While Martinez was blowing away opponents with near-triple-digit heaters, Wakefield was tossing them 68-mile-an-hour lollypops—a disparity in styles that could be particularly frustrating to hitters who faced them both during the same series (or even, on occasion, in the same game if Wakefield was pitching in relief).

Another big difference between them was that while Pedro had always been envisioned as a pitcher by scouts, Wakefield was once coveted for his bat more than his arm. A hard-hitting first baseman at Florida Tech, where he still holds school records with 22 homers and 71 RBI in one season, he was drafted as an infielder by the Pirates but struggled with a .189 average and no power in the minor leagues. The organization was meeting to discuss his possible release when a scout named Woody Huyke said he had seen Wakefield throw a decent knuckleball while goofing around—and that the team might consider grooming him to be a right-

---

[†] Taking this a step further, in 2000 the average ERA for all American League pitchers was 4.91, more than three full runs behind Martinez's 1.74. In 1966, when Koufax posted an ERA of 1.73, the NL average was 3.61. Clearly, Martinez was even more dominating than Koufax.

handed pitcher instead. Figuring they had little to lose, club officials decided to give it a shot.

The knuckler is at once baseball's most confounding and precarious pitch. Thrown from the fingertips, with little power behind it, it comes in at the batter with virtually no spin (the less spin the better) at speeds of just 60–70 miles per hour—25–30 miles per hour slower than most other pitches. At this speed and flatness it is easily impacted by the elements and can dart about unpredictably as it approaches the plate, making it very difficult to hit (or, in many cases, catch). Sometimes, however, it doesn't move at all, and in these cases it is essentially a "slow ball" that batters can crush into the next county.

Successful knuckleballers are those who can get lucky with the pitch more often than not, and this good fortune comes from self-confidence and repetition. Wakefield's conversion from infielder to pitcher began in 1989. He found almost immediate success in his new role, as he did three years later when called up to the majors in mid-season. Baffling National League hitters with an 8–1 record and 2.15 ERA over two months, he added a pair of complete game victories against the Atlanta Braves in the NLCS. Wakefield looked like the next coming of Phil Niekro, but the following spring his pitches stopped darting and he struggled to a 6–11 record with a woeful 5.61 ERA. Things got even worse in 1994 when he went 5–15 for minor league Buffalo, again allowing close to six runs an outing. Pittsburgh cut him loose the next April.

This is yet another instance of deposed Red Sox GM Dan Duquette making a great decision in a situation where others would not have taken a chance. Duquette scooped Wakefield up six days after his release, and after a few tune-up appearances at Pawtucket he won 10 straight starts for Boston in 1995 and was an incredible 14–1 with a 1.65 ERA during his first three months with the team. He fell a bit to earth after that, but still finished with an impressive 16–8 record to help the Sox win the AL East.

Wakefield had been pitching in Boston ever since, but his role was never quite the same from one season—or even one month—to the next. Because throwing a knuckleball causes very little strain on a pitcher's arm, he needed less rest between appearances than other hurlers, and was soon being called on in long relief, short relief, and even on occasion as a closer. Such is the beauty and danger of the knuckler and its unpredictable nature that at times Wakefield had stretches almost as dominant as in his first Red Sox season, while on other occasions he found himself throwing meatballs right into a batter's wheelhouse.

In 2002, with Lowe leaving his closer's role to join Martinez in the rotation and two additional starters picked up in John Burkett and Frank Castillo, Wakefield would prove invaluable to the club as a swing man splitting time as a starter and long reliever. Helping him in both capacities was a player who took Boston by storm that summer with a great blend of power and speed at the top of the order—as well as the type of dark good looks that made him particularly popular among female fans.

Known as a fun-loving guy who enjoyed skateboarding to the ballpark, Johnny Damon had spent the previous season with an extremely tight-knit Oakland A's team that partied its way to a 102–60 record. He was surprised that guys on the Red Sox didn't play more cards in the clubhouse or head out in packs to nightclubs on road trips, and he vowed to do what he could to loosen up his new mates—starting with carrying a boom box onto the team plane.

As a former AL stolen base champ still good for 25–30 swipes a year at a very high success rate, Damon also offered a refreshing change for a team long known as among the slowest in the majors. His speed enabled him to outrun balls hit into Fenway's deep-center-field triangle—420 feet from home plate—thus saving far more runs with his glove than he occasionally let in with his weak throwing arm. He could hit with 15-homer, 40-double power at or near the top of the order, and would see time in both of the first two slots during 2002.

Flanking Damon in the Boston outfield were two players who gave off completely different vibes to the Fenway fans. Right fielder Trot Nixon was a country boy from Wilmington, North Carolina, the well-mannered son of a doctor, drafted by the Red Sox out of high school in 1993 with a reputation as a gamer with a great attitude. The scouting reports, then general manager Lou Gorman recalled later, predicted that "this guy could be a leader. He was a type of guy who could be a mainstay on your ball club, give you 100 percent every day on the field. All the things about his makeup were so impressive that you said to yourself, this is the kind of guy you want on your club." Nixon was also heavily recruited as a college quarterback, but he transferred all of his toughness from the gridiron to the diamond after signing with Boston.

The reports proved right, as Nixon worked doggedly in the minor leagues to improve in whatever areas the coaching staff imparted. He got his first two major league hits on the last day of the 1996 season, at age 22, and battled difficult back injuries over the next several years to become Boston's regular right fielder and average 26 homers and 91 RBI over the 2001–02 seasons. His uniform and cap were always dirty, usually after the first couple innings, and he played the tricky vast regions of right field at Fenway with style—often making sliding or diving catches near or even in the stands. Popular with teammates and fans, he was seen as a team leader who got the best out of his ability and never dogged it.

On the opposite side of the outfield was a ballplayer who was Nixon's polar opposite: Manny Ramirez. A city kid all the way, Ramirez had moved to the United States with his family from the Dominican Republic at age 13, and spent his teenage years living in a high-rise apartment building just a few miles from Yankee Stadium in the gritty north Manhattan neighborhood of Washington Heights.[‡] He began grabbing attention and headlines in New York's daily newspapers as a senior at George Washington High who hit 14 homers in 22 games—including one 400-foot bomb that he reportedly struck one-handed after an ump failed to acknowledge his raised back arm as a request for time. Major league scouts routinely showed up at his games, along with people of all ages from the mostly Dominican neighborhood who saw him as the embodiment of their own dreams for success in the United States.

Ramirez's high school coach and reporters who covered him during this period say he was a very determined athlete, the type who would awaken at 4:30 A.M. and run up hills with an automobile tire tied to his waist in order to increase his foot speed (a favorite Dominican training method). He was already displaying some of the flakiness that would become his trademark—forgetting to show up to a team photo, for instance—but his talent was undeniable. Baseball was his

---

[‡] As a player at George Washington High, Ramirez could see the lights of Yankee Stadium from his school's home field.

ticket out of the tenements and his singular focus in life. By the end of his senior year, during which he turned 19, he had dropped out of school and signed a $250,000 bonus with the Indians.

While Nixon worked his way up methodically through five years in the minor leagues, Manny skyrocketed to the majors within two and was runner-up for Rookie of the Year. He had 31 homers and 107 RBI his sophomore season, along with a .308 average, and from 1998 to 2000 *averaged* .324 with 42 homers and 144 runs batted in per year—even though injuries limited him to just 138 games per season over the span. Twice, in 1995 and '97, his booming bat helped Cleveland to an American League pennant.

In watching Ramirez play, however, it didn't take fans long to notice something that power stats didn't always show. Somewhere along the way, long before signing his eight-year, $160 million contract for Boston, Manny apparently lost his tire-pulling drive. He often seemed to be taking it easy during games, stroking line drives deep into the outfield corners and jogging to second base with a double—when in some cases a hustling runner like Nixon might have stretched the same hit into a triple. One Boston sports talk radio host, Mikey Adams of WEEI, still points to Ramirez's suspiciously low triples total (20 over 19 seasons) as proof of his uninspired play.

On defense, Manny could be at varying times amusing and frustrating. After making a fine running catch on one play, he might later in the same game (or even inning) bobble or misjudge a ball as it bounced toward him off the left field wall. In an incident that went viral online, he once ran full-tilt at the outfield fence in Baltimore while pursuing a fly ball, caught it over his shoulder, scaled the wall after the grab to high-five a front-row fan, and then spun and threw the ball into second to complete a double play. His laughter and "What Me Worry?" demeanor surrounding these adventures irked the coaching staff far more than teammates, who claimed they loved the guy and were apparently willing to look the other way as long as he kept producing.

Sporting long dreadlocks and baggy pants, Ramirez seemed to be a 30-year-old kid playing among men, and like a petulant teenager challenged authority by begging out of the lineup with undetectable injuries and declaring his need to make emergency family visits to the Dominican (prompting sportswriters to come up with quips like "Manny's grandmother died again"). While in Cleveland his attitude prompted Indians manager Mike Hargrove to first make the declaration that his superstar's actions were just an example of "Manny Being Manny," and after sporadic usage over the next several years this catchphrase caught fire upon the slugger's arrival in Boston.[§]

Colorful athletes like Ramirez, Damon, and Martinez were tremendously popular with Red Sox fans, but when it came to achieving iconic status among the Fenway faithful, nobody could match Nomar Garciaparra. The shortstop was considered one of three elite performers then manning the position in the major leagues—Derek Jeter of the Yankees and Alex Rodriguez of the Rangers being the others—and Garciaparra's Cooperstown-worthy early seasons had former Boston players like Johnny Pesky and even the tough-to-

---

[§] The first time the "Manny Being Manny" phrase made the newspapers, according to one article, actually related to an off-the-field incident. Ramirez forgot about cashing a rather hefty paycheck, and it was later found by his clubhouse stall—inside one of his boots.

please Ted Williams gushing about his once-in-a-generation talent.

Garciaparra was a Southern California native with a Mexican background and hard, angular features that made him look like he could have walked right out of Boston's North End. His unique name—that of his father, Ramon, spelled backward—was perfect for leather-lunged fans to scream at Fenway Park, and the Boston-accentified variation of "NOMAH!" quickly became the subject of T-shirts and bumper stickers. A popular recurring sketch on *Saturday Night Live* during this era centered on a teenage couple from the Boston area named Sully and Denise who were huge fans of "NOMAHHHHH!" In one episode they even got to meet their hero when Garciaparra made a cameo appearance, a brief foreshadowing of another Red Sox–obsessed character that Sully actor Jimmy Fallon would portray down the road, this time on film.‖

Nomar was no great shakes as an actor, but as a ballplayer he was Oscar-worthy. He had a beautiful swing and a graceful stride that in both cases reminded old-timers of Joe DiMaggio, the last right-handed hitter to win back-to-back batting crowns before Garciaparra's eye-popping .357 and .372 titles in 1999 and 2000. Like DiMaggio, Ted Williams, and other supreme batsmen of yesteryear, he managed to hit 20 or more homers a season while keeping his strikeout totals low, even though he was notorious for swinging at the first pitch. In the field he was not quite in Jeter's and Rodriguez's class at getting to balls, but his accurate, from-the-knees

---

‖Fallon's film character was Ben Wrightman, the Sox–crazed fan and main protagonist of *Fever Pitch*—filmed during the 2004 season at Fenway Park.

throws on grounders deep in the hole were regular sightings on *SportsCenter* and other highlight shows.

The primary spokesman for the team at charitable events and the runaway leader in endorsements, Nomar was probably the most revered Red Sox player since Carl Yastrzemski had retired twenty years before. As with Yaz, kids throughout New England copied his elaborate set of rituals at the plate—which included stepping out of the batter's box to tap his helmet and pull up his batting gloves before each pitch. Youth baseball coaches would regularly chastise their players for "going Nomar" at the plate, although many of them did the exact same thing in their over-40 leagues. If fans in 2002 were asked which current Red Sox player had the best chance to make the Hall of Fame and have his number retired to the right field facade at Fenway, Garciaparra would have been the consensus choice.

This was the core group that new manager Grady Little had to work with when he took over the team for the 2002 season. Since the purchase of the franchise had not been made official until late February, there was little time for Lucchino and interim GM Mike Port to do anything major in terms of tweaking the roster. The biggest new additions brought in by Dan Duquette during his last days were Damon in center field and Tony Clark, a fine slugger with the Tigers, at first base. While the former would prove a wonderful asset and the latter a bust, the biggest keys to a successful 2002 season would be keeping Garciaparra, Varitek, and Martinez healthy and having Lowe—replaced as closer by Ugueth Urbina—make a smooth transition to being a full-time starting pitcher.

For a while, despite the wild 12–11 setback in the home opener at Fenway, it looked like the first team of the post-Yawkey era had the goods to accomplish what had eluded

Tom, Jean, and John Harrington's clubs during the previous 70 years. Lowe pitched a no-hitter in April (the first at Fenway since 1965), Pedro was back to his dominating self, and Garciaparra and Ramirez shined as a one-two power source in the middle of the lineup. Boston was 24–8 entering play on May 11, the best record in baseball, but Manny broke his left index finger that day and the Red Sox went just 21–19 in his absence to fall into their familiar second-place spot behind the Yankees.

Ramirez's return in late June sparked another strong stretch for the team, highlighted by a 22–4 win over Tampa Bay on July 22 in which Garciaparra celebrated his 29th birthday with three homers and eight runs batted in. But an August slump by the Sox enabled New York to widen its lead, and in the end the Yanks cruised to their fifth straight AL East title while Boston finished second—10 and a half games back—also for the fifth consecutive time. The 93–69 record by the Red Sox did mark an 11-game improvement from 2001, but an unusually unbalanced American League featured four teams with at least that many wins, denying Boston a spot in the playoffs for a third straight year.

Despite missing postseason play, it had been an encouraging first year for Little and the new owners. Garciaparra and Ramirez each finished with more than 100 RBI, Manny's .349 average led the American League, and Nixon, Damon, and Varitek all turned in fine seasons. More balanced than previous Boston teams, the Red Sox finished second in the AL in batting and runs scored and third in pitching, thanks in large part to Lowe (21–8) and Martinez (20–4)—the first 20-game-winning duo for the Sox since 1949.

These impressive stats, along with the selection of seven Boston players to the All-Star team, masked the real Achilles' heel of the club: the bullpen. Sox relievers went 15–22 with 17 blown saves in 68 chances, and the team's record in one-run games was a dismal 13–23. All-Star Urbina's 40 saves did not accurately portray his season; when things were tight, he and his mates in the pen had wilted too often. Even normally friendly Fenway Park couldn't help Boston in the close ones, for although the Sox had a .630 winning percentage in road games, they were barely above .500 on Yawkey Way.

Off the field, the owners fulfilled their promise to do everything in their power to modify the ballpark so it could be saved from the wrecking ball. They got started before the '02 season even began by adding a combined 400 seats at various spots throughout the park, as well as 10 new food and beverage stands to help clear up congestion. A more dramatic change came early in the campaign when the wire fencing separating bleacher seat patrons from the rest of the park was torn down—allowing every ticket holder freedom to roam the park at will. It was as if the third-class passengers of the SS *Fenway* were finally being allowed to stroll around the first-class deck.

"We wanted people to be able to wander in and out and circumnavigate the ballpark," says Lucchino. "In the previous ballpark we had built in Baltimore, and the one we designed in San Diego, the notion of moving around the ballpark was an important consideration and an important element of what we thought fans would want and enjoy. So when we came here and saw this gigantic wire fence, it came down quickly."

Later in the year, there were other opportunities for fans

bearing tickets to boldly go where few had gone before—onto the field at Fenway.

The Red Sox held their first-ever Father's Day Catch at the ballpark, during which patrons at that Sunday's contest could stay after the final out and enjoy a game of catch on the hallowed Fenway grass. A similar opportunity was presented in August, when, for a sizable charitable donation to the Red Sox Foundation, fans could spread out a blanket and picnic on the field just like Tom and Jean Yawkey had done a half-century before. The difference was that the Yawkeys had done it in an empty ballpark, their only companion a radio with which to listen to Curt Gowdy describe a Red Sox game on the road. This was a less intimate affair, but also more memorable to fans who never imagined they would be on the other side of the green fences surrounding the Fenway playing field.

These one-day events were very popular, and would become annual affairs, but the biggest change came on September 5. On that afternoon, Yawkey Way—which, formerly known as Jersey Street, had fronted the ballpark and its main entrances since 1912—was turned into an in-game concourse area. Portable fences and turnstiles at the corner of Yawkey Way and Brookline Avenue assured that only ticket holders could now traverse the street for two hours before as well as during games. Patrons would no longer be relegated to spending every moment at Fenway confined within the walls of the actual ballpark, and in the days to come visitors to Yawkey Way could feast on a giant Cuban sausage from El Tiante's Grille (and maybe meet legendary pitcher Luis Tiant himself); watch pre- and postgame TV reports live from behind a NESN soundstage, and sometimes even get on the air if they could leap in front of the roving cameras; shop in Twins Souvenirs (which would be renamed the Yawkey Way Store) without fighting through huge postgame crowds; and let their kids enjoy the juggler, face painters, brass band, stilt walker, and other family-friendly attractions.

Helping fans around the new amenities was a group of smiling, red-jacketed "Fenway Ambassadors," ranging in age from college kids to retirees, who would become fixtures at the ballpark. The park, long praised but little utilized beyond its role as a playing field, was becoming an entity unto itself—one that fans could enjoy and the owners could use to generate additional revenue. Year-round tours of Fenway, which were first started in the mid-1990s, were expanded so that participants had the opportunity to sit in the Red Sox dugout, walk atop the Green Monster, and look behind the left field door to see the dark, dank room where scorekeepers worked their metal-plate magic.

A few things the new guys tried did not work. Promotional giveaways, which Steinberg had used in Baltimore and San Diego to draw bigger crowds, were met with suspicion rather than excitement by jaded Red Sox fans worried about the "outsiders" coming in and trying to win them over. "In 2002, we figured a player-themed T-shirt or hat would be very well received, and we wanted to have Nomar, Manny, and Pedro T-shirt nights," recalls Steinberg. "We started with Nomar, and people were admonishing the people giving them out, saying things like, 'What are you trying to do here? If I want a shirt, I'll get it across the street [at Twins Souvenirs].' They were actually not taking the free shirts."

What went a long way in winning over skeptics at the turnstiles was how Steinberg and his colleagues responded to one of the saddest events in Red Sox history. On July 5, 2002, fans at Fenway for that night's game against the Tigers were asked to rise and observe a moment of silence for Ted Williams, who had died at age 83 earlier in the day. Over the next several weeks, a macabre drama played out in which Williams's two younger children had his body transported from Florida to a cryogenics facility in Arizona and then frozen, supposedly at his request, to be regenerated at a future date. His oldest daughter disputed the move, as did many of his former friends and teammates, as something Williams would never have wanted, and this fracas combined with a tasteless string of related jokes appearing in the print and broadcast media threatened to sully the memory of a legendary war hero, humanitarian, and hitter.

Then came what was billed not as a memorial but a "celebration" of Williams's life, held at Fenway on July 22. Under three huge photographs hanging above the Green Monster he once guarded in left field—showing Ted in his roles as a fighter pilot in two wars, a pioneering champion of the Jimmy Fund of Dana-Farber Cancer Institute, and as the greatest player in Red Sox history—a two-part event took place. During the morning and afternoon, fans were invited to roam through the silent ballpark and observe a series of artifacts depicting Williams's incredible life, including his Hall of Fame plaque brought in from Cooperstown. Then, in a poignant evening ceremony, former teammates and friends sat casually in lawn chairs on the field and shared their memories of Williams for a crowd of about 20,000.

Little touches, like the "9" lovingly carved into the left field grass and adorned with flowers by head groundskeeper Dave Mellor, and the "USMC" imprinted on second base to honor Ted's status as a Marine, were clear signs that the new regime understood just how special this icon, the Red Sox franchise, and its history were to the fabric of New England.

As former Williams teammates like Johnny Pesky, Dom DiMaggio, and Earl Wilson strode out to their positions on the diamond, joined by current players like Garciaparra and the opening music from *Field of Dreams*, it was as if one era at Fenway was ending and another beginning.¶ More than 40 years had passed since Williams homered in his final Fenway swing—a moment captured on the video screen as a spotlight shone down on the pitcher's mound and the very man who had delivered the pitch in 1960, former Orioles hurler Jack Fisher—but Boston baseball was at last entering the modern, post-Yawkey era.**

Of course the new owners could not truly distinguish themselves until they returned the team to the postseason and accomplished what the Yawkeys could not by winning a world championship.

To identify and bring aboard players who could help with this goal, president Lucchino and his partners wanted a sea-

---

¶ Although Ted's left field successors—Carl Yastrzemski and Jim Rice— were among those who took the field during this portion of the ceremony, that position remained empty out of deference to Williams. Once all the players were assembled, they walked as a group to left field and lit candles at the "9" floral arrangement.

** The video footage shown at the event of Williams's final home run was yet another dramatic touch at the ceremony. It was not the stock black-and-white version of the hit fans had seen countless times, but a color movie shot by a fan at Ted's last game that had never been shown publicly before. "A fan approached us with it, and we thought it was wonderful; it gave you a glimpse into that historic moment as seen by people who were there, including Ted waiting in the on-deck circle rubbing down his bat," explained Charles Steinberg.

soned pro with a proven track record to step in as general manager. Interim GM Mike Port had filled the role capably for the 2002 season, but his title and lack of experience—he had been Duquette's assistant for nearly a decade, but never a GM—made him an unlikely contender for the permanent position. For this Boston brass zeroed in on a man considered by many to be the greatest baseball mind then working outside of a dugout: Oakland A's general manager Billy Beane.

Despite the challenge of having one of the smallest payrolls in the major leagues at his disposal—$39,679,746, compared to $108,366,060 for the Red Sox (second-highest in the game) and $125,928,583 for the Yankees (first—naturally), Beane found enough gems among lower-salaried players through trades and free agency to lead the A's to 100 victories in both the 2001 and 2002 seasons. His philosophy involved seeking out players with strong intangibles like patience at the plate and an ability to get on base, rather than gaudy "traditional" stats like 30 homers or 100 RBI. The technique, which came to be known as Moneyball, would eventually become the subject of a bestselling book of the same name by Michael Lewis and a movie starring Brad Pitt.

The Red Sox had for decades employed the old method, stacking their lineup with players who regularly churned out 30/100 seasons at hitter-friendly Fenway, but they had just four American League pennants and no world championships since 1918 to show for it. Lucchino was willing to try the new approach, and fans and sportswriters enjoyed speculating about what Beane could do with nearly three times as much cash to spend on players than he had in Oakland. He had matched the Yankees with 103 victories on a shoestring budget in 2002; certainly he could outmaneuver them if given the chance to compete on much more equal financial footing.

Getting his man would be a challenge for Lucchino. Beane had signed a long-term contract with the A's, meaning that Oakland ownership was not required to grant the Red Sox an interview with him. Lucchino, who loved a good legal challenge as much as a good ball game, pursued the matter relentlessly—treating it like a case that could be won by cunning and determination. He interviewed other candidates, and J. P. Ricciardi, GM of the Toronto Blue Jays and once an assistant to Beane, got a lot of attention in the media as a possible hire. Ricciardi decided to stay put in Toronto, however, and it became clear that the man in Oakland was always Boston's first choice.

The A's finally granted the Red Sox permission to talk with Beane, provided Boston was willing to pay the standard compensation fee of a few players of fair market value if he took the job. Take it he did—at least for a few hours. After the two sides had apparently agreed on a contract for five years and $13 million, the largest deal ever given a GM, Beane changed his mind and like Ricciardi opted to remain in his current post. Beane cited "family reasons" as the key factor in his decision; as a divorced dad with a young daughter who lived on the West Coast, staying put would allow him to see her more often. Perhaps the drive to finish what he started in the Bay Area was a reason as well.[††]

Out of this disappointment came a series of decisions that

[††] Beane was still in Oakland through the 2013 season, and although his 17-year tenure has included eight 90-win seasons, he has yet to win an American League pennant.

would, like the Varitek and Lowe trade of five years before, go a long way in determining the fate of the Red Sox franchise.

The first came when Lucchino, Henry, and Werner ended their external hunt and turned to a very familiar face as Boston's new senior vice president and general manager. Theo Epstein had met Lucchino and Charles Steinberg when, as an 18-year-old summer intern, he first came to the Orioles in 1992 after his freshman year at Yale. He had impressed the two executives with his maturity, baseball acumen, and an idea he had for honoring the history of Negro League baseball as part of the MLB All-Star Game festivities at Camden Yards the next July. He saw that project through to fruition, and the three had worked under the same masthead ever since—for three years in Baltimore, seven years in San Diego, and now in Boston.

"After a thorough and extensive search of candidates throughout baseball, we concluded that the right person was right before our eyes," Lucchino said at a Fenway Park news conference on November 25. Tom Werner added, "Our common goal is to bring a world championship to Boston. Irrespective of his age, we are confident Theo is among the best and brightest in baseball. We believe that the team he'll assemble will achieve results for which we so yearn."

Although he had never previously held a GM post, Epstein was certainly no novice to major league front offices. His roles had rapidly grown over time, from a member of the media relations staff in Baltimore to director of player operations with the Padres and then to assistant general manager with the Red Sox, and while most people assumed he was being groomed for an eventual shot at the GM job in Boston, few imagined it would come this soon. At just shy of 29, he was the youngest to ever hold the position in Major League

Baseball history. Reporters began referring to Epstein as "The Kid" almost immediately after his appointment, but he had the poise of a veteran; with his handsome features and cool, confident demeanor, he looked equally at ease addressing reporters at a press conference or playing guitar in a charity rock band.

For those covering the team, it was a welcome change. Dan Duquette had been just 36 himself when he took over the GM post in Boston back in 1993, and like Epstein was a local boy made good who had grown up rooting for the Red Sox. Duquette possessed the strong work ethic, passion, and intellect needed for the role, but his history-professor glasses and awkward, at times strained relationship with media representatives—a key part of the job in baseball-obsessed Boston—often made him appear uncomfortable and aloof. Had he and Epstein squared off in a reenactment of the 1960 televised presidential debates, Duquette would have played the haggard and uncomfortable Richard Nixon, Epstein the self-assured and dashing Jack Kennedy.

Like Kennedy, albeit on a much smaller scale, Epstein's family history was one of both privilege and pedigree. His grandfather Philip and great-uncle Julius wrote the Oscar-winning screenplay for *Casablanca*; his father, Leslie, ran the Creative Writing Program at Boston University; and his sister, Anya, penned episodes of Emmy-winning TV shows like *Homicide: Life on the Street*. Born in New York City, Theo had moved with his parents at age five to Brookline—a suburb about a mile from Fenway Park—in the fateful Bucky (Bleeping) Dent year of 1978. This seemed fitting, for Epstein's formative years were spent living and (mostly) dying with the Red Sox through some of the worst near-misses in their history.

Perhaps the best illustration of Epstein's early devotion was a story he told about the October night when he and his twin brother, Paul, had watched Game 6 of the 1986 World Series as 12-year-olds home alone in their family's apartment. After Boston went up 5–3 in the 10th inning, the boys planned to leap off the living room couch and into the air precisely as the final out of the series was recorded a few minutes later—thus allowing them to experience their first moments of joy while in suspended animation. Three Met runs and one Bill Buckner error later, the long night ended with them still waiting on the couch. They never got the chance to jump off it in Game 7, either.

Now Epstein was making the biggest leap of all. While his brother kept a low-key profile as a social worker, guidance counselor, and girls soccer coach at their alma mater, Brookline High School, Theo was taking on one of the highest-profile positions in New England—and one of the most scrutinized. He had a sense of what he was getting into, having grown up watching the heat that then Red Sox general manager Lou Gorman came under in newspapers, on talk shows, and around water coolers for trades like Jeff Bagwell for Larry Andersen.[‡‡] Just as a politician made decisions that carried the potential to directly impact citizens and businesses

---

[‡‡] The Bagwell for Andersen swap was made on August 30, 1990, as Boston was pushing for its third AL East title in five years. GM Gorman sent Bagwell, then a minor leaguer with six career home runs, to the Houston Astros for veteran reliever Larry Andersen. While Andersen helped Boston to the East title with a 1.22 ERA in 15 games, the Sox were swept in the ALCS by Oakland, and Andersen (a free agent) signed with San Diego after the season. New England native Bagwell debuted with the Astros in 1991, was named NL Rookie of the Year, and went on to hit 449 homers for Houston.

within a region, Epstein knew that the moves of the Red Sox GM could have a profound effect on the psyche of New Englanders—and in many cases their financial livelihood as well.

Reporters pontificated on Epstein's youth with jokes and stinging barbs, just as they had criticized Henry, Werner, and Lucchino a year earlier as the "outsiders" and "carpetbaggers" who knew nothing of Boston baseball history or how to run a big-market team. Epstein was called everything from "Wonder Boy" to "The Rookie" in newspaper headlines; trying to lighten things up, Epstein's father joked that "At his age, Alexander the Great was already general manager of the world." Still the jokes continued.

Boston Herald sports columnist Steve Buckley, however, wasn't jumping on the bash-the-kid bandwagon. He had seen too much in more than four decades of watching the Red Sox—first as a born-and-bred fan, then as a reporter—to rush to judgment.

"I was thrilled by it. He talked a good game and he just seemed sharp," Buckley recalls of the surprise announcement of Epstein's hiring. "He struck you as a guy who was going to work 70 hours a week.

"Nothing the Red Sox had done in 85 years had worked. Why not bring in a 28-year-old kid?"

5. COWBOYS DO CRY

Kevin Millar was no more a cowboy than he was an astronaut, but sometimes such details don't really matter—especially when they get in the way of a good story.

The 2003 Red Sox were starting a crucial 12-game homestand when Millar, a fiery first baseman and team leader picked up that winter from the Florida Marlins, uttered the phrase that would become a rallying cry for the team and season.

"Derek Lowe left a game with a blister after six innings, and we lost to the Oakland A's," Millar recalls. "At that point we were just a game behind the A's for the Wild Card, and there were still six weeks left in the season. We went into the locker room, and there's 50 media guys all over Derek Lowe. I kind of cussed a little bit at them, and I said 'Get your ass over here!' so they all came over to my locker.*

---

*Lowe had shut out the A's on two hits over six innings when he developed the blister, which left him unable to throw a sinkerball—his best pitch. Reliever Scott Williamson gave up a three-run homer to Ramon Hernandez in the seventh, and Oakland won, 3–2.

"I said 'Listen, y'all just need to appreciate the group of guys that are in this clubhouse. We're not a 1980s team, we're not a 1970s team, we're not a 1990s team. We're just a bunch of guys that appreciate being here and play as hard as we can.' And then at that point, I just kind of said 'Y'all need to f***ing cowboy up!'"

His comments, Millar says today, "came out of nowhere"— just the angry rantings of a guy sticking up for his teammate and sick of people speculating in print and on the street about when this team was going to choke like so many Red Sox clubs before it. When one reporter asked him exactly what he meant by "cowboy up," Millar was truthful. "I don't know," he said. "It's just a bunch of guys who fall off their horse but get back on." What could have been a throwaway phrase caught fire, and the rush to assumptions began.

"In my bio [in the Red Sox media guide], it said I 'reside in Beaumont, Texas,'" Millar explains with a laugh. "So obviously cowboy up, Beaumont, Texas, redneck, hillbilly, everybody starts putting it together. Soon we have cowboy hats and country music in Boston and everybody thinks I own a big ranch and drive a horse for a living. Really I grew up in Los Angeles, with fake teeth and highlights in my hair. I didn't *live* in Beaumont, I *resided* in Beaumont. That's where I went to college, so we had a house there. I didn't have a horse. I lived in a neighborhood with a quarter-acre lot."

Millar may not have kept a saddle in his garage, but one thing was certain about the first roster put together by the front office group nicknamed "Theo and the Trio"—the 2003 Red Sox had more fun, more success, and more giddy-up in their step than any Boston club in a generation.

The first moves in this transformation took place in the days and weeks immediately after Theo Epstein was named general manager on November 25, 2002. "We're going to become a championship organization and win a World Series," Epstein said with confidence at his first press conference, and later added that he was sure there was room in his parents' den for a World Series trophy to sit alongside the Oscar his grandfather and great-uncle had won for the screenplay to *Casablanca*.

Many experts—and fans—were skeptical as to whether an unproven 28-year-old deemed "Boy Wonder" by a combative media corps could deliver on such a promise. Epstein emphasized in his opening address that it was going to take a group effort, and the Red Sox assembled a richly diverse and knowledgeable brain trust to help with the task and (hopefully) quiet the naysayers.

The first to come aboard was Bill Lajoie as special assistant to the general manager in scouting. The consummate baseball lifer with nearly a half-century of professional experience entering 2003, Lajoie had put in 28 of those years—as long as Epstein had put in on earth—serving with the Detroit Tigers in a variety of roles including general manager. He was the architect of a great 1984 Tigers club that led the AL East wire-to-wire en route to a World Series title, and most recently had been special assistant to GM John Schuerholz of the Atlanta Braves, one of the past decade's most successful and respected franchises.

"I remember Theo telling me that Bill Lajoie is 'in my extreme inner circle, and I like that he disagrees with me,'" says the *Herald*'s Steve Buckley. "If you like being disagreed with, in my opinion, that's the mark of a good leader."

Lajoie was actually one of *three* former general managers on Epstein's incoming staff. Lee Thomas, GM of the Phillies from 1988 to 1997 (including the NL pennant winners of '93) was also tapped to be a special assistant to Epstein, and Theo's predecessor, Mike Port, would be available for counsel as vice president of baseball operations. Port's professionalism in handling a potentially sticky situation—having one of his top lieutenants suddenly become his boss—went a long way in making Epstein's first months on the job run smoothly. Since Port had served for nearly a decade under former GM Dan Duquette, he could offer plenty of advice on how to handle the pressure of being a local kid running the Olde Town Team. Josh Byrnes, who had served the previous three years as assistant general manager with the Colorado Rockies, would fill the same role with Boston and focus on personnel decisions, negotiations, scouting, and player development.

On the opposite side of the spectrum from these "baseball lifers" on Epstein's incoming crew was senior adviser Bill James. The author of a widely popular collection of books that looked at the game and its history from a research-oriented perspective known as sabermetrics, James had never played professionally and with his gangly build and scruffy beard looked like he belonged in a computer lab rather than the front office of a major league team. Once again the jokes began, along the lines of the Red Sox bringing aboard a geek who played baseball board games to help run their team.

In reality, however, James was an ideal hire.[†] The father of

---

[†] James had a surprisingly similar background to his boss's boss. Like John Henry, James was born late in 1949, grew up on a farm, and became a baseball fan by listening to Harry Caray broadcast St. Louis Cardinals games over the radio. Just as Henry used batting averages and other statistics to develop the keen analytical math skills he would later use to become a billionaire commodities trader, James began crunching numbers from the game at an early age and loved the process so much he found a way to make it into an enjoyable (and, after some lean years, lucrative) career.

sabermetrics understood better than anyone that certain offensive and defensive statistics—including many he had devised himself through decades of trial and error—were far better than others in measuring past and predicting future player performance. Assembling lineups that could be as productive as possible both at Fenway Park and on the road was a key goal for Epstein, who had seen many Fenway-focused Red Sox teams filled with All-Stars fail in the past because they couldn't win away from home. James could help find the missing pieces by looking past the big numbers at players whose "win shares" and "runs created" numbers were the best fit for Boston.

Epstein's first shot at a high-profile signing, however, focused on a player for whom no prior minor or major league statistics were available. When Cuban pitching ace Jose Contreras defected from his homeland and announced his intentions to play in the majors in December 2002, the only numbers teams had to go on were those he had compiled pitching for the Cuban national team. Still, scouts who had seen him play raved about his skills, projecting the 31-year-old to be a number one or number two starter, so Epstein and Lucchino set out to get him for Boston. Their biggest rivals in doing so were the only MLB franchise for whom money was truly no object—the New York Yankees.

Bombastic New York owner George "The Boss" Steinbrenner was no big fan of Boston's new president, dating back to the days when Lucchino, then with the Orioles and Padres, voted against Steinbrenner on a variety of economic and player personnel issues that cost the Boss money. Once Lucchino took on the top job in Boston, Steinbrenner saw an opportunity to get back at him on the biggest stage. Even though Epstein flew to Cuba and joined Boston's director of international scouting, Louie Eljaua, in an all-night meeting with Contreras during which they enjoyed cigars with the pitcher and felt they were close to signing him, the Yankees wound up getting the right-hander for four years and $32 million in a deal announced in time for Christmas.

"The evil empire extends its tentacles even into Latin America," Lucchino told Murray Chass of *The New York Times* for an article that prompted numerous Steinbrenner-as-Darth-Vader illustrations on the front and back pages of the *Times*'s tabloid rivals, as well as on fan Web sites devoted to both teams. Although Lucchino added that the Yankees were "formidable adversaries, make no mistake," the lightsaber had been thrust. Steinbrenner responded by claiming Contreras actually turned down *more* money from Boston because he wanted to play for the Yankees, and told the New York *Daily News* that Lucchino was "not the kind of guy you want to have in your foxhole." The war of words took some of the pressure off Epstein for not signing Contreras, but heated up the Red Sox–Yankees rivalry to a new level before a single pitch of the 2003 season had been thrown.

By the time Boston took the field on Opening Day, March 31, Epstein managed to make quite a few changes in the wake of the Contreras affair. He let 40-save closer Ugueth Urbina leave as a free agent and on the advice of Bill James opted for a "bullpen-by-committee" in which any number of relievers— new signees Mike Timlin, Ramiro Mendoza, and Chad Fox, among others—might be called upon to finish off a ball game. Urbina's gaudy saves total had hidden the fact Boston's pen was a weakness in 2002, so Epstein was willing to take the risk. The starting staff, strong up top with Pedro Martinez, Derek Lowe, and John Burkett, and with Tim Wakefield ever ready as a swing man, was primarily left alone once the Contreras deal fell through.

Hard-hitting outfielders Johnny Damon, Manny Ramirez, and Trot Nixon were all back, as were Jason Varitek and No-mar Garciaparra at catcher and shortstop. In an effort to have a lineup capable of providing firepower from top to bottom, however, Epstein brought in several new infield faces. Doubles-machine Todd Walker replaced light-hitting Rey Sanchez at second base, steady pro Bill Mueller took over for undisci-plined Shea Hillenbrand at third, and first base and designated hitter were put up for grabs among a group that included Hillenbrand, Jeremy Giambi, Minnesota Twins castoff David Ortiz, and Kevin Millar. Although Epstein was enamored of Giambi and his high OPS (on base percentage plus slugging) of .919, compiled in part-time duty for Oakland and Philadel-phia the previous year, it was Millar who would wind up getting the most preseason press.

A favorite of John Henry, for whom he had played in Flor-ida, Millar was a scrappy athlete who called himself "a real blue-collar player" and whose value as a positive force in the dugout and clubhouse went way beyond his .296 lifetime av-erage. After the Marlins traded for up-and-coming first base-man Derrick Lee prior to the 2003 season, thus projecting Millar out to be an expensive part-time player on their roster, they swung another deal to sell Millar to the Chunichi Dragons of the Japan Central League for $1.2 million. It was seen as a great move for all involved, since Millar would get a two-year, $6.2 million contract with the Dragons and an op-tion for a third year—a far bigger contract than he'd likely get were he to stay in the majors (where he made $900,000 in 2002).

The only snag was that such a move required the player in question be put on waivers. This meant that any of the 30 MLB teams could put in a claim for the player, with the team with the worst record getting first chance to sign him. Epstein was also a Millar fan, so although he knew such a move could be seen as breaching baseball etiquette—since the Marlins and Dragons had worked hard to make the deal happen, it was assumed teams would just go along out of courtesy—Theo put in a claim. It was a bold move for the new kid in town, and it paid off.

"I was like 'Wait a minute, I want to stay in the States to play for the Red Sox,'" recalls Millar of finding out about Epstein's bid. "Japan wouldn't let me out of the deal, and suddenly you're on the phone every night at different hours because of the whole time change thing, trying to work it out. The president of the Japanese league flew into New York and we needed to meet with him. It was an honor thing with them. The guy who signed me said he was going to kill himself if I broke the deal. The whole thing was crazy.

"I was thankful that the Red Sox fought for me for six weeks. Thank goodness that John Henry had been with Florida because at some point, Kevin Millar is not that great of a player to be this big of a headache. We had a relationship, and I think he understood the intangibles I brought to a team enough that he thought 'Hey, we'll keep going after this guy no matter how bad it gets.'"

In the end, the three teams involved worked out a compromise. The Marlins returned $1.2 million to the Dragons, the Red Sox paid $1.5 million to the Marlins (including $300,000 in tickets for underprivileged Florida youth, a portion of it paid by Millar), and then the Sox signed Millar to a two-year, $5.3 million contract with an option for a third year. "The best news," Millar says, "is that the guy who signed me for the Dragons didn't end up killing himself. I saw him a few years later and he was fine."

Millar was officially purchased by the Red Sox from the Marlins on February 15, just in time to make the start of spring training by driving 1,000 miles all night in the rain from his Beaumont, Texas, home to his new team's training camp in Fort Myers, Florida. By the time he arrived, fortified by an estimated 15 vanilla coffees and inundated with cameras and reporters in the parking lot, he had barely slept in a day and a half. Still, he was all smiles. "It's unbelievable," Millar said of being with Boston. "It's definitely a dream come true, and that's the honest to God truth."

That Millar pushed himself to arrive punctually, and that he would wind up winning the first base job outright, was no surprise given his background. This was a guy who appreciated what he had because it had not come easily. A Los Angeles native who admittedly "wasn't that good until my junior year of high school," he impressed folks enough to make the team at L.A. City College, a two-year school, and then earn a scholarship to Division I Lamar University in Beaumont. Continuing to grow, he led Lamar in homers and runs batted in during 1992 while helping spark a 14-win improvement for the team, the best turnaround of any NCAA school.

For MLB clubs, it was not enough.

"I wasn't a big-toolbox guy with all the size and speed, but I thought maybe I'd get drafted in the middle rounds after my senior [1993] year at Lamar," he recalls. "We won the Sun Belt Championship and I had been a three or four hitter, but I didn't get drafted at all. At that point I was bummed out, thinking 'What do I do now?' I wasn't done playing baseball."

As luck would have it, that summer of 1993 was the inaugural season for the Northern League, then the only independent, unaffiliated professional baseball circuit.[‡] Not directly connected with major league franchises, independent teams give undrafted players a chance to showcase their talents and hope an MLB club takes notice. Millar's college coach helped arrange a tryout for him in St. Paul, Minnesota, and Kevin wound up making the St. Paul Saints. "It turned to be one of the best summers in my life," says Millar, who made $600 per month during the season. "We won the championship there, and that was when the Marlins bought my contract and I had the opportunity to go on to spring training with them."

Millar would endure five more minor league seasons and a broken bone in his left hand that sidelined him for most of one year before he finally earned a regular big-league job with Florida in 1999. He would use the long apprenticeship as a motivating force the rest of his career. Even when he didn't play as much as he wanted with the Marlins, he made the most of his opportunities, hitting .314 and .306 in 2001 and 2002 and becoming a favorite of teammates, coaches, and fans. This was the type of player Epstein and the Red Sox front office staff were looking for—character guys who played the game hard and well even if their numbers didn't scream off the page.

David Ortiz was another one. It's hard to imagine after a decade of Hall of Fame–caliber seasons that Big Papi was once seen as an underachiever, but that's exactly what the Twins thought of him when they released Ortiz after the 2002 season. The 6-foot-4, 230-pound Dominican Republic native had put together some monster seasons in the minor

---

[‡]While the Northern League had previously operated from 1902 to 1971, it had been dormant since then.

leagues for Minnesota, but in parts of six years in the majors had peaked at 20 homers and 75 RBI in 2002. Ortiz did show flashes of the power and toughness that would come to define his later career in Boston, including one 400-foot homer he hit in Kansas City in 2001 after breaking a bone in his right wrist earlier in the game. Asked after an MRI confirmed the break how he had managed the feat, Ortiz explained simply that he had to hit because "there was a man on third and one out. I hadn't had an RBI in like a week."

The pressure to produce, Ortiz would explain later, was the biggest problem he faced during his time with Minnesota. Even after he had made the big-league team and spent a full year in the majors, he felt he had to have a great spring training to make it again. He never believed he had the full support of management or the Twins coaching staff, which he says tried to change his sweeping left-handed swing so he would hit more homers. Three big stints on the disabled list in four years with wrist and knee surgeries didn't help, nor did playing his home games on the artificial turf of the Metrodome—which wreaked havoc with the big man's knees. Only twice in this period did he reach more than 400 at-bats in a season.

Even after he helped the Twins reach the ALCS with 32 doubles and his first 20-homer season in 2002—despite missing almost a month after surgery to remove bone chips in his left knee—Minnesota management didn't see Ortiz as part of the team's future. After trying unsuccessfully to trade him (his age and sizable contract didn't help), they released him on December 16, shortly after his 27th birthday. For more than a month, any major league team could have signed him as a free agent. None did.

Then Pedro Martinez, who had faced his Dominican countryman often enough in the majors to know what he could do, sold Ortiz's case to the powers that be in Boston. Big Papi could slam balls off and over Fenway's left field wall with regularity if given the chance, Martinez insisted, and Epstein decided it was worth making an offer to Ortiz's agent, Fernando Cuza. According to Tony Massarotti of the *Boston Herald*, the Yankees also had an interest in signing the man who would become their biggest tormentor, but Ortiz chose the Red Sox because he wisely surmised that he had a better shot at regular playing time if the primary man to unseat at first base and DH was Jeremy rather than Jason Giambi.[§]

One of the things that appealed to Epstein about Ortiz, as with Mueller and Millar, was his oversized personality. Despite all the frustration he endured in Minnesota, he was very popular with teammates and seen as a clubhouse leader. "In girth and mirth," Tom Verducci wrote in a *Sports Illustrated* profile, "Ortiz evokes Babe Ruth, Santa Claus, and your favorite stuffed animal from childhood . . . a 230-pound Teddy Bear who speaks like a California surfer with a thick Spanish accent." This would be a fun guy to have around, Epstein figured, even if he didn't play every day.

It was Kevin Millar (at first) and Jeremy Giambi (at DH) who were in the starting lineup, and not Ortiz, when the Red Sox faced the Tampa Bay Devil Rays in their first game of the 2003 season. Despite seven sterling innings from Martinez, Epstein's biggest nightmare scenario ensued when the bullpen-by-committee allowed five runs in the bottom of the ninth—the last three coming on a two-out, game-winning

---

[§] While the Giambi brothers combined to hit 490 homers in the majors through 2013, 438 of those were slammed by Jason—who had 41 for the Yankees in 2003 while his younger sibling was notching just five with the Red Sox.

homer by Carl Crawford off Chad Fox. "I know what a big deal has been made about the committee, and there will be even more now," Fox said after the game. "I'll take it. We'll take it. Because I know what kind of guys we have down here, and I know we'll get the job done."

Fox was right on the money. For although the bullpen experiment would continue to be problematic in the weeks and months to come, this Red Sox team displayed a never-say-die attitude and camaraderie that enabled it to rebound quickly from setbacks. The first case in point came just the next day, when Boston blew another late lead against Tampa Bay but wound up grinding out a 9–8 win on a home run by Millar in the 16th inning.

Fans who made it to Opening Day at a cold, wet Fenway Park a week later were treated to a fantastic pregame show when Lou Rawls sang the "The Star-Spangled Banner" and Ray Charles belted out "American the Beautiful" on a piano near home plate. Everybody in the ballpark was doing double- and triple-takes as they looked out to left field, where 174 "Monster Seats" were being installed to replace the net atop the left-field wall—39 feet above the playing field. The view would cost fans $50 a pop for a reserved seat, $20 if they wanted one of the 100 standing-room admissions.

The home opener wound up being rained out, but the Red Sox would heat up along with the weather. By May 26, when Tim Wakefield bested Roger Clemens in front of 55,000 at Yankee Stadium, they were 31–19 with a two-and-a-half game lead over the Yanks in the AL East. The vaunted offense Theo and the Trio had put together was doing its part, scoring more than six runs a game, and strong starting pitching led by Wakefield and others was making up for the bullpen struggles and nagging injuries to Martinez and Lowe. Mueller was smoking the ball while splitting time at first, designated hitter, and the outfield, and six other regulars were batting close to or above .300. Only Giambi (.198) was not carrying—or even hitting—his weight, and when the team ran into a dry spell that stretched into June he was relegated largely to pinch-hitting duty.

Epstein continued tinkering, trading Hillenbrand to Arizona for relief pitcher Byung-Hyun Kim on May 31. The move raised eyebrows since Hillenbrand was a young, productive .300 hitter and Kim was most famous for blowing back-to-back saves in the 2001 World Series against the Yankees, but Theo felt it solved two problems: the logjam at first base and designated hitter and the lack of an experienced and effective closer. Despite his playoff struggles, Kim had rebounded as a closer in 2002, and also had experience pitching middle relief and even starting—which he would do for the Sox while Lowe and Martinez returned to full health.

Hillenbrand, for all his promise and production (he was 10th in the AL in RBIs at the time of the trade), was an undisciplined hitter who did not follow the Red Sox edict of working counts and tiring out opposing pitchers. He also didn't fit the good guys/good karma atmosphere in the clubhouse, seen as more of a "me-first" type of player. Epstein had always envisioned trading Hillenbrand for pitching depth when he had the chance and necessity, which is why he had signed Mueller as a possible replacement for him at third. This was the opportunity he had been waiting for, and he took it.

The move, like the majority Epstein made in his first two years as general manager, worked well. Kim started five games during June, pitching well, and then stepped into a new role as Boston's closer. The bullpen-by-committee experiment was largely scrapped, and Kim would go 6–4 with 16 saves and a 2.28 ERA from July through September. Opponents hit just .193 off him, and he blew just three saves. Fellow relievers like Timlin, Fox, Alan Embree, and Scott Williamson were all now able to pitch where they were most effective, and the return of Lowe and Martinez to the rotation boosted a shaky starting staff that was largely ineffective beyond these two and Tim Wakefield.

The real story of the 2003 Red Sox, however, was their hitting. Statistically, fans had never seen anything like it.

Boston led the major leagues in batting average, runs scored, on-base percentage, and slugging percentage, setting MLB records in all but the first category.[‖] They also had 238 home runs, shattering the former team standard of 213 set back in 1977. Balance was the key to the onslaught; eight Red Sox players had 85 or more RBI, six had 25 or more home runs, eight had 30 or more doubles, and four regulars hit .300—led by league leader Mueller at .326 and runner-up Ramirez at .325. One memorable Friday night in June, the Sox scored 14 runs *in the first inning* of a 25–8 victory over the Marlins at Fenway, including 10 runs before the Marlins could record a single out. A few weeks later, after getting picked up from the Colorado Rockies, reserve outfielder Gabe Kapler immediately caught the bashing bug by going 7-for-9 with two homers, two doubles, a triple, and seven RBI at Fenway in his first two games in a Boston uniform.

The biggest surprise about Boston's amazing offense was who joined Ramirez as one of the club's two 30-homer men.

‖ Boston's team slugging percentage of .491 topped the old standard of .489 set by the most immortal offense of them all—the 1927 "Murder's Row" Yankees of Ruth, Gehrig, and Co.

Playing sparingly, David Ortiz was jokingly dubbed "Juan Pierre," by his new teammates when he entered June with two home runs—an average season's total for Pierre, a speedy singles hitter for the Marlins. Ortiz accepted the ribbing good-naturedly, but told his agents he wanted them to find a way to get him traded.[*] Then the Hillenbrand-for-Kim deal, Millar's outstanding production and solid defense at first base, and Jeremy Giambi's continued struggles and wrist injury in late June combined to open up a spot for Ortiz at DH, and Big Papi ran with it—hitting 27 home runs in just 75 games from July through September. His final totals of 31 homers and 39 doubles helped him to a .592 slugging percentage, third-best in the American League and right in front of teammates Ramirez (.587) and Trot Nixon (.578).

The calls to his agents to arrange a trade stopped. Thriving under the pressure and the attention, Ortiz was now one happy Papi.

"I love the fans here," Ortiz said after hearing chants of "M-V-P! M-V-P!" in the latter stages of the 2003 season. "It doesn't matter what time you walk onto the field down there, you have people screaming at you and wishing you the best. That puts you in a situation that you want to go up there and perform and do your best."

Just as impressive as the production turned in by Ortiz and his teammates was the team's emerging personality. This was perhaps the most endearing Red Sox club since the young Impossible Dream team that came out of nowhere to capture

[*]Ortiz told the "Juan Pierre" story in his autobiography, *Big Papi*. He still had only four homers entering July, but wrote that after he hit five in a three-game stretch near the start of the month, "nobody in the clubhouse was calling me Juan Pierre anymore."

the AL pennant back in '67 behind a mix of rookies, retreads, up-and-comers, and superstar Carl Yastrzemski. The 2003 bunch, unlike the Dreamers, had been expected to contend, and were doing so with star-quality players who also possessed big personalities like Ortiz, Damon, Millar, and Ramirez. As a group, they seemed to have great fun with the game and each other.

Fondness for the team beyond the box scores really took off after Millar's "Cowboy Up" comments, which led first to homemade posters in the stands and eventually to bumper stickers, T-shirts, and even boxer shorts Ortiz was caught wearing beneath his uniform. "Cowboy Up" was the title to a song by former minor leaguer Ryan Reynolds that used to play at Angels games in Millar's native Los Angeles, and its lyrics symbolized the team's never-say-die attitude: "Cowboy Up, dust yourself off, get back in the saddle, give it one more try."

It turned out the term was actually trademarked by a Western clothing company, but Wyoming West Designs was happy to work out licensing arrangements with a variety of Boston retailers—and eventually the Red Sox themselves—as demand for items bearing the phrase grew. Eventually there was a "Cowboy Up!" banner hanging from the Massachusetts State House and on the electronic message boards usually reserved for traffic information along the Massachusetts Turnpike.

The "Cowboy Up" message was personified by an unusual number of late-game comebacks and walkoff hits. "That was a very likable team, and the fans never left early," veteran peanut vendor Rob Barry remembers. "Before that I would usually leave after my shift was done, around the seventh inning, but not in '03. That year I starting going back into the stands to watch the end of the games. You never knew what might happen."

On those occasions when the Red Sox needed a late-inning comeback, Barry and other Fenway faithful could count on seeing another staple of the 2003 season—"Rally Karaoke Guy." The "guy" was Millar, who as a teenager had made a home video of himself singing and dancing to Bruce Springsteen's "Born in the USA." A huge hit the first time it was played, the video became required viewing as the season wore on. In a funny coincidence, the real Springsteen and his E Street Band played two sold-out concerts at the ballpark in September, the first-ever rock concerts at the venue.

The debate over Fenway's long-term future had still not been decided, as Lucchino, Henry, and Werner wanted to continue seeing how attendance and revenue could be improved with changes at the venue. There were plenty in 2003.

The most popular alteration was the café-style swivel seats atop the Green Monster. Designed by Janet Marie Smith in a way that made them look as if they had been there all along, the Monster Seats took nothing away from the magic and majesty of Fenway's most famous feature and proved immensely popular with fans. The sight of fans juggling concessions to catch home runs became commonplace, and patrons enjoyed yelling down at Manny Ramirez and other left fielders who took up position beneath them. From the day they debuted shortly after the home opener, the Monster Seats were among the hottest and hardest-to-get tickets in Boston.

Another major (and welcome) change was the Big Concourse, 25,000 square feet of new concession space including numerous food choices and picnic seating beyond the center field bleachers and right field stands. The locale eased congestion throughout the ballpark upon its August opening, which was helpful because additional lower-box seats had also been added—and more fans were piling into Fenway than ever before. On May 15 a capacity crowd of 33,801 saw Pedro Martinez beat the Texas Rangers, and from that point through the end of the season, every game on Yawkey Way was an official sellout. The Sox set a franchise attendance record for the fourth straight year with a total of 2,724,162, which ranked them fourth among the 14 American League teams—quite an improvement from their ninth-place showing during the late 1990s.

The large throngs had plenty to get excited about down the stretch, as the Red Sox battled for their first postseason berth in four years. A 17–9 September including a pair of wins in three games at New York was not quite good enough to catch the Yankees—who finished first to Boston's second in the AL East for the sixth straight year—but the Sox secured a Wild Card berth with several more late-game wins in the final weeks. Boston's 95–67 record marked its most wins since 1986, and set up an intriguing first-round playoff matchup with the AL West champion Oakland A's and general manager Billy Beane, who had taken and then reneged on the GM job with Boston two years before.

Could Theo Epstein and the team he was reshaping in his image beat the guy who could have had his job? Early on, it didn't look like it.

Oakland took the first two games of the best-of-five series at home. Martinez pitched well for Boston in the opener, and the Red Sox had a 4–3 lead heading to the bottom of the ninth, but then the team's biggest problem all year—bullpen breakdowns—became a factor. Byung-Hyun Kim, so strong for most of the regular season, reverted to his 2001 Arizona playoff form with a walk and hit batsman as the A's tied the score, and Oakland went on to win, 5–4, in 12 innings. Game 2 was never that close, as Oakland ace Barry Zito shut down Boston's big bats in a 5–1 victory, and the teams headed to Fenway with the Red Sox in a must-win situation.

Then a funny thing happened. Boston's bullpen corps suddenly found its mojo.

After starters Derek Lowe and Tim Hudson pitched seven brilliant innings in Game 3, leaving the game tied at one, the Sox got three perfect innings from Mike Timlin and one from trade deadline pickup Scott Williamson before Trot Nixon staved off elimination with a two-run, walkoff homer in the bottom of the 11th. As fans sang along to "Dirty Water," a Boston-themed rock song from the 1960s that had become yet another musical standard at Fenway as a post-victory anthem, the atmosphere had the feeling of a title-winning celebration. The Red Sox still trailed the series two games to one, and needed to win again at home and once more in Oakland to move on to the ALCS, but the confidence the team had played with all year had people believing that outcome was very possible.

In the end, they were right. Boston rallied to win Game 4, 5–4, with the help of three and a third more innings of scoreless relief (this time courtesy of Tim Wakefield and Williamson), and then completed their three-game comeback with a 4–3 decision at Oakland's Network Associates Coliseum highlighted by another strong start from Pedro Martinez, a three-run homer by Ramirez, and one more bullpen rescue—a pair of strikeouts by Game 3 starter Lowe with the winning runs on base in the bottom of the ninth. The Yankees had finished off the Twins in the other first-round playoff the previous day, meaning that just like in 1999, the Sox would have a shot at their bitter rivals in the ALCS with a World Series berth on the line.**

Home field advantage, of course, went to the division winners, so the teams met at Yankee Stadium for Games 1 and 2. The "1918" chants and banners were out in full force as Tim Wakefield, who had been kept off the roster for the '99 ALCS because of his unpredictable knuckleball, showed he certainly belonged this time with a terrific start—hurling six two-hit innings in a 5–2 win. Todd Walker, Ortiz, and Ramirez all homered off Yankees starter Mike Mussina, and Alan Embree, Timlin, and Williamson pitched shutout relief. Byung-Hyun Kim, after struggles against the Yankees in the regular season and versus Oakland in the ALDS, was now an afterthought.

The Yankees took Game 2, 6–2, as veteran left-hander Andy Pettitte bested a shaky Lowe, but most fans were already looking ahead to the dream matchup in the third game at Fenway: Pedro Martinez vs. Roger Clemens. When they previously faced one another in the 1999 ALCS at Fenway, "Cy Young" Martinez had beaten his "Cy Old" rival in a 13–1 laugher that was Boston's only win of the series. This time it was the 42-year-old Clemens who got the win, 4–3, in a game that proved more memorable for what transpired in the fourth inning.

New York was hitting Martinez hard, and he tried to get back control by pitching behind Yankee outfielder Karim

---

** A downside to Boston's thrilling Game 5 win in the ALDS was when Johnny Damon and reserve second baseman Damian Jackson collided in pursuit of a fly ball during the seventh inning. Damon lost consciousness, left the field in an ambulance after being revived, and missed the first two games of the ALCS with a concussion. He hit just .200 with one double and one RBI vs. New York.

Garcia. The pitch grazed Garcia in the shoulder, prompting a warning from the umpires, and when Clemens led off the bottom of the inning by throwing a bit too high and inside for Manny Ramirez's taste, the Boston slugger stepped toward the mound, cursing, with his bat in his hand. Both benches emptied, and 72-year-old Yankee bench coach Don Zimmer—who had almost died after being hit in the head by a pitch during his playing days—rushed across the diamond from the New York dugout to confront Martinez. Pedro stepped back, awkwardly pushed Zimmer to the ground, and in doing so pushed this already epic series to a new level of intensity.[††]

Nobody liked seeing an elderly man humiliated in such a way, but the fact it was Zimmer—manager of the '78 Red Sox team that blew a 14-game lead to the Yankees and Bucky (Bleeping) Dent—made it seem almost surreal. New York fans screamed for Martinez's head, even after Zimmer took blame for the incident in a tearful press conference, thus adding even more anticipation to another possible Martinez-Clemens matchup in Game 7 at Yankee Stadium.

"When this series began," said Grady Little after Game 3, "everyone knew it was going to be quite a battle, very emotional, with a lot of intensity, but I think we've upgraded it from a battle to a war."

The dream pairing would indeed come to pass. The Red Sox took two of the next three contests, including another excellent performance from Wakefield in Game 4 (seven innings, five hits, one run allowed) and a gut-wrenching 9–6

[††] As if this wasn't wild enough, Game 3 also featured a fight in the Yankee bullpen before the ninth inning, when three New York players got into a tussle with a member of the Boston ground crew. Karim Garcia, one of those involved, had to leave the game with a cut on his left hand.

decision in a win-or-go-home Game 6 at the Stadium. The bullpen was the star again in this one, as five Red Sox relievers pitched shutout ball over the final four innings while Boston rallied against Pettitte and New York's pen. Epstein and Lucchino had to especially enjoy watching rebuffed recruit Jose Contreras blow the save and the game with a seventh-inning meltdown, and the symbolism of the moment had Sox fans thinking this might finally be the year Boston got the best of New York.

So it came down to Pedro-Rocket III, the winner-take-all Game 7 battle for the right to represent the American League in the World Series. By this point Clemens's photo was already hanging upside down in several Boston bars, his fall from grace secure for defecting to Toronto and then New York after telling Red Sox fans he simply wanted to be closer to his family down in Houston. Beating the "Texas Con Man" in this game, arguably the biggest in the century-long rivalry between the two teams, would be the ultimate payback.

Adding additional drama to the situation, Clemens had announced his intention to retire—making it possible this could be his final game. For Pedro, the pressure was immense for an entirely different reason. Because of the fight with Zimmer in Game 3, he had become a marked man in New York City. One newspaper headline after the incident had labeled Martinez "Fenway Punk."

"I had to leave my family in Boston," Martinez recalled a decade later. "I was under a lot of security, with agents in front of my [hotel] room to protect me. I was really concerned about myself."

His teammates, however, looked loose. In a show of solidarity, and perhaps to distinguish themselves from the well-groomed Yankees—Steinbrenner didn't allow his players to sport beards or long hair—several Red Sox including Millar had shaved their heads. "I'll never forget stretching before the game, hats off, and Joe Torre looking over," said Millar. "He was kind of like, 'Wow.' I think it was the first time the Yankees knew we were at their level.

"It was like, 'We got these guys.'"

Early on, the scoreboard matched their swagger. The Red Sox went up, 3–0, in the second on three hits—including a two-run home run by Trot Nixon—and an error, and added a fourth run when Millar slammed a first-pitch fastball into the left field seats leading off the fourth.[‡‡] Then came a crucial turning point in the game; when the next two batters after Millar (Nixon and Mueller) reached on a walk and hit-and-run single, Yankee manager Torre removed Clemens and brought in Games 1 and 4 loser Mike Mussina.

It was the first time Mussina had pitched relief after exactly 400 starts in the majors, and the situation could not have been dicier. The Red Sox had men on first and third and nobody out, and were threatening to bust the game open. If they could get the lead to 5–0 or 6–0, a distinct possibility given the situation, the Yanks would be all but cooked.

Mussina, however, kept things right where they were, striking out Varitek on a knuckle-curve and then inducing Johnny Damon to hit a hard grounder to short that Jeter smoothly turned into a 6–3 double play. The Yankee captain pumped his fist as he ran off the field, knowing his team was still within

---

[‡‡] Millar's homer was the 11th of the series for the Red Sox, an ALCS record. Clemens would wind up not retiring, finally "going home" by signing with the Houston Astros for 2004—and winning his seventh Cy Young Award with an 18–4 record. He would eventually pitch through 2007, returning to the Yankees for his final season.

breathing distance. Torre's decision to put sentimentality aside and not let Clemens try and work himself off the ropes, despite the fact it might be his last game, had proven huge.

While Mussina rewarded his manager's decision by pitching three shutout innings, the only one in the Yankee lineup who could solve Pedro most of the night was Jason Giambi. He homered in the bottom of the fifth for New York's first run, and then—with his brother Jeremy, inactive for Boston due to shoulder surgery, undoubtedly feeling conflicted—hit another shot with two outs in the seventh to make it 4–2. At this point, Martinez had allowed just four hits and a walk, had notched seven strikeouts, and still had his good fastball. But Yankee Stadium had come to life, and when the next two batters after Giambi singled, pitching coach Dave Wallace came out to talk to Martinez. This was the first time it seemed possible Pedro would come out; he did not, and struck out Alfonso Soriano on a 94-mile-an-hour heater to end the inning.

Martinez pointed to the sky as he left the mound, his usual sign that his work was done. Certainly most people watching the game on TV or in person felt the same way; Pedro had to that point thrown exactly 100 pitches, and it was common knowledge that his effectiveness curtailed sharply after reaching the century mark (opponents hit .215 off Martinez overall that year, but .298 after 100 pitches). Mike Timlin had warmed up during the latter stages of the seventh, so it was assumed that he would come in for the eighth. In the dugout, Pedro put on his jacket and hugged longtime teammate Garciaparra.

There was every reason for Wallace and manager Grady Little to feel confident about their bullpen. Up to that point in the series, Red Sox relievers had compiled a 1.17 ERA, allowing just two runs and a .173 batting average over 15 and a third innings. Jon Tatelman, one of many Red Sox fans who had braved ridicule or fistfights by coming to the game, walked down from his bleacher seat to about 10 rows behind the Boston bullpen so he could get a photo of Timlin coming out to pitch.

But Ortiz homered off David Wells in the top of the eighth to make it 5–2, and with the added breathing room, the decision was made to send Martinez back to the mound to start the bottom of the inning. "When I went out in the seventh, I was told I was done," Martinez attested. "But [reliever Alan] Embree had trouble getting Nick Johnson out. If I could start that [eighth] inning and get Nick Johnson out with two or three pitches . . . Then nobody came out after I got Johnson out."

Rick Swanson, the "superfan" who had exchanged e-mails with Tom Werner and Larry Lucchino since shortly after they took over the team, was in the right field upper deck at Yankee Stadium. He had recently lost his teaching job after 15 years, but had purchased tickets to Game 7 through Werner.

"His last words to me were, 'Bring me back a souvenir,'" says Swanson. "So I took a mini–video camera with me, but in New York back in 2003, so close to September 11, you definitely weren't allowed to bring anything in. So I had to smuggle it in my pants, and my plan was that when the Red Sox won, and celebrated on the mound, I would have an image that I could send to Tom the next day.

"When the eighth inning started, I stood up and yelled full-throttle, 'FIVE, FIVE, FIVE OUTS TO GO!' Then things kind of went downhill."

Tim Wakefield, who was in the bullpen, was also among those surprised to see Pedro back out there. "I thought he was done after seven innings," he recalls. "Normally his telltale sign is that when he pointed to the sky, we knew that he was probably done, so all of us got up and started moving around. Embree and Timlin were up and ready and they sent him back out . . . and then it just happened so fast."

Number nine hitter Johnson sent a weak pop-up to short, and Martinez stayed in to face the top of the Yankee lineup. First was Jeter, who quickly fell behind 0–2 but then doubled over the head of right fielder Trot Nixon—who, possibly misjudging the ball off the bat, had started to his right before backtracking toward the fence. Bernie Williams stepped in, with left-handed Hideki Matsui on deck. Logic dictated that Embree, a lefty, come in to face Matsui, regardless of what Williams did. When Williams lined Pedro's 115th pitch to center for a single, scoring Jeter to make it 5–3, Embree's entry seemed a virtual certainty.

As Yankee fans waved signs like "Cowboy Down and Out" and "DestiNY," and Matsui got ready to bat, manager Little jogged out to the mound and gathered with several infielders around Martinez. Matsui had doubled off Pedro earlier in this game, as well as in Game 3.

"He asked me if I had enough left in my tank," Martinez said later. "I said yes. I never say no. I always want to stay in there. I did what I could. I will refuse to give the ball if you ask me."

Fans, watching from the stands or on TV, saw Martinez nod his head yes several times and cringed. Little patted him on the back and retreated to the dugout.§§

---

§§ Although Little has been almost unanimously derided outside the Boston clubhouse for his decision to leave Martinez in, he may have been thinking about Game 3 of the ALDS—when Pedro threw 130 pitches over seven innings and held Oakland scoreless over the final four frames.

"I can't pinpoint my thinking at that moment, but we'd been hitting and missing with the bullpen all season," Little would explain. "They did a great job in that series, but I'm not just reflecting on two or three games. I'm reflecting on one hundred and seventy. That's where the thinking of stretching Pedro came in."

Larry Lucchino may not have agreed with the decision at the time, but hindsight has made him more sensitive to Little's dilemma.

"The bullpen had been so exceptional that the conventional wisdom makes the decision look like it was a no-brainer," Lucchino says, "but when you have a singular kind of performer and big-game pitcher like Pedro, it was not as much of a no-brainer as many people thought it was."

Matsui stepped to the plate, took two strikes, stepped out to take a breath, and then ripped the ball down the right field line and off the hand of a fan for a ground rule double. The fan interference meant Williams had to return to third (he had reached home easily), but the tying runs were now both in scoring position. Jorge Posada was next up, and Little never moved in the dugout. He was sticking with his ace all the way, despite the fact Pedro was now up to 118 pitches.

Back in the stands, freelance cameraman Kevin Vahey—who worked 40 to 50 Red Sox games per season for NESN, but was at this one as a Boston fan—couldn't believe what he was seeing. He had learned that winter that he and Grady Little were born the exact same day and year, but he felt nothing but disdain for March 30, 1950, right now. If Little had never been brought into this world, maybe Pedro would be back in the dugout where he belonged.

"The Yankee fans around me were all laughing when Little went out to talk to Pedro, and then left him in," recalls Vahey. "I was keeping basic score but not pitch counting. I figured he was getting near or over 100. Can you imagine if there was Twitter back then? It would have exploded."

Throughout New England and beyond, Red Sox fans yelled at Little through their televisions and radios, knowing he could not hear them (and probably just as well, given their choice of words). And in a private suite at Yankee Stadium, where Red Sox senior staff had gathered, the atmosphere was just as heated—and just as loud.

"I was there with John Henry and a bunch of the other owners," remembers Frank Resnek, a Boston baseball fan since the 1940s who had bought a little more than a 3 percent share in the team when the new ownership group came aboard in 2002. "Somebody from the Red Sox came to the suite during the seventh and said, 'Pedro is done this inning,' so we were shocked when he came out for the eighth and couldn't believe he stayed in so long. People were screaming, 'Take him out! Take him out!' It was your worst nightmare come true."

At a darkened Fenway Park, Pam Ganley had gathered in a function room with other younger members of the front office and support staff to watch the game. She recalls that the atmosphere changed "from a feeling early on that you had already won to slowly watching something die. Everybody loved Pedro, so we were torn. It seemed kind of obvious that he was done, but he was *Pedro*. It was surreal, really."

Martinez got the count to 2-and-2, with Posada swinging and missing at a nasty curve, and then induced him to hit a weak flare to shallow center. Three Boston fielders converged on the ball, but if fell between them for a game-tying double. Now, finally, Little came out to get Martinez while the

Yankees celebrated outside their dugout as if they had already won the series.[III]

Did Little leave Pedro in too long? Kevin Millar doesn't think so.

"I will stand by it [Little's decision to let Martinez face Matsui and Posada] until I die," says Millar. "We were all good with it. We had no closer that year; we were bullpen-by-committee. We had Alan Embree and Mike Timlin, but Pedro Martinez is the best pitcher in baseball; if we're going to lose a game, we're going to lose it with our best pitcher. If we bring in Alan Embree or Mike Timlin and there is a walk or, God forbid, a three-run home run, you know the question that Grady would have to answer after that game would be, 'How do you take out Pedro Martinez in Game 7?'"

Any questions would sting far less if the Red Sox managed to win, and they had their chances. After Embree and Timlin finished off the eighth with no further damage, Boston got the go-ahead run to second base in both the ninth and 10th against Yankee closer Mariano Rivera. They failed to take advantage, but Timlin pitched a scoreless ninth and Wakefield—likely to be named MVP of the series if Boston won for his two earlier victories and 2.08 ERA—came on for a perfect 10th. It remained 5–5.

By the time Rivera retired the Red Sox one-two-three in the 11th, marking the first time he had pitched three innings in a game since 1996, the Stadium was rocking on every pitch. "My friend Joe said I became comatose after that, like I lost a lot of energy after the game was tied," says Swanson.

[III] Matsui's tying run meant both teams had now scored 29 times in the series. Counting the regular season, the Yankees led the season series, 13–12. You can't get closer than that.

"He kept saying, 'It's not over!' and I said 'It's over.' But I continued to film the game, pitch by pitch."

As Wakefield warmed up for the bottom of the 11th, FOX-TV cut to a shot of broadcasters Tim McCarver, Joe Buck, and Bret Boone in their booth discussing the game. Forgoing any deep analysis, Boone simply said, "Tell you what, I've just enjoyed watching it." His partners laughed.

A moment later, his brother Aaron—batting .105 for the Series, and in the finale only as a defensive replacement—stepped in against Wakefield. High above right field, Rick Swanson's camera battery died. There would be no victory celebration footage for Tom Werner after all, and no need to worry about it.

On the first pitch of the 11th inning, at 12:16 A.M., Aaron Boone swung and lifted a fly ball to deep left. Before it even landed in the stands, a series-winning home run, Wakefield was walking off the mound and into the Red Sox dugout. Police in full riot gear emerged from the tunnel and passed him just as he turned in toward the clubhouse and what he knew to be his certain fate.

Aaron Boone was the new Bucky (Bleeping) Dent. Wakefield was sure he had just become the new Bill Buckner.

6. AFTER-BOONE PLANS

As Yankee Stadium loudspeakers belted out Frank Sinatra's victory anthem of "New York, New York" and a tearful Tim Wakefield broke down in the visitor's clubhouse, stunned Red Sox fans headed for the stadium exits after Aaron Boone deflated their hopes with one well-timed swing in Game 7 of the American League Championship Series.

It was no walk in the park.

Rick Swanson had a Red Sox sweatshirt on depicting Boston's 1915 World Series champs, which drew plenty of attention as he walked out. "People were taking pictures of me," he says, "kind of like somebody coming out of a fire. It was tough to take."

Kevin Vahey, the Fenway cameraman born on the same day and year as suddenly infamous Red Sox manager Grady Little, had an equally traumatic exit. "I took off my cap and stuck it in my pocket; I could not put up with the taunts," he recalls. "I went to a watering hole in Manhattan where they know me. It was a Red Sox–tolerant club. The bartender looked at me and said, 'You can have whatever you want, and it's on the house. You've been through too much.'"

Jon Tatelman, the bleacherite who had waited in vain to photograph Mike Timlin emerging from the bullpen in the eighth, thought he had disguised himself well by wearing a shirt that only *hinted* of Boston, one depicting his favorite band, the Dropkick Murphys. He got out of the stadium okay, but somebody noticed his shirt on the subway and put two and two together. "He asked me if I was from Boston, and I just said 'yeah,'" says Tatelman. "I didn't want to talk about it; I was stunned. I felt our own manager had taken the game away from us."

Those who had seen the nightmare of Boston's 6–5 loss unfold from afar were equally distraught. Ronni Gordon, a recovering cancer patient watching at home in South Hadley, Massachusetts, with her teenage son, Ben, had grown tired during extra innings and went upstairs—turning on her bedroom television just in time to see Wakefield give up Boone's series-ending homer. The next day she made the 90-minute drive to Dana-Farber/Brigham and Women's Cancer Center for a checkup. Whereas she was used to trading smiles with caregivers and other patients on such visits, that would not be the case on this day.

"As we got into Boston, we saw the newspaper boxes filled with papers that had this front-page headline: DAMN YAN-KEES," she recalls. "Inside the clinic, I sat alongside people with life-threatening diseases, silently hanging their heads. I guessed that at that moment, many were thinking not about their health but about baseball. Dan, an Oakland fan, said he had already mourned his loss. But the normally cheerful Lauren, who had gone to almost every Red Sox home game that season, was unusually subdued.

"When I got home," Gordon continued, "I read an e-mail that my son, Ben, had written at about three in the morning, after the loss: *'I guess I now know what it's really like to be a Red Sox fan. A bullpen ERA of less than 2 is to Pedro what Dave Stapleton was to Buckner.* I'm changing my name to something that doesn't start with a B. I don't want to have anything to do with Babe, Boggs, Bucky, Buckner, or Boone.'"

Buckner. That was the name Wakefield couldn't get out of his head either in those first awful hours after the loss. During the 85 years since the Red Sox last won a World Series in 1918, Buckner—he of the infamous error that ended Game 6 of the '86 Fall Classic—was perhaps the most vilified on a short list of Boston players whose part in poorly-timed miscues led to crushing defeats and decades of unfair ridicule.

Now, after surrendering Boone's shot that allowed New York to advance to the World Series instead of the Red Sox, Wakefield felt certain he was about to join Buckner, Mike Torrez (who gave up Bucky Dent's homer), and the others on Boston's roll call of losers. Despite the fact he had pitched brilliantly in winning two games earlier in the series, one flat knuckleball would be how he was remembered.

"It was heart-wrenching, it really was," says Wakefield. "You know, we felt like we were so close to bringing joy and happiness back to the city of Boston after, at that point, 85

---

* Stapleton had replaced a hobbling Buckner for defensive purposes at first base in the ninth inning of every Red Sox win in the 1986 postseason. In Game 6 of the World Series, Red Sox manager John McNamara let Buckner stay on the field for the Mets' final at-bat, with Boston leading, 5–3. Some speculate McNamara made the move so Buckner could be in the victory photos.

years, but now I'm standing in the same footsteps that Bill Buckner had stood in. I felt like I was going to be the goat. I was worried about that. I was worried about a lot of things."

Wakefield's wife, Stacey, was pregnant with their first child. He had heard the stories about the abuse Buckner had endured in the Boston area after the 1986 World Series, and how he had moved his family to Idaho to get them away from the memories and cruelty. Convinced that Stacey and his future children would be forced to go through a similar ordeal, Wakefield felt powerless to stop the wrath headed his way.

But as he was consoled by teammates in the clubhouse, and later on the bus and plane rides home, sound bites and story lines were already emerging from Yankee Stadium that would make it clear the world—and the Red Sox front office—had other scapegoats in mind.

Grady Little's decision to leave a tiring Pedro Martinez in the game deep into the eighth inning, when the Yankees rallied for three runs to tie the score, was getting far more scrutiny in postgame discussion than either Wakefield or Boone. Pedro was a gamer who wanted to stay in despite the warning signs; Little let him, and Martinez went double-single-double-double to the last four men he faced.

A player's manager all the way, Grady defended his move by praising his pitcher. "Pedro is our man. In situations just like that all season long, he's the one we want on the mound," Little told FOX right after the game. "He made the pitches like he wanted to, the ball just got in a little bit on Posada, and he squeezed it out over the infield. That was the game."

Others would not be as kind.

Dan Shaughnessy of *The Boston Globe,* author of the most

fatalistic Red Sox history of them all, *The Curse of the Bambino,* leveled no scorn at Wakefield but had plenty for Little and Pedro. "The Sox aren't going to the World Series because Grady fell asleep at the wheel and Pedro couldn't perform like a star when it counted," Shaughnessy wrote. His colleague Bob Ryan, while acknowledging there were plenty of additional reasons for the loss, offered similarly stinging commentary: "The problem is that the Pedro Martinez of 2003 is not the Pedro Martinez of 1999. Check that: the problem was that Grady Little thought that the Pedro Martinez of 2003 *is* the Pedro Martinez of 1999."

The *Boston Herald,* the *Globe's* scrappy rival, selected Little's decision to stick with Martinez for 123 pitches as the biggest "dud" of the series, and callers to Boston sports radio talk shows were especially vicious. One went so far as to deem Grady "the worst manager in the history of baseball" despite his 95-win regular season.

New York writers predicted a dreadful future for the Boston skipper. "For Sox manager Grady Little, the derisive chant of '19-18' may echo in his head for the rest of his managing life," wrote Anthony McCarron in the *Daily News.* "Why didn't he take out Martinez and use the bullpen that had been so effective throughout the series? Little could become as much of a rivalry icon as Ruth or Dent. For Yankee fans, anyway." Dave Anderson of *The New York Times* put it more bluntly: "Among improper Bostonians now, Little will be subject to the second guess. Not just today or tomorrow or next week. Forever."

Pedro, heroic in defeat, tried to put the blame squarely on his own tired shoulders.

"I wouldn't put Grady in a spot," said Martinez after the game. "I am the ace of the team. You have to trust me. I wasn't thinking about pitch counts. This was not the time to be thinking about pitch counts.

"There's no reason to blame Grady. He doesn't play the game. We did. I did. If anyone wants to point a finger, point it at me. I gave up the lead. If you want to judge me, curse me for that, I'll take that."

Martinez praised his manager for doing "a great job all season," but it wouldn't be enough. Wakefield, Martinez, and everybody else among the playing ranks would be exonerated for the Game 7 loss, but there needed to be a fall guy—and Grady was it.

Team president Larry Lucchino and general manager Theo Epstein began getting questions regarding Little's job status as soon as the game ended, and while they said all the right things about needing time to fully assess what had transpired, most people assumed that Grady's role with the organization was in serious jeopardy.

They were right. On October 27, just 10 days after Boone's post-midnight homer, the clock struck 12 on Little's two-year tenure as Boston manager. The official word was that he was not being fired, but rather that his contract was up and not being renewed; he was even given $310,000 in severance pay and bonuses on the way out the door. The end result, however, was the same:

Grady was gone.

The decision hit many people in the organization hard, especially the players. They had stuck up for Little until the end, part of a mutual respect between the manager and his men that was apparent in his postgame remarks about Martinez. Grady didn't appear to have a malicious bone in his body, and even when things were at their worst he was thinking about others.

After Game 7, for instance, when he had to know his job was in jeopardy, nobody would have blamed Little if he brooded and kept to himself on the silent team charter home from New York. Instead, he got up and approached Uri Berenguer, a member of the Red Sox Spanish Beísbol Network.

As a teenager receiving bone cancer treatment in the Jimmy Fund Clinic at Dana-Farber a few years before, Berenguer had befriended longtime Sox radio voice Joe Castiglione during his visits to the clinic. Soon he was helping out in Castiglione's booth at Fenway, and by the time Uri graduated from Boston Latin High School he was occasionally getting on the air during games. Now, less than three years later, he had just finished his first full year as the youngest regular broadcaster in the major leagues—and the Red Sox manager wanted to congratulate him on a job well done.

"For the last part of the flight, Grady came and talked with me, commending me on the season," recalls Berenguer. "He was telling me how I had started out right, and to stick with it. We didn't talk at all about the game. As a 21-year-old, that really stood out."

Class had never been the problem with Little, but it couldn't keep him employed in Boston. Lucchino, Epstein, and principal owner John Henry were all quoted as saying the decision to let Grady go was *not* made simply because of his failure to remove Martinez earlier in Game 7, and an official release stated that Henry "took the position well before the postseason that the club may need to question a long-term commitment to its manager." While many fans figured this was just the party line, those close to the situation say there is truth to it.

"One of the most misreported historical facts in Red Sox history, and something that is continuously misreported, is that Grady got fired because of that game," says Steve Buckley of the *Herald*. "That's just wrong."

As proof, Buckley tells the story of when he was covering the 2004 baseball playoffs a year later and fishing for material to use in his pregame notes. Approaching Henry, he jokingly asked him to "tell me something that makes me sound smart." Henry laughed and started to walk away, but then turned back and told Buckley he'd grant his request.

"'What is it?'" Buckley asked.

"The whole thing about Grady Little getting fired because he left Pedro in? That's not true," Henry replied. "We were going to fire him anyway. We weren't bringing him back."

Buckley probed deeper. "But what if you won the World Series?"

"You know that Disney commercial—'We just won the World Series, and I'm going to Disneyland'?"

Buckley nodded.

"Well, if the camera had been on me, it would have been, 'We just won the World Series, let's fire the manager.'"

The problem, Buckley and others attest, is that while Little was great at handling both young and veteran players, he had failed to embrace the new Red Sox organizational style that placed a heavy emphasis on statistical analysis. He reportedly ignored many of the lengthy reports prepared for him by Epstein and the baseball operations team, and went with his gut more than the numbers—Exhibit A being his decision regarding Martinez in Game 7.[†]

[†] Asked whether, after all these setbacks, the front office was beginning to wonder if a "Curse of the Bambino" really did exist that had kept the Red

There was no guarantee, of course, that the Red Sox would have won the finale even if Little *did* take Pedro out. Alan Embree, Mike Timlin, and the rest of the Boston relief corps had pitched extremely well during the ALCS, but had struggled much of the regular season. In recent Red Sox managerial history, Don Zimmer had kept his job after the monumental breakdown and Bucky Dent game in 1978, and '86 skipper John McNamara held on for parts of *two* years after not removing a hobbling Buckner for defense in the last inning of World Series Game 6 at Shea Stadium. There had been precedent for giving Little another shot.

The fact that Red Sox senior leadership was not willing to do so, and Henry's admission that Grady would have not kept his job even if Boston *won* the 2003 World Series, emphasized the fact that the front office was fully invested in finding a new manager committed to its way of thinking. For all the good feeling and "Cowboy Up" brotherhood surrounding the '03 Sox, Grady-Gate was a reminder that this was still a business, and that Henry and Co. were willing to do whatever it took to get those five more wins needed to stop the "19-18" chants.

"This is not going to be a stat-geeks organization," Lucchino said when asked what qualities they were looking for in their next manager. "Nor is it going to be an organization that is going to be run by old, salty-dog traditionalists. There will be a lot of Grady Little in our next manager."

Some early names floated about included veteran big-league

Sox from winning a World Series since 1918, Epstein offered a definitive reply: "It doesn't exist. Just give us a couple of years and we're going to win a World Series and that'll satisfy those troubled people who continue to believe in curses."

skippers like Jim Fregosi, Charlie Manuel, and Bobby Valentine, as well as popular former Red Sox like Glenn Hoffman and Jerry Remy who were short on experience. Whoever they chose, he needed to be more wedded to their ideas of strategy and game preparation than Little had been.

One thing Lucchino was not going to let stand in the way of this and other upcoming transactions was financial limitations. Almost immediately after what he called the "bitter and very crushing" end to the '03 season, Lucchino met with John Henry, Tom Werner, and the rest of the Red Sox ownership group at the team's annual partner's meeting. There they discussed making a greater fiscal commitment to catching the Yankees once and for all.

"One of the behind-the-scenes effects of 2003 is that we added $35 or $36 million to our payroll," says Lucchino. "We went into that next season with a budget saying 'We're not going to come this close again and let this happen to us again.' We wanted to have greater financial flexibility than we had before, and we wanted to win desperately. I remember one of our limited partners saying, 'Well, if we do this, Larry, are you able to assure us that we're going to win the World Series next year?' I said of course not, but we want to do anything we can to increase the probability."

Given this renewed commitment, the next major move the Boston brass made, just two days after letting Little go, was especially shocking: They put their best overall hitter—Manny Ramirez—on waivers.

This was done with the knowledge of Ramirez's agent, Jeff Moorad, as well as the full understanding that the move might cost them the services of a future Hall of Famer who had finished first and second in the American League batting race the past two seasons while bashing 33 and 37 homers. What they hoped was that Manny's oversized contract—which still had about $100 million owed to him over the remaining five years of an eight-year deal—would keep teams from claiming him and assuming the contract, but might prompt interest in a possible trade.

Money was not the prevailing issue. The new-era Red Sox were about teamwork, respect for the game, and a burning desire to win. In the case of the unpredictable, undisciplined Ramirez, it could be argued, all three of these attributes were missing. He lacked focus, often seemed to not be hustling, and was prone to begging out of games with mild or phantom injuries. With the record-setting offense Boston management had put together, they felt they could afford to let Manny leave in his prime—despite his outstanding statistics—if the offer was right.

In the end, the move worked as hoped. No team claimed Ramirez, and the Red Sox heard from a very interested potential suitor: Texas Rangers owner Tom Hicks. Alex Rodriguez, the Rangers' all-world shortstop and defending American League MVP, had an even loftier contract than Manny's: $252 million over 10 years, of which he had completed just the first three. The consensus was that Rodriguez, a Gold Glove fielder who had led the American League with 52, 57, and 47 home runs the previous three years, was baseball's best all-around player, but the Rangers had still finished last each year he had been with the team. A-Rod wanted to be with a contender, and the thought occurred to the executives of both the Rangers and Red Sox—why not swap superstars?

The problem was that Boston already had someone playing shortstop, a fellow by the name of Nomar Garciaparra. One of the most popular players in team history, he had compiled tremendous statistics over six healthy seasons, batting .326 with an average of 27 homers and 107 RBI, and was a fan favorite still in his prime at age 30. But Garciaparra had struggled in the '03 postseason with a .265 average and just one RBI over 12 games, and there was concern that his range on defense was beginning to slip.

On top of that, Nomar and Boston ownership were miles apart on how they assessed his value. Garciaparra's seven-year contract, signed after his stellar Rookie of the Year season in 1997, was due to expire in 2004. He had rejected a four-year, $60 million offer from the team prior to the '03 season, feeling that he was worthy of a deal closer to that of fellow AL super-shortstops Rodriguez ($25.2 million per year) and Derek Jeter ($18.9 million), with whom he was often compared. Garciaparra and his agent Arn Tellem believed there was room for negotiation, but Henry and Boston ownership felt their offer was fair and did not plan on raising it. Nomar spent much of 2003 scowling at the media when discussion of his contract came up, and the consensus was that he would test free agency after 2004.

Boston's front office had no desire to let Nomar walk without compensation, and was very interested in an A-Rod-for-Manny swap. The stage was set, therefore, for a pair of mammoth deals: Rodriguez for Ramirez, and Garciaparra to another team for an outfielder to replace Manny. The first piece of the puzzle, given the magnitude of the money involved, would require the permission of commissioner Bud Selig and some salary restructuring by both clubs, with the players union carefully watching on to make sure nothing was done to cost either player any of his millions.

Negotiations were supposed to be kept quiet, but word leaked to the press and eventually the public. Garciaparra saw the headlines while on a Hawaiian honeymoon with new wife, Mia Hamm—an icon in her own right as a U.S. women's soccer star—and was understandably upset that the Red Sox were seeking someone to take his job. He even called a sports radio talk show and the *Herald* from paradise to air his concerns. "I know there's always been this speculation that I'm unhappy there [in Boston]," Garciaparra told the *Herald*. "No words have ever come out of my mouth—publicly or privately—that I don't want to be there."

Epstein found a team willing to deal for Garciaparra in the Chicago White Sox, whose All-Star outfielder Magglio Ordonez was also in the final year of his contract. White Sox GM Kenny Williams and Epstein met at the baseball winter meetings in Dallas and agreed to an even-up swap, contingent upon the Rodriguez-Ramirez trade. Ever thinking ahead, Epstein and Lucchino felt they could more easily replace Ordonez with comparable outfield talent were he to leave for free agency after '04 than they could Garciaparra, since the only shortstops on par with his overall skill set were Jeter and A-Rod.

While the particulars of this two-step, three-team swap were being worked out, a process that would take approximately six weeks, the Red Sox went about filling their other needs—which were similarly multilayered.

In seeking a new manager, Boston officials identified one candidate as a finalist for his pedigree and leadership qualities as well as for his connections. Terry "Tito" Francona had grown up in baseball, first as the son of a 15-year MLB veteran, and then as a player who experienced both the heights of being one of the nation's top young talents and the challenge of hanging on for a decade in the major leagues after a pair of significant injuries.

He had managed for four years in the minors and then four more with the talent-poor Philadelphia Phillies, never posting a winning record in the City of Brotherly Love but developing a reputation as a hardworking player's manager who could handle youngsters as well as stars—one of the latter being his ace pitcher, Curt Schilling. Boston brass had a longtime interest in trading for Schilling, a former Red Sox farmhand who had been an All-Star in Philly and then a World Series hero with the Diamondbacks. Arizona, looking to unload Schilling's hefty contract in its final $12 million year, was hoping to trade him during the off-season. Because of Francona's past relationship with the big right-hander, Lucchino and Co. were thinking that Francona may be just the guy who could get Schilling to Boston.

This would not be easy. By virtue of his 16 years of big-league service, Schilling could veto any trade. In an interview with Jayson Stark of ESPN.com, he said he was interested in playing for only two teams besides the Diamondbacks—Philadelphia and (gasp) the Yankees. By mid-November, a trade to New York had already been proposed in private and the press: Schilling and Arizona second baseman Junior Spivey going east in a deal for second baseman Alfonso Soriano and first baseman Nick Johnson (with the Yankees also assuming the last year of Schilling's contract). What was not in the papers was that Theo Epstein was also working with Arizona general manager Joe Garagiola on a possible trade for Schilling, contingent of course on the pitcher's approval.

So in zeroing in on Francona as a managerial candidate, Lucchino and Epstein were in part thinking a step ahead. They would never hire him or any manager solely as a means of getting a player, but if Tito *did* get the job, he may just have an ace—and a Diamondback—in his pocket.

"There was a pretty exhaustive [managerial] search that took place," says Lucchino, "but he [Francona] had a couple of important things going for him. One, he had major league experience. Two, he was very hungry, because his major league experience was not that successful. Three, we thought he had some of the personality traits that were essential; he had a reputation of being an easygoing, players-kind of manager who had a sense of humor and an ability to limit the problems and distractions. On-the field, he sort of bought into the philosophy that we were trying to establish here—the sort of grind-it-out, on-base percentage, quasi-Moneyball style. I would never say 'Moneyball style' because I don't believe we can ever be that easily characterized.

"And four, we thought he could help us bring in some high-quality players given the reputation he had and the pre-existing, strong relationship he had with Curt Schilling. We were very aware of the impact a decision like that [hiring Francona] could have in the Curt Schilling sweepstakes."

Francona's knowledge of the "quasi-Moneyball style" had come right from the source itself. Fired by the Phillies in 2000, Francona had been a bench coach with first the Rangers and then the A's, teaming up with Oakland skipper Ken Macha against the Red Sox in their five-game ALDS battle of '03. Francona's boss with the A's was none other than Billy Beane, the father of Moneyball. When Francona came in for his interview with the Sox on November 6, 2003, he was perhaps more ready than anybody for the type of number-crunching and analysis club officials put him through—including game simulations played out on video.

Boston's other primary candidates at this point were all coaches with no big-league managerial experience: Glenn Hoffman of the Dodgers, Joe Maddon of the Angels, and DeMarlo Hale of the Rangers. Francona had gotten the thumbs-up as a manager from Red Sox assistant GM Lee Thomas, general manager of the Phillies while Francona was there, so when Epstein said that Francona "kind of blew us away," the job was all but his. Epstein, Lucchino, John Henry, and others who met with him were confident he could handle the pressure of managing in Boston, since Philadelphia is also generally considered one of baseball's toughest media markets in terms of scrutiny by the press and fans.

Before making an official offering to Francona, the Red Sox brass wanted to see how having him ready and willing would help them in landing their top off-season priority. The week of Thanksgiving, after working out a deal with the Diamondbacks to trade young pitchers Casey Fossum and Brandon Lyon and a pair of minor league prospects for Curt Schilling, the Red Sox sent a power trio of Lucchino, Epstein, and assistant GM Jed Hoyer down to Schilling's home in Arizona to try and convince the big right-hander that Boston—where he had started his career as a minor leaguer before being traded to the Baltimore Orioles—was the place for him.

Schilling, never at a loss for words, had admitted to the press that he was only interested in talking to the Red Sox about a trade because of the possibility that Francona would be Boston's next manager. He went so far as to say, "Terry is the number one attraction there for me. If he's not the manager there, my interest in going to Boston would diminish drastically."

Now, hearing from Sox brass that Tito's appointment was

The K Men, shown here in the Fenway Park bleachers around 2000, were a popular, red-faced presence at ~~rly~~ nearly every home start made by Pedro Martinez for the 1998–2004 Red Sox (and many road games as well). ~~ro's~~ Pedro's strikeouts were recorded by the group in true scorekeeper fashion, including those batters caught ~~king~~ looking—noted with a backwards "K." *(Courtesy of the K Men)*

~~ton~~ Boston manager Grady Little (in jacket) talked to Martinez late in Game 7 of the 2003 ALCS at Yankee Sta-~~m.~~ dium. Jason Varitek, Bill Mueller, and Kevin Millar apparently didn't like what they were hearing; Sox fans ~~ldn't~~ wouldn't like what came next. *(Courtesy of The Boston Red Sox)*

Terry Francona (left) and Theo Epstein enjoyed a light moment during their first spring training together in March 2004. After bringing in Francona, Curt Schilling, and Keith Foulke, GM Epstein hoped for a different finish than the previous year. (Courtesy of Brita Meng-Outzen/Boston Red Sox)

Ellis Burks (left), here with Jim Rice in 1992, was the only member of the 2004 Red Sox to have played for the team during the Yawkey years. Although two knee surgeries kept him off the field almost the entire '04 season, the savvy veteran would prove a key force in the dugout and clubhouse. (Courtesy of The Boston Red Sox)

Directors Peter (left) and Bobby Farrelly took in the view at Fenway Park, where they spent the late stages of the 2004 regular season shooting scenes for their cinematic ode to Sox-obsessed fans, Fever Pitch. Soon the brothers would need a new ending for their film. (Courtesy of The Boston Red Sox)

Babies born during 2004 became living talismans as the Red Sox entered the playoffs, with parents keeping them awake through many late nights of the postseason. After Rachel, shown here with her father, was born on August 16, the Sox promptly won 20 of 22 games. *(Courtesy of Saul Wisnia)*

e home dugout exploded as Da-
Ortiz's walk-off homer cleared
he Green Monster in left-center
ield, completing Boston's ALDS
eep over the Angels. *(Courtesy of Julie Cordeiro / Boston Red Sox)*

Johnny Damon was first to congratulate Ortiz as he neared home plate after putting away the Angels. Next stop — Yankee Stadium and the ALCS. *(Courtesy of Julie Cordeiro / Boston Red Sox)*

By the 2004 postseason the K Men had moved their cheering-and-posting site to atop the Green Monster, senior member Kevin McCarthy (in bandana) had taken to praying as Big Papi and the Red Sox sought the t McCarthy first dreamed of while hiding out at Fenway back in 1967. *(Courtesy of the K Men)*

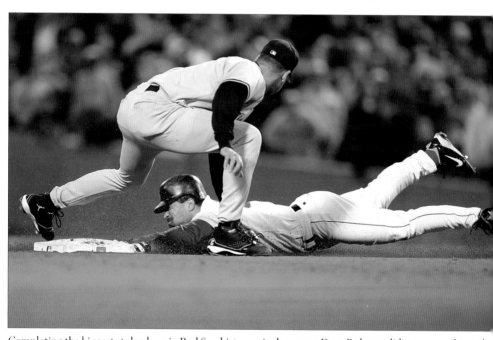

Completing the biggest stolen base in Red Sox history, pinch-runner Dave Roberts slid into second just ah of Derek Jeter's tag in the ninth inning of ALCS Game 4 at Fenway Park. Moments later, Bill Mueller sing in Roberts with the tying run — setting the stage for more extra-inning heroics by David Ortiz. *(Courtes The Boston Red Sox)*

Curt Schilling, blood clearly visible on his injured right ankle, followed through at Yankee Stadium during Game 6 of the ALCS. Schilling's performance in the "Bloody Sock Game" proved both courageous and clutch. *(Courtesy of Julie Cordeiro/Boston Red Sox)*

x Rodriguez slapped the ball out of reliever Bronson Arroyo's hand in the eighth inning of ALCS Game aising his status as Yankee Enemy #1 to a new level. A-Rod would be called out for interference, helping a Yankee rally. *(Courtesy of Julie Cordeiro/Boston Red Sox)*

Above: The Red Sox let loos[e] [at] Busch Stadium after beating [the] Cardinals in Game 4 of the W[orld] Series, capturing their first w[orld] championship since 1918. *(Cou[rtesy] of Jack Maley / Boston Red Sox)*

Above: David Ortiz (**rear**) hammed it up in the victorious visitor's clubhouse with (from left) World Series MVP Manny Ramirez, Kevin Millar, and Gabe Kapler. Their T-shirts and hats told the story. *(Courtesy of The Boston Red Sox)*

Owners (from left) John Henry, Tom Werner, and Larry Lucchino savored the moment in St. Louis. They fulfilled their primary commitment of delivering a World Series title to Red Sox fans in just three seasons. *(Courtesy of The Boston Red Sox)*

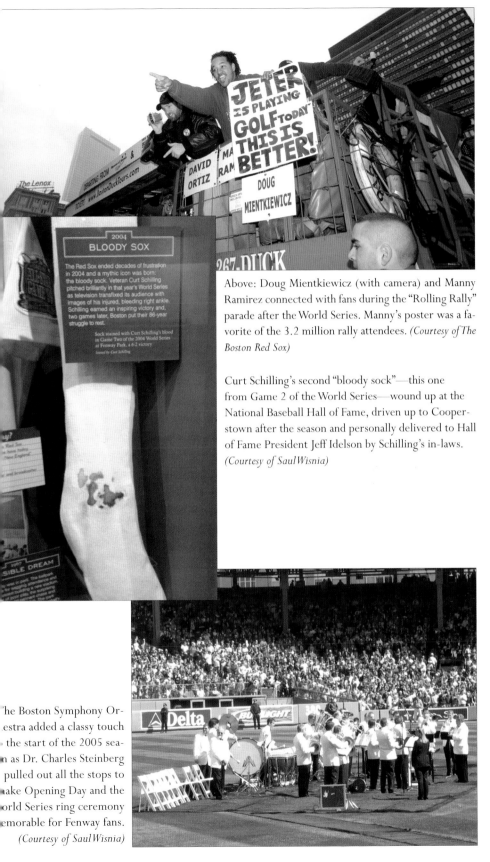

2004 BLOODY SOX

The Red Sox ended decades of frustration in 2004 and a mythic icon was born: the bloody sock. Veteran Curt Schilling pitched brilliantly in that year's World Series as television transfixed its audience with images of his injured, bleeding right ankle. Schilling earned an inspiring victory and, two games later, Boston put their 86-year struggle to rest.

Sock stained with Curt Schilling's blood in Game Two of the 2004 World Series at Fenway Park, a 6-2 victory.
loaned by Curt Schilling

Above: Doug Mientkiewicz (with camera) and Manny Ramirez connected with fans during the "Rolling Rally" parade after the World Series. Manny's poster was a favorite of the 3.2 million rally attendees. *(Courtesy of The Boston Red Sox)*

Curt Schilling's second "bloody sock"—this one from Game 2 of the World Series—wound up at the National Baseball Hall of Fame, driven up to Cooperstown after the season and personally delivered to Hall of Fame President Jeff Idelson by Schilling's in-laws. *(Courtesy of Saul Wisnia)*

The Boston Symphony Orchestra added a classy touch to the start of the 2005 season as Dr. Charles Steinberg pulled out all the stops to make Opening Day and the World Series ring ceremony memorable for Fenway fans. *(Courtesy of Saul Wisnia)*

The Opening Day crowd gasped, and then cheered wildly, as the 2004 championship banner was unfu[rled] over the Green Monster — covering smaller banners denoting the 1903-12-15-16-18 titles. The theme f[rom] *2001: A Space Odyssey* proved the perfect accompaniment. *(Courtesy of Saul Wisnia)*

By the time the 2013 Red Sox marked their latest World Series championship with this Fenway Park cele[bra]tion, owners Lucchino, Henry, and Werner had produced three titles in ten seasons — and saved Fenway [for] future generations. *(Courtesy of Brian Babineau / Boston Red Sox)*

very likely, Schilling was more intrigued than ever about a deal—especially with all the turkey talk about how he could help the Red Sox finally get past the Yankees and win a World Series title for the first time since 1918.

Schilling knew what it was like to beat New York, having teamed with Arizona rotation-mate Randy Johnson to dismantle the pinstripers in the '01 World Series—a feat that earned him series MVP honors and selection (with Johnson) as *Sports Illustrated* Co-Sportsmen of the Year. Achieving such a feat for Boston, however, would be monumental; Schilling didn't believe in "that curse thing," but he did believe in history. He knew the team that broke through for Boston would be immortalized in New England forever. He'd never have to buy a meal there again.

After breaking bread with Epstein and Hoyer, Schilling—who served as his own agent—agreed to the trade and a two-year, $25.5-million contract extension through 2006 that included an option for a third year. Then, once that signing was done, he signed on to the Red Sox fan Web site known as the "Sons of Sam Horn" to let fans know how excited he was to be joining the team. Using the screen name "Curt38," the fervent video "gamer" had to convince some initial skeptics that they were indeed conversing with Boston's newest ballplayer.

Schilling, a 6-foot-5, 205-pound horse in the Roger Clemens mold, had pitched more than 250 innings in both 2001 and 2002 while going 22–6 and 23–7 and notching 609 strikeouts in 516 innings. Although an appendectomy and hand injury had limited him to 24 starts in 2003, he still registered a 2.95 ERA and was considered completely healed.

Statistically, he was one of the best control artists in MLB history, with less than two walks issued per nine innings pitched over his career and a strikeout-to-walk ratio second all-time to only 19th-century hurler Tommy Bond. Schilling's regular season record of 163–117 gave him a tidy .582 winning percentage, but what was even more impressive were his postseason numbers—a 1.66 ERA and 91 strikeouts in 86 and two-thirds innings. In his 11 playoff starts, his teams were 8–3.

"There are three types of fans. Yankees fans, Red Sox fans, and everybody else. I guess I hate the Yankees now," Schilling said once the deal was done, immediately endearing him to countless New Englanders. "Many of the fans tell me about the history of this franchise. The Red Sox have brought me here to change that history."

Although Schilling also brought to town a reputation as an outspoken guy who liked to talk a lot—his nickname in Arizona was "Red Light" for the way he perked up when the TV cameras were around—he also wanted the ball every four days and wanted to go nine innings when he got it.

"He's a power pitcher but he's smart," said new teammate Kevin Millar, who had faced Schilling in the past. "He doesn't just overpower you. He elevates his fastball whenever he wants. He spots his split finger whenever he wants. I'm thrilled to death about this move. I'm as excited as I've been. Knock on wood, but a healthy Pedro, Schilling, and Derek Lowe? I would hate to be a right-handed hitter facing those guys in a three-game series."

Once Schilling's signing was made official, the Red Sox went about doing the same with Francona. Introduced to the Boston media on December 4, Tito was immediately tested when he was asked if, as the newest Red Sox manager, he realized it was just a matter of time before he would end up just like Grady Little—another guy out of a job.

Not skipping a beat, Francona responded perfectly.

"Think about it for a second," he said. "I've been released from six teams. I've been fired as a manager. I've got no hair. I've got a nose that's three times too big for my face, and I grew up in a major league clubhouse. My skin's pretty thick. I'll be okay. . . . This is the most exciting day of my baseball life."

That life in the game, both as his father's son and as a player, had gone a long way in preparing Francona for the task that lay ahead. His nickname came from his dad, Tito, who as an outfielder with nine teams over 15 MLB seasons also gave his preteen son the ultimate hardball apprenticeship in the mid- to late 1960s—letting him spend his summers hanging around big-leaguers, shagging fly balls during batting practice, and occasionally getting the chance to hit himself. Terry learned the game by playing and observing, both at the ballpark and on the car rides home, listening from the backseat as his father and teammates discussed that night's pitcher or key plays.

After a stellar collegiate career at Arizona, where he batted .401 in 1980 to win both the Golden Spikes Award from USA Baseball as the nation's top amateur player and College Player of the Year honors from the *Sporting News,* the first baseman/outfielder was selected in the first round (22nd overall) by the Montreal Expos that June. Francona sped through the minor leagues in just over a year, and was an everyday left fielder batting second for the Expos in June 1982 when he caught his spikes in a piece of wet turf at Busch Stadium and crashed into the outfield wall pursuing a line drive. He suffered a torn anterior cruciate ligament (or ACL) in his right knee, and just like that, his season was over—his average forever frozen at .321.

Pushing himself through a grueling rehabilitation, Francona was back with Montreal the next spring. Primarily a part-timer in '83, he got hot late in the season and won back a starting job for 1984. Then, while having his best year yet with a .346 average and a league-leading 19 doubles, another mid-June disaster derailed him. Now batting third in the Expos lineup, he twisted his good (left) knee in the first inning of a home game against the Pirates, trying to avoid colliding with pitcher John Tudor while running down the first base line. Two innings later, while in the field, Francona felt something pop in his knee and collapsed—unable to get back up.[‡]

Although he was optimistic, telling reporters that "I don't think it's as bad as the last time I hurt my knee, my season isn't over," this turned out to be the case. He didn't play again in '84, and at age 25 his near-glory days were gone. Never a home run hitter, he now had no speed either; although he stuck it out through parts of six more years in the majors thanks to hard work and a high pain threshold, he was never again an everyday player.

Longing to stay in the game when his MLB days ended with the Milwaukee Brewers in 1990, Terry turned to managing in the White Sox system and within three years was skipper of a championship club with the Class AA Birmingham Barons. While with the Barons in '94 he managed a raw but athletic outfielder who had been away from baseball since high school, and Tito's ability to maintain a sense of normalcy on the team while helping along this player—NBA

[‡] Eerily, Francona's two major injuries occurred almost exactly two years apart—on June 16, 1982, and June 14, 1984—and on both occasions he was second in the National League in batting at the time of the incident.

superstar and .202 hitter Michael Jordan—showed he was capable of dealing with even the oddest clubhouse challenge that might come his way. He also wasn't afraid to talk to or bench Jordan if the situation warranted it, a trait he carried to the major leagues. If Pedro Martinez wanted to keep pitching in a game, but Francona didn't think he was up to it, he would have no trouble overruling his ace and taking the ball from him.

This didn't mean Francona lacked heart. Like Grady Little, he always had his players' back, and would do a superlative job presiding over the many strong personalities in the Red Sox clubhouse. One of the very first things he did after the press conference at which he was officially named Boston's manager was to call every player on the roster to let them know how excited he was to work with them.

There was, of course, still time to tweak that roster—and one big hole left to fill.

Although Byung-Hyun Kim had done well as the Boston closer for long stretches of the 2003 regular season, he had fallen apart in the playoffs just as he had with Arizona two years before. Scott Williamson had stepped in to save all three Boston wins in the ALCS, but there was a free agent on the market who was not only far more experienced at the role than Williamson, but was arguably the best in the game at it. Even better, he was someone Francona knew very well from their time together on the '03 Oakland A's squad on which Tito had been bench coach.

Keith Foulke.

The reigning American League leader in saves with 43, Foulke had gone 9–1 with a 2.08 ERA in 2003 before faltering against (ironically) the Red Sox in the ALDS. A smart pitcher who didn't have triple-digit speed but could get batters out with his fastball, change-up, or curve, he was a bit of a throwback as a closer who often came in before the ninth. He had thrown more than one inning 22 times in '03, including 11 appearances of two or more, and had outstanding control with 20 walks and 88 strikeouts over 86 and two-thirds innings.

As with Schilling, Francona's likely hiring—and the respect Foulke had for him—would play a key role in the reliever's decision to come to Boston. When Foulke heard that Francona was apt to be the next Red Sox manager, it made a big impression; he was excited about the prospect of being reunited with Tito.

"I love the guy to death," Foulke still says of Francona today. "He wants his players to go out there and be individuals, to go out there and do things their own way."

The feeling was mutual. While Francona was still awaiting word on whether he had gotten the Boston job, he was asked by the Red Sox what he thought about Foulke as a possible free agent signing. As he would later write in his own book, *Francona: The Red Sox Years,* Francona felt awkward discussing a player who was still officially on an Oakland team to which he was still officially employed as a bench coach. Certainly he hoped whichever team he was with in 2004 would have Keith Foulke on it.

Foulke felt the same way.

"When Tito was talking to them [the Red Sox], and when that process was getting close, my agent told me, 'Don't be surprised if one of these [free agent] calls comes in from Boston,'" explains Foulke. "And when we found out that Tito was hired, that's when things started getting heated up. I came up to Boston for a visit, and I remember Theo [Epstein] took us to a [Celtics] basketball game, and we were up on the big video screen. People cheered; I think everybody knew why I was there."

Another nice touch by Theo in the push for Foulke was finding out he was a hockey fan and getting him a Bobby Orr jersey. Epstein even arranged for the hockey great to call Foulke's home and leave a message on his answering machine. "I was standing in a closet, picking out clothes for the day, when I heard it," Foulke recalls with a laugh. "I was like, 'holy shit.'" He was too scared to call Orr back, but this gesture also made an impact.

In the end, it was the chance to go to a contending team in a big market that sealed the deal for Foulke. He had enjoyed the intensity of playing at Fenway Park as a visitor, despite his struggles there in the '03 ALDS, and was amazed that even as an opposing relief pitcher he could walk down the street in Boston and be recognized. These people really took their baseball seriously. "Nobody knew me [out of uniform] in Oakland and Chicago even when I played for their team," he says. "This was a legit chance to be with a winner."

When Foulke decided to sign with Boston, in early January of 2004, the first person he called was Oakland GM Billy Beane. For Beane, it was becoming a familiar refrain. He had already lost a top coach (Francona) to the Red Sox a month before; now he was losing his top reliever to them as well. "I told Billy I appreciated everything he did for me, but I felt like this was part of my career, something I wanted to do," says Foulke.

Going for the brass ring seemed a natural step for Foulke, who had already seen how unpredictable and uncertain a baseball career can be. Born in San Diego and raised in the Houston area, he jokes that "I didn't even know what a reliever was growing up. When I was in high school you started a game, and you finished the game." Signed by the Giants, he started all 85 games he pitched in their minor league system as well, and his first professional relief appearance was his major league debut in mid-1997.

His San Francisco stay was not a long one. The Giants, who were battling for a division title in '97, used him predominantly as a starter, but after he fell to 1–5 with an 8.26 ERA by late July they sent him to the White Sox as part of a nine-player swap at the trade deadline. In Chicago he went right to the bullpen and stayed put, and after being a National League fan all his life he found the AL—and relief pitching—to his liking.

Primarily a set-up man for such undistinguished closers as Bill Simas and Bob Howry in his first several seasons with the White Sox, he was good enough in the role to garner a 2.22 ERA and several Cy Young votes in 1999. The next year he was handed the finisher's spot and thrived in it—saving 34 and 42 games over two seasons (and 84 chances) while keeping his WHIP around 1.00 and helping Chicago to an AL Central title.

Was it then he developed the tough mentality of a closer?

"I never bought into that," says Foulke. "To me, pitching is pitching, and the only thing that changes the style of pitching is the score. I never really called myself a closer."

In 2002 Foulke learned the fragility of the role he deemed nameless. He suffered the mysterious pitcher's enemy—a "dead arm"—early in the year, and lost his closer's spot after his ERA ballooned to 5.26 in mid-season amidst a slew of losses and blown saves. While he pitched better out of the late-game spotlight, by the end of the year he was deemed expendable and sent to Oakland in another multiplayer trade.

"Chicago wanted people in their bullpen throwing 95 [miles per hour], the typical closer type," says Foulke. "I didn't fit in their plans anymore, so Billy [Beane] made a trade for me—and the next thing you know I'm an All-Star."

In Boston, signed to a contract that with incentives could pay him as much as $26.5 million over four years (three of them guaranteed), he would be expected to have a similarly successful season. Given a starting rotation that included Curt Schilling, Pedro Martinez, Derek Lowe, and Tim Wakefield, he was bound to get plenty of save chances provided middle relievers like Mike Timlin, Alan Embree, and Scott Williamson—strong points on the '03 team—could do their job.

Then again, given Foulke's ability to pitch two or more innings out of the pen, he might not always need them.

"Keith had great numbers last year [2003], but I think his importance goes beyond that," said Francona, alluding to Foulke's ability to even pitch multiple innings in back-to-back games—a throwback to former Sox bullpen bulldogs like Bob Stanley and Dick Radatz. "He does a lot of things better than the numbers show."

How the numbers shook out for Foulke, Schilling, and Francona would go a long way in determining if the Red Sox could end the Yankees' six-year reign atop the AL East—and/or get back at their rivals in the postseason. For historian Richard Johnson, the busy first months since Game 7 and

Grady-Gate had proven one thing: when it came to the past, the new Red Sox ownership was both willing to accept it and committed to changing it.

"The '03 season has *everything* to do with '04—because of the shock and awwwwwwww of that finish," says Johnson. "All I could think of that night as we were all suffering through that last game was, 'Welcome to Boston, Misters Lucchino, Werner, and Henry. Welcome! You're one of us now! You've endured this. You're writing the paychecks for these guys. Now, even though you knew from an abstract standpoint sort of what the fans had undergone through the years, and some of the disappointment we had suffered, you got your tattoo and did your blood handshake. You are now part of the gang. How are you going to deal with that?'

"Well," Johnson continues, "how they dealt with it was sending Theo [Epstein] out to Arizona for Thanksgiving dinner with Curt Schilling. You were talking about an ownership where these guys were all Alpha wolf kind of males who were not taking no for an answer and weren't taking second place. They didn't spend much time feeling sorry for themselves and licking their wounds. They went and started to put the final pieces in place."

Except one.

In the end, the proposed Manny-Ramirez-for-Alex-Rodriguez deal between the Red Sox and Rangers did not come to pass. Boston wanted to restructure A-Rod's massive contract so that it would pay him $21 million a year rather than $27 million; although Rodriguez and his agent, Scott Boras, agreed to the measure, the Major League Baseball Players Association had authority to turn down the swap—and did so shortly before Christmas because, as union representative Gene Orza stated, "It was clear it crossed the line separating restructuring and reductions—and by a huge margin."

Orza did say they would look at other offers from the Red Sox, but a frustrated Lucchino said the deal was "dead." This would have been exasperating enough for the Red Sox, but what came next was truly cringe-worthy. On Valentine's Day, Yankee boss George Steinbrenner made himself a sweetheart of a deal with the Rangers—trading second baseman Soriano to Texas for Rodriguez, with Texas paying $67 million of the $179 million left on A-Rod's contract.[§] The swap started another war of words between the Yanks and Sox, with an agitated John Henry claiming that "baseball doesn't have an answer for the Yankees" and Steinbrenner snorting back that Henry "chose not to go the extra distance for his fans" (with a more lucrative offer for A-Rod).

The deal was met with groans throughout Red Sox Nation, but after the initial shock a different sort of feeling set in among Boston fans and players. Yes, the Yankees had outmaneuvered them again, but maybe they had done so because they knew the Sox had gotten stronger themselves—and were hungry for revenge.

Boston backup catcher Doug Mirabelli stated that "just because he's [Rodriguez] there, doesn't mean we're scared," a likely unintentional piece of prose that might have made for a

---

[§] What enabled the Yankees to make a play for A-Rod, ironically, was that their own incumbent third baseman, Aaron (Bleeping) Boone, had torn up his knee in a pickup basketball game that offseason. In the end, the Rodriguez deal would wind up being so monumental—and enduring—a moment in the Yanks–Red Sox relationship that it would be the subject of an ESPN documentary that first aired in February 2014 on the tenth anniversary of A-Rod's signing with New York.

nifty slogan (although "A-Rod Sucks" fit much better on bumper stickers). Alan Embree had an even more positive way of spinning things, saying that Steinbrenner and Co. were "worried about us in a big way. They know we have a very good ball club this year and it's exciting."

The gauntlet for the 2004 season had been thrown by the Red Sox, and picked up by the Yankees. Twelve other American League teams hoped to have a chance at grabbing it as well before the year was over.

First, however, Tim Wakefield had to put the previous October behind him, and that opportunity came when the Boston chapter of the Baseball Writers' Association of America held its annual dinner in January. The BBWAA dinners, once a staple in many big-league cities, have largely fallen by the wayside in recent decades—but in baseball-crazed Boston they continue to routinely sell out as fans, media, and players come together for an unofficial jump start to spring training. Players regularly accept or present awards at the event, giving fans a chance to applaud them for their previous year's work.

Wakefield was being honored at the '04 dinner for his community service work, and he was nervous about getting called up. The man who had silenced 56,000 fans at Yankee Stadium with his brilliant win in the previous fall's ALCS opener was now worried about a roomful of folks with a soft spot for the Sox.

"I didn't know how I was going to be received," Wakefield recalls. "I had just given up the [Boone] home run in October, and I didn't know where I stood."

He found out soon enough. As Wakefield was introduced and walked to the stage, 1,200 attendees stood up at their tables and clapped for what felt to him like 20 minutes.

"It was one of the biggest ovations I've ever gotten in my

life," says Wakefield. "It bought me to tears, it really did. That was when I felt like I was part of the culture here. I wasn't going to be the next Bill Buckner."

A month later, Wakefield, new teammates Schilling and Foulke, and the rest of the organization's pitchers and catchers reported for the start of spring training in Fort Myers. So did their new manager, a man burdened with the knowledge that after a year that couldn't have ended worse, this one was expected to end a whole lot better.

Still in late October, but this time without Frank Sinatra.

7. FAST BIKES AND FAST STARTS

Ellis Burks just had a feeling. Something about this team felt right.

Burks had played for the Red Sox what seemed like a million years before. A fan favorite in the late 1980s and early '90s, he was at his best a Silver Slugger and Gold Glove winner touted as a future MVP candidate. Injuries, however, seemed to haunt the young center fielder from Vicksburg, Mississippi, around every corner; 60 games missed in 1989 with problems in both shoulders, hamstring woes he played through in '90, tendinitis and disc troubles in '91 that cost him 30 more contests. When he wasn't on the disabled list, he frequently played hurt.

He also played under unusual and at times uncomfortable circumstances—especially given the time period. After the departure of Jim Rice, Lee Smith, and several other black players on the Red Sox, there was a period when Burks was the *only* African American on Boston's entire 25-man roster. It wasn't a stellar roster either; after popular manager Joe

Morgan was fired, his successor Butch Hobson presided over back-to-back sub-.500 clubs.

In his bright white home uniform, Burks stood out from his teammates on the Fenway Park grass much like Jackie Robinson had at Ebbets Field as a Brooklyn Dodger rookie— only this was 1992, not 1947.

The number of African American players throughout the majors would dip greatly in later years, but at this point they were strongly represented on other teams and constituted a large proportion of the league's most productive and popular performers. This made the Red Sox situation all the more troubling. Management assured fans and probing reporters that Burks's unusual circumstances were only a coincidence, and that race was never a factor in the team drafting or signing players. Still, the Sox never seemed to sign African American free agents in their prime, despite actively pursuing the likes of Kirby Puckett and Tim Raines. According to Burks, many black players in the early 1990s viewed the Red Sox as a team that didn't embrace athletes of color, and Boston as a difficult city for them to play in. Given the choice, they chose not to do so.

"I'd be in the outfield warming up, and guys on other teams would ask me, 'Man, how do you deal with Boston? How do you stay knowing how it is up there?'" says Burks, looking back. "I was like 'Man, it really is not that bad.' I never had a problem with anybody on the team or in the front office. But they had that reputation, you know? There was a stereotype of playing in Boston for so many years, because of what had happened to them in the past."

Burks did not complain about his situation, and always represented the team with hard work and class. But he could not stay healthy, and by the time a cracked back shut him down midway through 1992, management had seen enough. Burks had just turned 28, an age when most players are entering the prime of their careers, but in his case the great speed that had been at the center of his game was all but gone. When his contract was up that fall, general manager Lou Gorman called Burks to say the Red Sox were not re-signing him. Ten years with the organization, ended by a phone call.

Was Burks hurt? Surprised?

"A little of both," he admits. "I was hurt by the fact that this was the team I came up with and to which I had given my all. I just thought it was a bad way to show your support for a player when he gets hurt doing his job and you just get rid of him. That was when I figured out this game was more of a business than anything personal."

Over the next dozen years, although still plagued by injuries, Burks had emerged when healthy as the MVP-caliber player fans had first seen blossoming at Fenway. He never lost his confidence, and got back his speed. He hit 40 homers and stole 32 bases in one year, twice hit .344, and became a quiet, steady leader of teams in Chicago, Colorado, and San Francisco. While he never won the World Series ring all players covet, and still had a tough time getting on the field more than 130 games a year, he felt he proved something to the Red Sox for giving up on him.

Clearly he had; in the winter of 2000–01 Boston expressed interest in bringing him back as a free agent, but he didn't feel quite ready. Among other things, the same ownership group—John Harrington representing Mrs. Yawkey nearly 10 years after her death—was still running the show. Burks signed with the Cleveland Indians instead, and put up his usual 25–30-homer, 80–90-RBI numbers for the next two seasons.

Now Harrington was gone, and the new guys in charge contacted Burks in the winter of 2004 asking him to come aboard as a part-time outfielder and designated hitter.* Things had changed in a lot of ways since he felt isolated as the only African American suiting up for the Sox and Fenway a place with peeling paint and a losing club. He got along with his teammates okay back then, but after the games everybody just said "see you tomorrow" and went their separate ways. Scandals like the Wade Boggs–Margo Adams affair didn't help matters, nor did the team's failure to win in the postseason. Memories of the 1986 World Series and the "Buckner Game" had still been fresh on fans' minds when Burks and his mates went up against a deeper, more talented Oakland A's team in the 1988 and '90 ALCS, and two straight four-and-out sweeps further hardened the hearts of the Fenway Faithful.

From coming in with the Indians the past few seasons, Burks could feel the transformation under way at Boston. Fenway was refurbished and alive, with '86 a bit farther in the rearview mirror, and the team had become a melting pot of whites, blacks, and Latinos who seemed to have fun together in and away from the clubhouse. In 2003 they also learned how to win, and he had a hunch this might be the year they found a way to beat those damn Yankees.

"The Red Sox were very sincere about bringing me back," says Burks, who remembers being amused by the fact that the guy recruiting him, GM Theo Epstein, had watched him

---

*Making the offer all the more impressive is that Burks had been injured yet again in 2003, limited to 55 games due to a right elbow injury that required surgery. The Red Sox clearly wanted his presence in the clubhouse as much as at the plate.

play for the Sox as a kid back in the '80s. "You know how you just get a good feeling about something, a *really* good feeling? I just knew this team was going to win, so I turned down a much higher offer at Seattle to come here."

What Burks saw when he joined the team for spring training a couple weeks after his signing in early February reinforced his first impressions. "It was carefree; more of a family atmosphere," he says. "A lot of the guys went out together for dinner after the games, or to movies together. Eight or 10 guys would end up at the same place, easy. Everybody got along; everybody hung out."

Then there were the motorcycles.

"Six or seven guys on the team had these damn motorcycles in Florida," Burks recalls with a laugh. "You would see them riding to the ballpark in Fort Myers, [Johnny] Damon with his long mane flowing out from under his helmet. I don't know if there was a clause in anybody's contract, but Tito [Francona] said it was fine as long as you guys are careful. He allowed them to do it and it was another thing that brought the guys together."

Damon, who had vowed he would loosen up the quiet Boston clubhouse upon joining the club in 2002, took things to another level this time around. The "long mane" Burks saw under Johnny's motorcycle helmet was a constant topic of conversation during spring training, as Damon showed up in Florida with shoulder-length hair and a thick beard that caused schoolgirls to swoon and old-school sportswriters to snicker. According to Dan Shaughnessy of the *Globe*, "Fans couldn't decide if caveman Johnny looked more like Jesus or Charles Manson," although judging from the signs and T-shirts that started appearing around Fenway in the summer of '04—the most popular of which were variants on "What Would Johnny

Damon Do?"—more folks felt he favored the preacher-carpenter of Nazareth. When he visited local salons for a trim, it made the gossip columns.

Other Red Sox were also wearing their hair long, and/or sporting beards, and the contrast to the clean-shaven Yankees was clear. While George Steinbrenner still employed a "no facial hair, no long hair" policy in New York, Boston players were free to do as they pleased, often with humorous or frightening results—e.g., Pedro Martinez's jheri-curled perm, which made him look like Eriq La Salle's character in the 1980s Eddie Murphy movie *Coming to America*.

Long locks and fast bikes aside, spring training was not completely devoid of speed bumps. Given what had happened over the winter with the near-trades of Manny Ramirez and Nomar Garciaparra for (respectively) Alex Rodriguez and Magglio Ordonez, new manager Francona was prepared for both Nomar and Manny to show up with ruffled feathers.

Ramirez gave Tito the biggest initial headaches. As Francona recalled in his autobiography, the day Manny came into camp and met his manager for the first time was not a kumbaya moment. "I went up to him and introduced myself, and it wasn't good," the manager wrote in *Francona*. "He wouldn't talk to me, and he wouldn't shake my hand. I tried to talk to him, and he said, 'You just want me to like you.' I said, 'No shit. You're right.' It's not what I expected."

Francona was frustrated, but he didn't let it consume him. He made sure David Ortiz—one of Ramirez's closest friends on the club—got Manny to the first big team meeting on time, and learned to expect the unexpected from Ramirez on a daily basis. Soon Manny was smiling and laughing and telling Tito he'd do whatever necessary to help the team win.

There was also the issue of Martinez, the team's proud star

pitcher for the past six seasons, who now—just a few months after letting a trip to the World Series slide through his masterful fingers—would no longer be the only ace in camp. Curt Schilling, a certified Yankee killer who had one World Series ring to Pedro's none, had been brought in to help put the Red Sox over the top. It was uncertain if Martinez would see Schilling as a valuable teammate or as the team's way of saying he no longer had what it takes, and while Pedro did grumble a bit privately, both players said the right things to the press and their teammates. "People thought there was going to be a clash with those two, but I never saw it," says Burks. "Those guys played well together, fed off each other, and it was good."

Yet another off-field challenge facing the team was the contractual status of some of its biggest stars. Although right fielder Trot Nixon signed a three-year, $19.5 million deal just before spring training, five other key players—Ortiz, Garciaparra, Martinez, Derek Lowe, and Jason Varitek—all had contracts that expired at the end of the 2004 season. Management made it clear it enjoyed hammering out a deal with Nixon because he didn't make unreasonable requests;[†] and, as Epstein was quick to point out, this fiscally conservative style had worked quite well in recent years for another local sports franchise that had gone from a regional laughingstock to the top of its game.

After decades of floundering in the National Football

[†] Interestingly, Nixon would have the least productive season of these six players in 2004—limited by back and other injuries to just 48 games (although he did hit .315). In the course of his three-year deal, he never exceeded 13 home runs or 67 RBI, figures far below his previous three years' output.

League, the New England Patriots had righted their ship under owner Robert Kraft and coach Bill Belichick and won their second Super Bowl in three years a few weeks before the Red Sox broke camp. Having stars like quarterback Tom Brady, kicker Adam Vinatieri, and defenders Rodney Harrison, Ty Law, and Richard Seymour certainly helped, but a big key to the Patriots' success was that they offered few guaranteed, multiyear deals. Even the team's best athletes seemed to be performing for their contractual lives each season, and nobody was kept around for sentimental reasons or past heroics. The result was a hungry approach that translated into championships.

Baseball and football were two entirely different games, of course, but who was to say that a play-for-your-pay style couldn't work on the diamond with pending free agents as it did on the gridiron?

"To do good business and execute a successful plan, at times you have to be prepared for players to go into the last year of their contract," Epstein stated in his first spring training press conference of 2004. "It's not a panic situation for the player, it's not a panic situation for the club. . . . It's unrealistic to think we could sign every one of them. The finances don't add up. That's life. There's change sometimes."

Theo and the Trio figured they had a team that was capable of competing for a World Series in '04 as currently constituted. What happened next could be worried about later, after the final game—and hopefully a victory parade. Epstein and Lucchino were open to discussing new deals with players and their agents, but not getting into prolonged negotiations. If they wound up with five stars playing the entire season in the last year of their contracts, so be it.

Epstein would not even say which of the potential free

agents would be the team's top priority to sign, a fact that particularly did not sit well with franchise icon Garciaparra. Nomar remained the most popular player on the team, and on a Hall of Fame trajectory, but his last season had not ended well—with a .170 average in September and a lackluster postseason output of one RBI in 12 games. He still figured he was worth a big payday, bigger than the team was willing to agree to, and talks had broken down between management and Garciaparra's agent, Arn Tellem.

Nomar grumbled his way through the early days of camp, and his mood went from bad to worse when he was hit by a line drive during batting practice on March 5—suffering an injury to his Achilles tendon that kept him on the bench for all but eight hitless at-bats of the exhibition schedule. He was expected to miss the beginning of the regular season as well, making Epstein look like a genius for signing a two-time Gold Glove–winning second baseman during the off-season—free agent Pokey Reese—as a backup at second and short.

Injuries had been virtually nonexistent on the Red Sox during 2003—when Jeremy Giambi was the only position player to go on the disabled list all season—but now guys were dropping like pop flies in the eighth inning of the '03 ALCS.

Nixon showed up to camp with a bad back that turned out to be a herniated disc; he went on the DL without ever playing—and was not due to return until May. Veteran Gabe Kapler took over in right field for the time being, but the loss of two big offensive guns in Nixon and Nomar for what looked to be much of the first month had folks fearing a slow start. Everybody knew Garciaparra's value to the team, and Nixon was one of the most underrated hitters in the league. His 28 homers and 87 RBI in 2003 were merely satisfactory output for his position, but he compiled them in just 441 official at-bats for an OPS of .975 that ranked fourth in the AL.

The state of the pitching staff further contributed to the MASH unit–like atmosphere surrounding the team as Opening Day approached. Relievers Lenny DiNardo, Reynaldo Garcia, and Jason Shiell were all on the DL to start the season, as was former closer Byung-Hyun Kim—who after his postseason woes in 2003 was projected to be Boston's fifth starter. Kim had a bad back and ankle that kept him out of exhibition action early on, and then developed an inflamed right shoulder. Young Bronson Arroyo, a minor leaguer with Boston in '03 whose experience in the majors consisted of a couple up-and-down stints with the Pirates a few years before, took advantage of the situation and earned the final spot in the Red Sox rotation (until Kim could return).

Then there was much hyped new closer Keith Foulke, who struggled mightily in Florida with a 15.00 ERA over eight appearances and nine innings. Opponents batted .395 against him in exhibition play, but there was something almost nobody outside the clubhouse, and even many inside it, didn't know: he was pitching in constant pain.

"Every year, at the end of winter, when I tried to fire it up again, my legs were hurting me—in the joints of my knees," he explains. "It was like I couldn't do whatever I did the year before. This started in '02. It was probably why I didn't throw as hard [in the spring]. My control, from what I can remember, wasn't as good. My breaking balls weren't as good, because I had a hard time getting my lower half into my mechanics."

Foulke was confident that, as in the previous two years, things would get better with time. His teammates, watching his fastball coming in at 88–89 miles per hour rather than the low 90s they had seen the previous year, were not so sure.

"We had a preseason game in Atlanta before we started the season," he says. "I was in the outfield, throwing with our trainer Chris Correnti, trying to figure out what's going on. Curt [Schilling] told me after the season that he and Kevin Millar were talking in the dugout when I was pitching, and Curt said, 'Holy cow, is this the guy we're putting the season on the line for?'"

Schilling was not the only one concerned with the roster situation, as by this point even the backups were falling down. Veteran Ellis Burks, so thrilled to be with his original club again, missed the first several spring games with a sore right elbow. Then, just as he was starting to come around late in the Grapefruit League schedule, a moment of indecision cost him during Boston's second and last exhibition matchup with their old friends from New York.

"I hit a ball in the gap and was going for two, when all of a sudden, I don't know why, I started thinking about going for three," he recalls. "It was spring training, what the hell. Then I changed my mind and slammed on the breaks, just as I passed second base. Jeter was taking the throw, and for some reason my [left] knee gave out on me, and as it went, my body went over my knee and I felt that little pop. I knew it was my meniscus that was torn right there.

"Figures it was against the Yankees."

Ah yes, the Yankees. Although Francona had made a conscious decision not to discuss the previous October's unfortunate turn of events with the team or reporters, the buildup to the regular season and another knock-down, drag-out battle between the two AL East powerhouses was bigger than ever. The fact New York had acquired Rodriguez after the Sox had seemingly already worked out a deal for the reigning MVP—only to have it thwarted by the Players Association—added even more fuel to the fire.

"Because A-Rod had been traded to the Yankees, that added an exciting element to spring training—and there were a gazillion New York writers around," Steve Buckley of the *Herald* remembers about Red Sox camp. "As many New York writers were covering the Red Sox in spring training in '04 as there were Boston writers. The *Post, Daily News, Newsday*—they were all there every day. There was a lot of anticipation on Red Sox–Yankees in the wake of what happened in 2003, and now with Schilling in the picture, and A-Rod adding an exciting new personality, it was the perfect storm."

It was also a chance for fans in both cities to get used to plenty of new faces. In addition to the acquisition of Rodriguez, the Yankees had made several other changes to their roster. Big-time starting pitchers Roger Clemens, Andy Pettitte, and David Wells (a combined 53–24 in '03) were all gone, but veterans Kevin Brown (14–9 with the Dodgers) and Javier Vazquez (13–12 in Montreal) had been brought in to fill the void. Mike Mussina (17–8) and former Cuban superstar Jose Contreras (7–2) were back in the rotation as well, along with Jon Lieber, a possible fifth starter trying to rebound from left elbow surgery.

It was unclear how the New York rotation would fare with all the changes, but the bullpen surely looked better. Mariano Rivera was back for another year as the game's best closer, and the bridge to the Sandman was vastly improved with the acquisition of two accomplished veteran relievers—Paul Quantrill and Tom Gordon. Both were former Red Sox, but would have no trouble remembering which side they were with now when they heard the boos at Fenway Park.

The Yankee lineup, as usual, would be an imposing one. Catcher Jorge Posada (.281, 30 homers, 101 RBI), first baseman Jason Giambi (.250, 41, 107), and left fielder Hideki Matsui (.287, 16, 106) were all back, and while second baseman Alfonso Soriano and his 38-homer bat would now be summering in Texas, A-Rod and his 47-dinger stick would be in pinstripes. So would free agents Gary Sheffield (.330, 39, 132) and Kenny Lofton (.296 with 30 steals), upgrades in right and center field respectively. Derek Jeter (a .324 average), the classy Yankee captain even many Red Sox fans found hard to razz, would be in the middle of the action at shortstop alongside new third baseman Rodriguez.

The first spring training game between the two teams on March 7 attracted more television crews and media members (250 in total) than many playoff contests, and players were peppered with questions about the past, present, and future. Tickets were going for $499 each on eBay the day before the contest at City of Palms Park in Fort Myers (Boston's home turf), leading Bob Ryan of the *Globe* to joke: "That's a nice price for the Final Four, but it's a preposterous figure for a spring training contest in which you will be very happy that you sprung for a program by the fourth inning. Of course, it's the Red Sox and Yankees we're talking about, so right away we've dispensed with rational thought." Some people called the matchup "Game 8."

Back in the world of reality, the Red Sox broke camp and headed to Baltimore and the April 4 opener. In a pregame interview with reporters, Francona told them "when I woke up this morning, I was right in the middle of an inning," a level of all-consuming intensity he said had never hit him that early but he expected to last the season. Amidst continued concern about the injuries to Garciaparra and Nixon, glass-half-full Kevin Millar reminded folks that the Yankees had played the first six weeks of the 2003 season with Derek Jeter disabled by a separated shoulder, and had gone a red-hot 26–11. "We've got great players in this clubhouse," said Millar. "We want Trot and Nomar back at full strength, but we'll hold the fort down."

Even Millar, however, would have a hard time putting a positive spin on the first regular season game of the 2004 Red Sox season, which ended just like the last playoff contest in '03—with a Boston loss and a Pedro Martinez subplot.

On a chilly, windy Sunday night matchup at Camden Yards, Martinez pitched okay, allowing three runs over six innings after a shaky start, but reliever Mike Timlin was roughed up for three more in the seventh and Boston left 14 men on base in an uninspiring 7–2 loss. After the game, it was discovered that Pedro had left the ballpark well before the final out. Coming on the heels of his 6.75 ERA in spring training, when he allowed 26 base runners in 16 innings, the incident worried fans. Could Pedro be cracking under the pressure?

The alarmists felt a little better after a pair of wins behind Schilling and Lowe, but the finale of the opening series went to the home club when the Orioles prevailed, 3–2, in a rainy, 13-inning marathon. The game ended well past midnight, after which Boston's chartered plane was kept grounded on the runway more than four hours due to mechanical trouble before finally taking off at 5:46 A.M. from Baltimore/Washington International Airport. This meant that Red Sox players, after flying in to Boston and then busing back to their cars at Fenway just before 7:30 A.M., had almost no time to go home and rest before having to return to the ballpark for the 3 P.M. opener against Toronto. Terry Francona, not seeing the point in such a trip just for a couple hours' shuteye, spent the wee early morning before his home debut as Red Sox manager curled up on his office couch.

As Tito was getting his bleary-eyed troops ready, fans whose Opening Day tradition included buying tickets on game day were getting a shock: scalpers were getting as much as $125 for bleacher seats (face value $12–$20) and $150 for right field grandstands (normally $27). The late-night loss in Baltimore and the team's injury concerns had done little to deter fans from their Sox obsession; despite the previous fall's excruciating finish, they were ready for more. "The same as the sun is shining, the demand is high, and expectations are high," said owner Jim Holzman of Ace Ticket, the area's leading broker. "I think that everyone believes this is the year."

Whether that was still the consensus four hours later is uncertain, but the home team certainly did nothing to instill confidence.

Everyone enjoyed a raucous pregame ceremony during which the champion Patriots trotted out their latest Super Bowl trophy for the crowd to see (a repeat of Fenway's 2002 debut), and then Pats owner Robert Kraft threw out a first pitch to Francona. Terry should have checked if Mr. Kraft was available to pitch later in the game; after Boston used five relievers in the extra inning loss at Baltimore, the bullpen was gassed going into this one and in need of a deep start from Bronson Arroyo.

He did his part, departing after six innings with a 5–4 lead courtesy of a Jason Varitek homer. Then the pen leaked again, as the Blue Jays scored six runs off three relievers over the last two innings for a 10–5 win. The last of these wasn't ever a "real" pitcher, as the strain on the relief corps forced

Francona to put first baseman/outfielder Dave McCarty on the mound in the ninth (he allowed a walk, double, and a wild pitch, but also induced two groundouts). McCarty enjoyed himself, as did the fans, but the postgame fallout was not as humorous.

The lopsided loss, and the oddity of having to pitch a position player on Opening Day, were the basis for widespread panic from reporters and sports radio talk show callers through the night. Epstein tried to quell the concern by explaining that it was an odd confluence of circumstances—a 13-inning game the first week of the season, and an abnormal number of players (seven) on the disabled list—that created the situation. Fans still panicked, with doomsayers writing off the season after six games.

One thing was clear: this was Theo's team. Twenty-one of the thirty-two players on Boston's Opening Day roster (including those on the DL) had been acquired since Epstein was named general manager on November 25, 2002, and the young GM—who had celebrated his 30th birthday in December of '03—was ready to sink or swim with this club. The early days of the season had them treading water, but then what Burks had anticipated started coming true. These Red Sox *were* different; faced with injury and adversity, along with the unspoken weight of the previous season's letdown, they refused to crumble. They didn't pay attention to the newspapers, the talk shows, or history. They just went out and played.

And started to win.

Starting with an impressive 4–1 victory by Martinez the next day (with Pedro looking much sharper than in Baltimore), Boston won 13 of its 16 remaining April games to finish the month with a major league best 15–6 record and a two-and-a-half-game lead in the AL East. Fenway fans, who had snatched up tickets at a record rate before the season—nearly 2.4 million sold before Opening Day—especially enjoyed three home wins in four days against the Yankees and .160-hitting Alex Rodriguez.[‡]

This was followed up the very next weekend by a three-game sweep at Yankee Stadium, the first for the Sox at their personal House of Horrors since September 1999. New York fans lustily booed their underachieving club, which with its $183 million payroll fell to 8–11 on the year. Derek Jeter, after extending his career-high hitless string to 0-for-25 in the series finale, said afterward, "The booing is directed at a lot of people, and it should be. We haven't played well. It shows that people care."

It was still very early, of course, but Boston players and fans were buoyed by this 10-day, six-of-seven takedown. One especially good sign was seeing Keith Foulke match Yankee ace closer Mariano Rivera by pitching a scoreless 10th and 11th at the Stadium on April 24, and then pick up the win when the Sox managed to plate a run in the 12th on a Manny Ramirez double, groundout, and sacrifice fly.

"Last year we didn't have that guy who could come in and pitch a scoreless [10th] and a scoreless [11th]," said reliever Mike Timlin, who picked up the save. "As strong as [Foulke] is, he probably could have thrown another inning."

Ramirez finished April batting .388, and he and Ortiz each had five homers, but the big story in the early going for Boston was pitching. The team staff compiled an MLB-best earned run average of 2.95 in March and April, and in one stretch hurled three straight shutouts and 32 consecutive

[‡] A-Rod went 0-for-16 at Boston in April, delighting the crowd that jeered him mercilessly, before singling in his final at-bat of the four-game series.

scoreless innings. Derek Lowe, Pedro Martinez, and new-comer Curt Schilling all sported 3–1 records, while Tim Wakefield was 2–0 with a 2.14 ERA.

The relief corps was a big part of the effort as well, with its best stretch of run-free support—also 30-plus innings—in more than 30 years. Foulke quieted those concerned by his dismal camp with a 0.60 ERA and five saves in April, while Alan Embree, who would prove to be a workhorse all season, appeared in 12 March and April games and allowed just three hits and two runs over 10 and a third innings. Scott William-son, over eight games and nine and two-thirds innings, had a 0.00 ERA.

Along with the absence of Garciaparra and Nixon from the lineup, the most discouraging piece of news from the first month centered around Ellis Burks. After trying to play through the pain of the meniscus tear in his left knee suffered in spring training, and managing to limp his way around the bases with one of Boston's first regular season home runs, Burks hit just .133 in nine contests and joined Nomar and Nixon on the disabled list April 26. Slated for arthroscopic surgery the next day, he was expected to be out at least four to six weeks nursing this and a sore elbow.

The move, while deflating to the teammates who had come to admire Burks's class and enthusiasm and value his 17 years of experience, left room for another fan favorite to rejoin the club. Brian Daubach had nowhere near the athleticism and all-around abilities of Burks, but the big-swinging, fun-loving first baseman could lay claim to being one of just four Red Sox players (in the impressive company of Ted Williams, No-mar Garciaparra, and Tony Conigliaro) to hit 20 or more home runs his first four seasons (1999–2002) in the majors. Daubach had been pushed out of his starting job with the arrival of Kevin Millar the previous season, and after making the '04 team out of spring training—and getting a big ovation when he pinch-hit in the ninth inning of the home opener—was demoted to Triple-A Pawtucket in mid-April. Like all the Red Sox of 2003, Daubach was getting another chance.

So was Fenway Park. In their latest creative effort to squeeze as many folks as possible into the 92-year-old venue, and thus justify giving it a reprieve from the wrecking ball, management handed out free green T-shirts on April 29 to 420 fans with tickets in bleacher Sections 34 and 35 behind Fenway's "triangle" in deep center field.§ These seats had long been covered with a black tarp during day games, out of concern that if people wore white shirts while sitting there, batters with the triangle directly in their field of vision would have trouble picking up the ball as it sped toward them at the plate. Green shirts eliminated the problem, and got 420 more people into the ballpark. By the end of that day's doubleheader sweep over Tampa Bay, the Red Sox had registered 75 consecutive home sellouts and had two more wins on the young season.

Players asked if they still thought about the 2003 season and how it ended were split; some used it as a motivator to try harder this year, while others like reliever Scott Williamson kept it out of their minds. "These are totally different circumstances," Williamson said. "The only thing that's the same is our uniforms."

Those who felt compelled to relive the high points and heartaches of the past had an excellent opportunity starting in late April, when the documentary *Still, We Believe: The*

§ The fans bearing seats for the section were originally scheduled to attend a night game that was rained out, thus presenting the dilemma.

Boston Red Sox Movie debuted in local theaters. Focusing on the relationship between the team and its fans with the backdrop of the '03 regular season and playoffs, the movie by local filmmakers Bob Potter and Paul Doyle Jr. received strong reviews from critics and Red Sox officials—although John Henry had one regret that showed the owner's unbridled optimism for how 2004 would turn out.

"They should have shot over two seasons," Henry said. "It would have had a great ending."

8. K MEN, ROLE MEN, AND RAIN

OUT OF ALL THE FANS WHO WERE WATCHING THE Red Sox during the early part of the 2004 season, it's hard to imagine one whose story better personified his passion for the team than Kevin McCarthy.

Grabbing another slice of pizza from the silver tray to his left, McCarthy laughs as he thinks about where his tale began: right here, in this restaurant, maybe in this very booth. It was at the Pleasant Café in Roslindale, Massachusetts, a wood-paneled, Formica-tabled diner virtually unchanged since his childhood a half-century before, where McCarthy first summoned the courage (with the help of several beers) to hatch a plan that he hoped would end with him celebrating a Boston championship on the Fenway Park grass.

It was the night of October 11, 1967. The young, underdog Red Sox had just beaten the mighty St. Louis Cardinals, 8–4, in Game 6 of the World Series. The seventh and deciding contest was set for the next afternoon at Fenway, and 20-year-old McCarthy and his college buddy Joe Whalen—who had gone to Sox games together all season—had no tickets and little hope of securing them.*

What they *did* have was knowledge of the walls in and around the ballpark. With a little climbing and a lot of luck, they surmised, they could find a way into Fenway under cover of darkness. They would find a hiding spot, wait until morning, and when the gates opened at eleven they would reemerge and blend in with the paying crowd.

One more well-pitched game from Gentleman Jim Lonborg and the Sox—ninth-place finishers just a year before— would have their first world championship since 1918.

"We jumped in my car and drove over to Fenway," explains McCarthy. "We parked on Van Ness and then started walking around the ballpark, trying to figure out how to get in. We were right over where the big brick wall and the statues [of Ted Williams and other Red Sox greats] are now, and all of a sudden this station wagon pulls up with an extension ladder on the top. These guys pile out, and we figure they are there for the same reason as us.

"'Hey, this is the short wall—bring it over here,' I yelled.

"So they brought the ladder over and leaned it against the wall. They even offered to let us go in first. Joe and I climbed up and over, and we were still hanging on the other side of the wall about to jump down when we hear the cops show up and kick them out. They never ratted us out, though, never

---

*They were at the last game of the regular season, when Red Sox ace Jim Lonborg defeated the Twins to clinch a tie for the pennant. As McCarthy remembers: "We were crouched along the wall—six of us—and we sprinted out and hoisted Lonborg up on our shoulders and tore his shirt off. I still have a piece of his undershirt."

said, 'Hey, there are two more guys hanging over the wall on the other side.' They just left, and we never saw them again."

McCarthy and Whalen jumped to the ground, about a six-to-eight-foot drop, and squeezed their way through the old wooden turnstiles. They were now officially inside the ballpark, behind the right field grandstands, and the hunt for a hiding place began.

"Well, first we walked onto the field and out to the bull-pens," McCarthy says with a laugh. "Remember, back then it was a big deal to be on the Fenway grass. Now all you need to do is be a mother on Mother's Day."

Once the pair had satisfied their childhood fantasies, they began looking around to see where they could stash themselves for the night.

"We saw the center field camera stand," he recalls. "We went up in the bleachers, and it was raised up. It was pretty filthy underneath, but we said, 'That's it.'"

They crawled into place beneath the camera stand, Whalen going in feet first and McCarthy headfirst so they could face each other and talk. Space was tight and sleep was too risky, but it was dark and they were well hid.

There they stayed, chatting quietly through the night. Then, just after dawn, Whalen—who was the only one of them who could see out from their hiding spot—alerted Mc-Carthy to stay still and not make a sound.

A security guard leading a huge German shepherd on a leash was strolling across the walkway in front of the bleachers, directly below them.

"My feet were sticking out near the edge of the camera stand; the dog walked up, sniffed them, and walked away," recounts McCarthy. "We got a big pass there."

Later that morning, Whalen whispered a warning again: another guard was coming.

"This guy was solo, without a dog, but you still tense up," says McCarthy. "He went on top of the camera stand, right above us, and then we heard him talking, saying something like, 'Camera 3, check,' into a walkie-talkie. We couldn't see, all we could do was hear. Then he said something else:

"'Are you boys comfortable down there?'

"We started groveling—'Please mister, don't turn us in! All the bankers are going to be in the bleachers.[†] We've been to 35 games this year.'

"'Kids,'" the guard said, "'as long as you're not here when I have to do my job, I'm okay.'"

The boys had gotten their second pass, but they weren't out of the woods yet. They had to hold out until eleven before they could emerge, but with about an hour to go they started getting extremely antsy. The beers from the night before had finally worked their way through their systems, and nature was calling them both.

"I still remember the debate; we wanted to hold off, but we just couldn't," says McCarthy. "It was real close to eleven, so we just decided to go for it."

Moving cautiously, so as not to attract attention from the growing number of workers now cleaning and readying the ballpark all around them, they crawled along the length of the short wall above the camera stand and then bolted downstairs to the restrooms.

[†] McCarthy was making a reference to the fact that World Series tickets often wind up in the hands of fans who don't normally attend games during the regular season.

"I went into a stall, and I was relieving myself when there was a pound on the door," says McCarthy.

It was Security.

"Unfortunately, my bladder was the third pass. They kicked us out, and then we came back here [to the café] and watched [Bob] Gibson beat Lonborg in Game 7."

Were McCarthy's story to end there, it would already be impressive. What makes it all the more is what happened 30 years down the road.

Kevin's girlfriend, Nancy, had managed to get tickets for all four '67 World Series home games, but wouldn't give any to him because they were fighting at the time. "I had to find my own way in," he says with a laugh, but he admired her spunk and asked her to marry him. They framed a pair of her tickets (bleacher seats, $2 each), had a son and daughter, and naturally raised them to be Red Sox fans. When their son, Ryan, grew into a good ballplayer, Kevin coached his summer league teams in addition to the team at the suburban Boston middle school where he worked for 35 years as a special education teacher.

Besides a love for the game, Ryan also picked up his father's passion for helping others. In high school he and teammate Kirk Carapezza built a Wiffle Ball "stadium" in Kirk's backyard that they modeled after Fenway Park—complete with its own Green Monster. They held annual "Opening Day" charity events to which they invited baseball celebrities like former Red Sox Rich Gedman and Mike Andrews, and raised $70,000 for the Jimmy Fund of Dana-Farber Cancer Institute.

Fueled by the bedtime stories they had heard of Kevin's near-successful Fenway break-in (as kids, they were told Kevin's "liquid courage" had come from lemonade), Ryan and

Kirk began half-jokingly plotting their own attempt with Kevin offering his help. The younger duo never got up the nerve, but more than 30 years after Kevin's original attempt they found another way to make their mark at the park.

In April 1998, as high school juniors, they were at Fenway for Pedro Martinez's first home game with the Red Sox. "He struck out 12 Mariners," Ryan McCarthy recalls, "but we looked up, saw the bleachers were practically empty, and realized nobody was putting up K cards [for Martinez's strikeouts] like they used to do for Roger Clemens. We didn't think that was right."

The next time Martinez pitched, Ryan and Kirk walked up on game day and bought bleacher seats. Inside their jackets they hid homemade K cards, and for each of Pedro's strikeouts—he had a dozen more that day versus the Indians—they taped one card to the wall at the top of the right field bleachers. They had so much fun they decided to do it again for his *next* home start, and bought seats in the last row of the bleachers so they could post their cards easier.

Thus the K Men were born.

For the rest of the '98 season, and each of Martinez's remaining six years with the team, Ryan and Kirk led a contingent of fans—including Ryan's father *and* mother, Kevin and Nancy—that posted K cards for every Pedro start at Fenway along with many of his road games. Nancy painted the faces of all the K Men and K Women red before each game, and the group designed its own silk-screened K cards. (They began laminating the cards after unruly New York fans ripped them up one night at Yankee Stadium.) Other fans, including a group of young Dominican men who brought flags to wave in honor of their countryman Martinez, applauded their efforts and started helping them post.

When Martinez's brilliance and the group's growing numbers made getting bleacher seats together an impossibility, the K Men started buying standing-room tickets. Pedro waved or otherwise acknowledged their efforts on several occasions, even autographing a couple K cards for them to raffle off for the Jimmy Fund. And when disaster struck and the right field wall on which they posted their cards was torn down as part of the first Fenway renovations in the early 2000s, the K Men found a way to keep going.

"That first game without the wall, we used clotheslines to hold up the cards." explains Carapezza. "They interviewed us on NESN, and we talked about how we were being forced to deal with unfair working conditions. Somehow Larry Lucchino heard about it, and the next thing you know we were invited in to the front office to meet with somebody on his staff."

The Red Sox worked out a deal with the K Men; as long as they paid their way in, there would be space for them to post their Ks on a small area of wall atop the Green Monster, right above the center field triangle and the camera stand where Kevin McCarthy and Joe Whalen had hid out that first night. The group's new high-visibility spot made them more popular than ever, and the K Men added additional creative flair to their act—including cards that spelled out "O-R-T-I-Z" and "N-O-M-A-R" as well as "Los Ponchados de Pedro" ("Pedro's Strikeouts"). They even designed custom-made T-shirts that they sold to raise money for a variety of charities.

Now, in May of 2004, the Red Sox and the K Men were still seeking Kevin's 1967 dream of a world championship celebration at Fenway—and the team looked like it might be up to the task. Boston began the month with the best record in baseball, endured a tough stretch of 13 road games in 16 starts, and was still in first place in the AL East with a 30–18 mark when Pedro blew away nine Mariners in an 8–4 victory on May 28. David Ortiz and Manny Ramirez, fast becoming one of the top power-hitting tandems in the game, each homered in the Friday night contest, with Ortiz's shot a grand slam.

Making the club's strong start all the more impressive is that it had been achieved without the services of two key performers—shortstop Nomar Garciaparra and right fielder Trot Nixon. Garciaparra's Achilles injury and Nixon's disc problems had not improved as quickly as hoped, and by early June neither had appeared in a game. The fact that Boston withstood their absence so well was a testament both to the strong leadership and comfortable, loose atmosphere manager Terry Francona and his staff created for the team, as well as the ability of role players to step up when needed.

Calvin "Pokey" Reese Jr. was a prime example.[‡] A starting second baseman for several seasons on the Cincinnati Reds, with whom he had earned two Gold Gloves, Reese had dropped off severely at the plate in recent years and was batting just .215 with the Pittsburgh Pirates in early 2003 when he suffered severely torn ligaments in his thumb while attempting to steal a base. He had season-ending surgery May 15, but Epstein took a chance and signed him to a relatively cheap one-year, $1 million free agent contract for '04 on the very same day (December 23) that incumbent

---

[‡] There are two stories for how Reese got his nickname as a young child. In one version, he had a belly button that stuck way out and people liked to poke—so his grandmother dubbed him "Pokey." The other tale is that he was a chunky boy whose grandmother called him "Porkie," but with her Southern accent made it sound like "Pokey."

second baseman Todd Walker defected from Boston to the Cubs.

Whereas Walker had been a strong hitter (with five homers in the '03 postseason) and a so-so fielder, Reese would be counted on primarily for strong defense while sharing second base duties with another new pickup—Mark Bellhorn of the Rockies. If Reese batted .250 with a few homers, it would be a bonus; Boston already had plenty of other players (including Bellhorn) who could hit. Besides, if the Sox couldn't win the pennant in 2003 with an offense that rivaled the '27 Yankees, maybe it was time to try a new approach.

That time came sooner than expected when Garciaparra's injury necessitated the Red Sox making Bellhorn the full-time second baseman for the start of the 2004 season while putting Reese at shortstop. There his acrobatic dives, spins, and leaps into the air to snag line drives drew chants of "Po-key! Po-key!" from fans, along with the admiration of his teammates and coaches.

"His first step and incredible range make him a guy who just comes around once in a lifetime defensively," said Boston third base and infield coach Dale Sveum. "I played against Ozzie Smith [a Hall of Famer generally considered the best defensive shortstop of all time], and I've still never seen anyone's range and first step quite like Pokey Reese."

The newcomer had a compelling life story. Reese was raised dirt poor in Columbia, South Carolina, and his boyhood home had no bathroom or hot water. He learned baseball on hardscrabble, rock-strewn fields, and picked up his great defensive abilities as a batboy for his father's team—chasing down balls with his bare hands. Finally getting a glove cut down on the pain, but not his drive. It kept him going for eight years in the minors and eventually a high salary of $3.2 million with the Reds.

Now, not only was Reese turning heads in the field, but he was also providing the bonus offense the Red Sox had hoped for in signing him. His average, which hovered around .220 during the first month, had risen all the way up to .270 by mid-June as Reese collected a surprising number of hits and RBIs (including an inside-the-park homer) from the bottom of the batting order. He knew he would lose his starting job when Garciaparra returned, and that's exactly what happened, but Pokey's efforts helped Boston stay afloat and in (or near) first place throughout the first half.

Bellhorn, the other half (with Reese) of the expected second base combo, played every day while Reese was holding down shortstop and produced at a level far greater than anybody could have expected. Batting primarily second in the order behind Johnny Damon, he shook off a slow start to collect 24 RBI in May. Although his high strikeout total and low batting average were not great figures for a number two hitter, he also walked a lot and was among the team leaders in runs scored. At the end of May he was hitting just .247, but his on-base percentage was a lusty .389.

"Every day he shows up and he plays the game right," Francona said of Bellhorn. "He works the count out and does things that are so important. He finds a way to win that maybe doesn't show up in the box score. We know that and appreciate it."

While Bellhorn and Reese helped solidify the infield in Garciaparra's absence, Gabe Kapler did the same in the outfield while right fielder Trot Nixon was out. Possessing a highly ripped physique that had landed him on the cover of numerous bodybuilding magazines, Kapler was one of those guys who don't put up big numbers but always seem to be in the thick of things. The former Minor League Player of the Year had never lived up to early expectations that he would be an elite power source—he had 146 RBI in 139 games one season in Double-A—and had bounced from team to team before joining Boston in mid-2003. Now, as a steady .270-ish contact hitter with a strong arm that proved quite useful in the deep corners of right field at Fenway, he was proving a fine complementary player.

Kapler was the one with the Adonis-like body, but another member of the Sox had the nickname that suggested muscle: rookie Kevin "Greek God of Walks" Youkilis. In fact, Youkilis wasn't Greek at all, nor did he have a physique that made anybody think of the Discus Thrower. He was big and beefy, and although the third baseman had yet to grow his trademark beard, he stood out in the Boston clubhouse as a guy who didn't particularly look like a baseball player.

He knew how to play, however, and what Youkilis could do better than almost anybody in the professional ranks was find his way to first base. In one stretch between Double- and Triple-A in 2003, he reached safely via a hit, walk, or hit by pitch in 71 straight games. When author Michael Lewis penned his bestselling *Moneyball* about the new approach to player analysis employed by Oakland A's general manager Billy Beane, he used Youkilis as an example of the type of on-base machine of a player Beane coveted—but one he could never get away from the Red Sox. It was Lewis, in fact, who came up with the "Greek God of Walks" moniker.

Youkilis's arrival in the big leagues came a bit earlier than expected, due to another unfortunate circumstance in what seemed to be a never-ending set of obstacles facing the Red

Sox. In mid-May, third baseman Bill Mueller, the defending American League batting champion, began experiencing pain in his right knee. He was expected to miss a few games, and the Sox brought up Youkilis to give Mueller a breather. The plan was that the rookie would return to Pawtucket—where he was hitting a ho-hum .258—once Mueller felt up to returning.

The new kid made the most of his opportunity. In his big-league debut at Toronto on May 15, the very day he was called up, he went 2-for-4 with a home run. Pedro Martinez, always one of the more mischievous guys on the club, implored his teammates to give Youkilis the silent treatment when he returned to the bench after his homer, and they did—ignoring him until it looked like he was going to burst. The ball, meanwhile, was retrieved from the stands to give to Youkilis, although he didn't plan to keep it long. His parents, Mike and Carolyn Youkilis, had rushed to Toronto from Cincinnati as soon as he told them of his call-up—and now he had the perfect welcome gift.

"My dad always talked about it—hitting a home run for your first major league hit," said Youkilis after the contest, a 4–0 Boston win. "He and my mom are the biggest influences in my life and for them to be able to come here on a minute's notice. . . . It'll be a good feeling to be able to give that ball to my parents."

Youkilis wasn't the only new kid on the block having a big day. The starting pitcher for the Sox on May 15 was Bronson Arroyo, a tall, trim right-hander who was going for Boston because of yet another injury: the back woes of fifth starter Byung-Hyun Kim. Arroyo had already filled in for Kim on a few occasions as the South Korean struggled to stay healthy, but this was by far his best effort—eight innings of shutout ball with six strikeouts, zero walks, and just three hits allowed. The Key West, Florida, native with the long, blond curls threw exactly 100 pitches, and Francona may have considered leaving him in to throw a complete game had the pitcher not been battling the flu for a week.

It was a great game all around, and another day in first place for the Red Sox. What neither Arroyo nor Youkilis knew at the time, however, was that their big performances would prove the launching points for a summer of opportunity.

Mueller's knee problems would soon land him on the disabled list, and Youkilis would hit .284 over 30 games while starting at third in his place. Along the way he'd reach base in 26 of his first 29 big-league games—living up to that nickname—and would prove invaluable as a role player once Mueller returned to the regular lineup. Kim, meanwhile, was off to Korea to see a back specialist, and management's patience with him was running out. Arroyo would thus stay in the rotation the rest of the year, and prove, despite a rough stretch in June, to be one of the best fifth starters in baseball.

All hands would certainly be needed on deck, because Boston's primary competitor in the AL East was not rolling over. After a lackluster April in which they went 11–10 with one of the worst team batting averages in the majors, the Yankees had rebounded to raise their record to 30–19 by the end of May. The turnaround certainly wasn't a surprise; with the talent manager Joe Torre had on his club, and the financial resources of George Steinbrenner at his disposal to make tweaks as necessary, nobody expected a New York slump to last long anyway.

As well as Boston's young guns were doing, it would be the veterans who Francona would most come to count on in crunch time. They were already coming through now—from Reese to Keith Foulke and his 1.01 ERA and 10 saves through May to Curt Schilling, whose 8–3 record and 3.03 ERA after two June starts had firmly established him as the staff ace. Pedro had a 6–3 mark himself to this point, but his 3.98 ERA hinted that his days of domination were passing; over his first six Boston seasons, his aggregate earned run average had been just 2.26. The bullpen crew of Mike Timlin, Alan Embree, and Scott Williamson was helping bridge the gap from starters to Foulke well.

The camaraderie around the clubhouse and dugout was infectious. Everybody wanted to be a part of it, even if they couldn't play. About a week after his knee surgery, Ellis Burks began coming to Fenway to do his rehab; watching the games on the TV in the trainer's room, he felt a natural urge to don his uniform.

"They asked me if I wanted to go home [after his surgery], and I said no," recalls Burks. "'I don't want to go home,' I told them. 'I am staying here in Boston, coming to every game, getting my rehab in, and trying to get back out there.' That's what I did. I stayed for every game, dressed and sat on the bench for every game, went on every road trip. If I wasn't able to play, at least I could be there to support them."

Among those Burks and everybody else enjoyed watching do their work the most was the Dynamic Dominican Duo of Ortiz and Ramirez. The 2003 season had not been a true representation of what these players could do together, because Ortiz was not even a regular until well into the summer. In 2004 they were penciled into the middle of the Boston batting order from Opening Day on, and the result was back-to-back production unseen in Boston since Fred Lynn and Jim Rice wreaked havoc on American League pitchers 25 years before. Ramirez was having a typical (for him) season with 14 homers and a .349 batting average entering June, and Ortiz was proving his breakthrough campaign of '03 was the real deal with 11 home runs and a .276 batting mark of his own.

What made this level of production all the more impressive was that it was being accomplished without Nomar Garciaparra and Trot Nixon. Both were expected back soon, however, leaving glass-half-full Red Sox fans to wonder, as June beckoned, just how much better their team was still capable of getting.

The answer did not come quickly, nor did it come when expected. June began with the Yankees and Red Sox tied atop the AL East, and with New York on a hot streak the cries for Garciaparra's return among casual fans were getting louder. More astute patrons, however, had been admiring the excellent glovework turned in at shortstop by his replacement Pokey Reese, and wondered whether rushing Nomar back was the best idea. (Nixon's return, on June 16, came with far less fanfare or drama—but also a home run.)

The Red Sox were 34–23 and riding a three-game winning streak after Martinez and Foulke two-hit the Padres, 1–0, in an interleague contest on June 8. Reese played at short in that game; the next evening, with Nomar back in the lineup, the Red Sox lost, 8–1, and looked sloppy doing it—making three errors and going 0-for-5 with runners in scoring position in a game delayed mid-contest by rain. Garciaparra received an ovation his first time to the plate, but although the box score notes he went 1-for-2 before being removed for a pinch hitter after the 2-hour, 20-minute delay, you had to dig deeper to find the details of a play that would serve as an eerie precursor of what was to come.[§]

In the top of the fifth inning, with no score and men on first and second, Brian Giles hit a ground ball that Garciaparra fielded cleanly but one-hopped to first. First baseman Andy Dominique (getting his first-ever start at the position) dropped the ball, and then in his frustration picked it up and made a wide throw home as two runs scored. It was a sign that Nomar was either rusty, not entirely healthy—when asked this by reporters, he had said he would "never" be at 100 percent—or, more alarmingly, might be showing on-the-job uncertainty. He had been noticeably (and understandably) frustrated by the team's courting of A-Rod over the winter, along with their refusal to meet his contract demands the previous season, but now the team needed him to move forward and focus on playing the best baseball he could.

On a variety of levels, it soon became clear that this was not going to be possible.

Garciaparra was immediately put back into the starting lineup upon his return, but struggled to regain his batting stroke and range in the field. His hitting was not quite as bad as it had been the previous September and October—when he batted .170—but after his first 15 games in June he was at .233 with one home run. He also appeared to be miserable, and while he would not discuss the situation with reporters, the consensus was that he was frustrated by three main things: his failure to play up to his potential upon his return,

---

[§] If the score and rain were not bad enough, Boston fans were forced to watch the final outs of a 7–5 Yankees win over the Colorado Rockies on the Fenway JumboTron during the delay.

his inability to work out a new contract, and lingering resentment over the botched A-Rod deal.

The team fed off his bad vibes, or more accurately starved from them. Beginning with that wet loss to San Diego, Garciaparra's first game back, the Red Sox went 18–21 over the next seven weeks. To be fair, it wasn't all Nomar; the team had been starting to slump before his return, and was just 27–28 in May and June combined. But seemingly overnight, the easygoing camaraderie appeared to have disappeared from the Red Sox clubhouse—and the guy who just yesterday had been the most iconic athlete in town was at the center of the tension.

Compounding the problem was that Pokey Reese had become immensely popular during his three months at shortstop, and, this being an election year, "Pokey for President" bumper stickers had started popping up around Boston. Now, as fans watched ground balls that Reese used to gobble up sneak by Garciaparra into left field, another sticker appeared that matched what was on the minds of many Fenway patrons (and on the boisterous lungs of a few): "Pokey would have had it."

"I think Francona put it best [after the fact]—Nomar was Bostoned out," says Steve Buckley of the *Herald*. "Nomar had to get out of there and they had to get him out of there."

As an example, Buckley mentioned the red line that ran through the home clubhouse at Fenway Park, in front of the players' lockers, to keep the media at bay. The rumor was that it had been Nomar's idea to add the line to the room a year or two before, and while most players didn't worry about making sure reporters and cameramen stayed behind it, he did.

"I remember that Nomar was talking to the writers one day, and one writer had his toe hanging over the line," Buckley says. "Nomar looked down and said, 'Careful, you got your toe over that line.' Everyone just assumed he was kidding and kind of laughed, but he said, 'No I'm serious.' And it was like 'Oh Jesus.'"

While the Red Sox were slumping, and Nomar was sneering, the Yankees kept winning. By June 29, when the two teams met in New York to start a three-game series, the Yanks had extended their lead in the East to five and a half games. New York won the first two games of the series, 11–3 and 4–2, with Garciaparra making three errors, and on the afternoon of the finale Nomar asked out of the lineup. This seemed an odd request, especially given the importance of the game; although the plan had been for him to skip every third game during the first several weeks after his return, he had played in 15 of 16 and the last eight in a row.

He was surely hurting, his manager knew, but Francona also knew the fans would not be very forgiving if they saw Nomar sitting out.

"I checked with him that night because I knew he was going to get crushed by the media," Francona said later. "So I went to him. He was in the whirlpool, and I wanted to get across to him that I wished he would play. The way we were playing, I thought people were going to start taking shots at him, and I didn't want them to."

The game wound up being one of the best of the regular season, and Francona's greatest fears for Garciaparra were realized. The Yankees took a 3–0 lead against Pedro Martinez, the Sox battled back to tie it in the seventh on a Manny Ramirez homer, and it stayed 3–3 until extra innings. Both managers played it like a playoff contest, switching up defenders and inserting pinch runners until their lineup cards were filled with ink. Kevin Millar saw time at first, third, and left—all in the same inning.

Two moments late in the game marked the unofficial beginning of the end of the Nomar Garciaparra era in Boston. At one point the TV cameras shot across the Red Sox dugout, and fans could see what appeared to be the entire team standing atop the steps cheering on a rally. Viewers quickly noticed Nomar was missing, and then they saw him—sitting quietly behind his teammates on the bench, by himself, staring blankly ahead.

Then, in the top of the 12th, with two outs and runners on second and third, pinch hitter Nixon hit a foul pop that Jeter set his sights on. He sprinted across the diamond and dove into the third base stands, making the grab. As he walked back to his dugout with blood gushing from his chin and the ball triumphantly held in his hand, Jeter symbolized the ultimate warrior. Where was Nomar? Still on the bench.

Manny did his best to turn the momentum around, hitting his second homer of the night in the top of the 13th, but this was just not destined to be Boston's game. Francona, taxed for pitchers, tried to get a second inning out of combustible Curtis Leskanic, and New York got to him for three hits, two runs, and the win in the bottom of the frame. After the game, it didn't matter that Francona explained how Garciaparra had told him he was available to pinch-hit in extra innings, and had been stretching out in the runway for a possible appearance. While Jeter needed stitches and X-rays, Nomar needed a major public relations overhaul.

"That game was the end of Nomar in Boston," says Buckley. "It was clear that was the end. He had to go after that."

With the Sox scuffling, and now a season-high eight and

a half games behind New York in the East, rumors started to fly about Boston attempting to trade Nomar and some of its other prospective free agents rather than risk losing them altogether. One deal had Garciaparra going to the Cubs as part of a three-way trade with Arizona that would bring pitcher Randy Johnson to Boston and a reunion with Schilling, his co-ace from the 2001 Diamondbacks squad that whipped the Yanks in the World Series.

"I think it all depends on what happens in the next month," said Derek Lowe, another player rumored to be on the block. "These guys, they know who they want to sign and who they don't want to sign and if we start falling out of this thing, then I think the guys they don't want to sign, they'll listen to trade talk."

Like the fans, Lowe figured Nomar was not long for Boston. "It's not the most pleasant thing when you see the writing on the wall and you know where your future's headed," Lowe claimed. "If he has a feeling they don't want him back, and if they're just trying to get rid of you, how much fun are you going to have at your job?"

Garciaparra was in the starting lineup at Atlanta the night after the Yankee series ended. He had three hits, but that was a lot like Bill Buckner getting two hits in Game 7 of the 1986 World Series.

It was too late—the damage was done.

9. FENWAY FIGHTS AND FLIGHTS

I<small>T HAD RAINED ALL NIGHT AND INTO THE MORN</small>-ing, leaving the Fenway Park outfield so damp that even an umpire who really *was* blind would have been tempted to call the game on account of squishiness.

This, however, wasn't just any game.

The Red Sox had fallen to the Yankees, 8–7, the night before. All losses to New York were tough, but this one really hurt, with ace Curt Schilling inexplicably blowing an early 4–1 lead and normally reliable Keith Foulke coughing up the winning run in the ninth on an Alex Rodriguez RBI single. Boston had gone 1-for-11 with runners in scoring position, and a three-homer game by Kevin Millar had been wasted. Worst of all, the Sox were now a season-high nine and a half games behind Joe Torre's pinstriped crew.

With the other three AL East teams all under .500, it was looking more and more likely that the Sox would finish second to the Yanks for a seventh straight excruciating year. Even with a division title all but an impossibility, Boston still needed every win it could get in a supertight Wild Card race—and every opportunity to gain confidence against New York in anticipation of a possible postseason encounter. After winning six of seven April games against their rivals, the Sox had lost three straight at the Stadium a few weeks before, including the "Nomar-Jeter" game when Garciaparra sat out with a lingering knee injury and watched his Yankee counterpart wrap himself in bloody glory. Last night made it four straight losses to the Evil Empire.

It wasn't just the Red Sox who had a big stake in this game, however. FOX had it scheduled as a nationally telecast, marquee matchup—with a 3:15 Saturday afternoon starting time. Boston–New York games always got strong ratings, and this year they had been through the roof both locally on NESN and nationally on FOX and ESPN. The intensity and intrigue established during the previous year's playoffs and built up during the winter-long A-Rod saga made for must-see TV. Sox–Yanks was like a soap opera and reality show rolled into one.

Those affiliated with the Democratic National Convention, scheduled to get under way a few days later at Boston's FleetCenter, were also eager to see the game go off as planned. Everybody from delegates to corporate sponsors to fundraising groups to politicians themselves had been seeking out tickets to the Sox–Yanks contests, along with trying to nab access to other Fenway specialties like batting practice, private tours, or reserved space in one of the ballpark's function rooms overlooking the field, which would remain open once the team headed out on the road after Sunday's series finale.

Nothing, however, trumped player safety. A group including managers Francona and Torre, Red Sox chief operating officer Mike Dee, and Fenway groundskeeper Dave Mellor all walked the field, and after feeling the soft, squishy grass and viewing the wide assortment of puddles, decided that the game should be canceled.

Out on Yawkey Way, Sox VP and event maestro Dr. Charles Steinberg was biting into a Rem-Dog from Jerry Remy's, waiting for the gates to open and the crowds to come pouring in, when his cell phone rang. It was Mike Dee.

"Hey, chief, where are you?'" asked Dee. (He called everybody chief.)

"On Yawkey Way."

"Listen, you've got to get an announcement out—we're banging the game."

"Banging? What does that mean?"

"We're postponing the game."

"I was suspicious," explains Steinberg of what he was hearing. "It's not raining. It's gray and it's raw with billowy clouds and yes, it rained overnight, but, man, you've got 30,000 people pouring in to eat hot dogs and drink and hang out for two hours before the game is even scheduled to start.

"So I said, 'Why?'

"'The field took a real beating last night, and they're not going to be able to play.'

"'Where are you?'

"'I'm in Tito's office.'

"'I'll meet you there.'"

As Steinberg rushed across the street into Fenway and down toward the manager's office, he made calls to three more ballpark insiders: public relations director Glenn Geffner in the press box, talking through a press release and passing on the edict to "not release it until I tell you"; to video/scoreboard production manager Danny Kischel in the control room, giving him a public address announcement and a similar request to "not read it until I tell you"; and to the scoreboard operator, with an announcement to "not show anyone until I tell you."

"All three systems were ready to go as soon as we called them back and said, 'Yes, go ahead. Postpone this game,'" recalls Steinberg. "We didn't know if there could be a double-header the next day, because the teams already had the ESPN Sunday night game scheduled."

Something felt strange to Steinberg. When he got to Francona's tiny corner office in the bowels of the ballpark, he found Dee, Tito, Mellor, Larry Lucchino, Theo Epstein, and special assistant Jonathan Gilula all crowded around Francona's desk.

Someone reiterated what Dee had told Steinberg about the field "taking a beating" the previous night, and Steinberg asked outright if a cancellation was absolutely necessary.

"I was worried that there was something dangerous going on," says Steinberg, looking back. "We're not that far removed from 9/11, we've got the Democratic National Convention coming up, so I asked, 'Is there more to the story than you're telling me?' Someone, maybe Larry, said, 'No, this is baseball driven all the way.'"

Realizing the kinds of questions they would be getting from writers as the ballpark filled up and the skies cleared, Steinberg continued pressing for more details he could pass on.

"Look, it's our [cancellation] call to make, not the umpires, if the game hasn't started yet," Lucchino said. "But Tito, go out with Joe Torre and the umpires and Dave Mellor and see if they also see what we see. It's our call, and they don't need to agree, but see if they all understand."

Lucchino's thinking was that if they could get more buy-in from some other key folks—Torre, the umpires—it would be easier to justify their decision to cancel such an important game when the writers started asking.

"So out to shallow left field walked that group, Terry Francona and Joe Torre and the four umpires and Dave Mellor," says Steinberg. "Mike Dee and I trailed behind, walking along the warning track. And humorously, they were stomping on the outfield grass in a way that splashed and elicited water reminiscent of Lucy stomping on the grapes [on a classic *I Love Lucy* episode]. This made it clear to everyone what we were dealing with here."

Francona came back to where Dee and Steinberg were standing. He explained that Torre had acknowledged that it was the Red Sox' call to make, and that they could do so whenever they wanted. The understanding was that the game would be canceled, so Torre was now presumably telling this to his team in the visitor's clubhouse.

"As we were walking, Mike Dee took a call in his ear, and Tito and I heard half of the conversation," recalls Steinberg:

"Hey, chief, what?"

"We're walking on the warning track."

"How many guys? A mutiny? Where?"

"All right, we're on our way there."

Then Dee turned to Francona.

"That was Jonathan Gilula, Tito. He says a bunch of players are in your office, threatening a mutiny if we don't play this game."

Without skipping a beat, Francona replied, "Well, it's the first sign of life I've seen from them in weeks."

The trio returned to Francona's office, where the same people from before were now reassembled and joined by four more: Jason Varitek, Johnny Damon, Pedro Martinez, and Kevin Millar. All were in uniform except Varitek, who had on a red T-shirt and a stern look. Steinberg doesn't recall whether it was Francona or someone else who started talking with Varitek, but he still remembers the words.

"We wanna play," said Varitek.

"Guys, I know that, but the field took a real beating last night."

"We wanna play."

"Right, I understand that, but it would take a super-human effort to get the field ready."

"Then do a super-blanking-human effort, we wanna play."

"Yeah, we wanna play, yeah!" That was Millar.

"Yeah, we're not afraid of these guys, I'll come in from the bullpen if I have to!" That was Pedro.

"Then we heard this thunderous thud of a door closing," says Steinberg. "There in the doorway is David Ortiz. 'What's going on?' he bellows. Somebody, I don't know if it was Millar or Varitek, tells him, 'They don't want us to play,' to which Papi says something like 'We want their asses! We want these guys! We want to play!'"

Millar says that at the time, the players in Francona's office thought that "the people upstairs" were behind the possible cancellation because they didn't like the pitching matchup: 3–7 Bronson Arroyo of the Red Sox against New York's Tanyon Sturtze (3–2), who had won the Nomar-Jeter game back on July 1 in relief. Boston players, however, wanted their crack at Sturtze, who came in sporting a 5.05 ERA.

"At that point, it's almost like the movie *Rudy*," says Millar.* "We took our jerseys off and said, 'We're playing.' Bron-

---

*In the movie, after the Notre Dame coach says he will not let Rudy suit up for a "real" game after four years as a practice player, the seniors on the varsity team all walk into the coach's office, one by one, and place their

son Arroyo was probably the most underrated guy on that team, and we just wanted to get out there and do it."

It was now 2 P.M., and it was clear the players were not going to back down. Lucchino instructed Mellor to work on the field for an hour and see what progress he could make; if he *was* making progress, then the team would consider delaying but not postponing the game. If it looked hopeless, they would cancel.

"So we start to disperse, and then poor Tito's phone rings," says Steinberg. "It's Joe Torre, and I get to hear another one-sided conversation."

"Yeah, I know. I know.

"I know I told you that.

"No, we're going to try to play."

"Joe, we all have bosses." That was Lucchino, chiming in.

Mellor and his crew went to work on the field. After an hour they had indeed made progress, so they kept going and the crowd was told the starting time was being delayed an hour until 4:20.

Veteran cameraman Kevin Vahey was working the game for FOX. "The truck had told us the game was called, and then five minutes later they called back and said, 'Wait a minute, don't take anything down yet!'" Vahey explains. "I actually heard that someone at the FOX network office called [baseball commissioner Bud] Selig and said, 'The Red Sox can't call this game, the weather is going to clear and all our people are there.'"

The subplot to all this is that while the field was being cleaned up, it was also being *set* up with a stage and equipment

---

jerseys on his desk and say they won't be playing either. The coach gives in, and Rudy gets to suit up.

for a short pregame concert. The Dropkick Murphys, the Boston-based Irish rock band whose trademark song, "Tessie," had become a hit at Fenway when it was played over the loudspeakers after Red Sox home wins, was planning to perform the piece live at the ballpark for the first time.

"Tessie" had originally been written at the turn of the 20th century for a Broadway musical, and was a favorite of Boston's Royal Rooters baseball fan club. The Rooters changed the words to make fun of the Pittsburgh Pirates, and heckled them with the song all through the 1903 World Series. Pirate players placed some of the blame for their series loss to the Sox (then the Boston Americans) on "Tessie," and the song became an official battle cry for the renamed Red Sox through four more World Series titles in 1912, 1915, 1916, and 1918.

Then the Sox sold Babe Ruth, fell into the American League basement, and the Rooters disbanded. "Tessie" was played only occasionally at Fenway during the '20s, and never after 1930. The story of the song and its connection to the team might have ended there, were it not for the curiosity of Steinberg. Ever a student of history, he kept reading in books on the Red Sox about the magic of this song he had never heard. In October 2003, with Boston and the Yankees squaring off in the ALCS, he found online a scratchy audio recording of "Tessie" from 1903. If the Sox beat New York, he hoped to clean up and play it during the World Series—100 years after its first use as a talisman for victory. Perhaps it could be a good-luck charm once again.

That didn't happen, of course, but over the winter a new plan emerged. Epstein, the general manager/guitarist, was holding his annual "Hot Stove, Cool Music" fund-raiser at which local bands performed as a sort of pre–spring training celebration. Would-be rock stars from the baseball world like

Epstein, ESPN analyst Peter Gammons (also a guitarist), and even ballplayers with musical talent like Arroyo joined in on the fun. Held in one of the bars across the street from Fenway, it was becoming a widely popular show that resulted in a CD that raised even more for charity.

At the January 2004 event, *Boston Herald* sportswriter Jeff Horrigan suggested that Steinberg talk to frontman Ken Casey of the Dropkick Murphys about redoing "Tessie" for a modern audience. Casey went for the idea, Horrigan helped rewrite the lyrics to make them relevant to the '04 Sox, and the Dropkicks recorded it with Arroyo and Damon singing backup vocals. The revamped "Tessie" had been playing at Fenway all summer.

But never live. Until the game the players saved, and history recorded.

First the Dropkicks did their thing, banging out their hit at full throttle from center field while young Red Sox employee Colleen Riley, dressed as "Tessie," danced onstage. Steinberg, watching the whole thing from the Red Sox dugout, looked over at Arroyo and thought how cool it was that the young pitcher, who had helped with the recording, was now getting the chance to see its live debut.

"Who's going for us today?" Steinberg asked, and Arroyo replied by giving him a crooked little smile. Realizing that he had been so consumed by everything going on that he had forgotten, Steinberg laughed and said, "Of course, it's you!"

Once the game finally started, before a full house loaded up on emotion, beer, and the 54-minute delay, the Yankees sought to make all the lobbying efforts and lucky songs inconsequential. They had jumped out to a 3–0 lead by the third inning, helped in part by a Millar error at first base, when Rodriguez stepped in against Arroyo. Few in the ballpark knew it, but this pair had first faced each other as high school players in southern Florida. Rodriguez, pumped about his game-winning hit the night before, crouched over the plate—leaving him little time to escape an Arroyo sinker that got away and hit him near the left elbow. A-Rod stepped out of the box, glared at his adversary as he took a few steps toward the mound, and started shouting at Arroyo.

In looking back at the incident, Arroyo said he never meant to hit Rodriguez, but did want to pitch him inside due to the results of their last face-off. Back in April, at Yankee Stadium, A-Rod had hit an outside pitch from Arroyo about 500 feet for a mammoth home run, but it had been quickly forgotten in the aftermath of Boston's 3–2, 13-inning win and subsequent three-game sweep.

Exactly who said what during this latest encounter varies depending on the source. In watching the replay, and talking to several folks near the incident, it appeared to go something like this:

A-Rod spun around after being hit, dropped his bat, and as he walked toward first yelled at Arroyo that he should "throw the fucking ball over the plate." Varitek stepped over and in front of A-Rod to keep him from doing anything physical to Arroyo, telling him to "just take your base." The two quickly exchanged "fuck yous," and then A-Rod bumped Tek and motioned with his finger—the universal language for "You want a piece of me? Come and get me!"

Tek did just that, shoving his glove into A-Rod's face and then grabbing him as both benches emptied. At first players sprinted over to break up the fight, but within a few seconds they had also started some new ones along the first base line in front of the Red Sox dugout. The biggest subplot was when Sturtze, who had grown up a Red Sox fan in Worcester, made the poor decision of grabbing Kapler from behind. The strongest guy on the team, Big Gabe soon had his attacker on the ground with an unnecessary (but appreciated) assist from teammates Ortiz and Nixon.

"I think the first base dugout had the best angle, but from center field [where he had his camera] you could tell something was happening," says Vahey. "Whether or not Varitek said, 'We don't throw at .260 hitters!' I don't know."[†]

Down in Florida, Joe and Donna Varitek were watching the Red Sox on at home like they always did. When they saw their son and A-Rod starting to go at it, they were not surprised. "He was doing his job, protecting his pitcher," reflects Donna Varitek today, the exact same response that Jason had given in interviews right after the incident. Joe remembers being afraid that Jason's old football instincts might backfire on him. "I got a little worried after the push incident; Jason went into his driving tackle thing and drove A-Rod to the ground. He could have really hurt himself."

Another guy who almost got hurt wasn't even on the field.

"That was the day I thought I killed Johnny Pesky," says closer Keith Foulke with a nervous laugh, speaking of the 85-year-old former Red Sox shortstop, coach, and manager who was still with the team that summer as a sort of legend-in-residence. "It was the fourth inning, so I was in the clubhouse, dressed and ready to go out to the bullpen. I'm sitting there watching it on TV, and you kind of see it [the fight] starting to go. When Jason stood up, and they started jawing at each other, I took off my pullover, headed for the door, and

---

[†] This is one of the many versions of the brief prefight conversation between Varitek and Rodriguez to circulate through the years; if it was true, it was a great on-the-spot retort by the catcher.

was just about to turn and run down the stairs [to the dugout and field] when I ran into Johnny. He fell back, and I caught him."

Another not-quite-so-old-timer was taking in one of the more unique views of the action in a suite high above the Red Sox dugout. *Herald* columnist Steve Buckley was interviewing former All-Star outfielder Fred Lynn for a book he was writing entitled *Red Sox: Where Have You Gone?*, and at the precise moment Lynn was describing for Buckley a three-homer game he had in Detroit as a rookie back in 1975, Arroyo hit Rodriguez—and sent Lynn, who had done some TV work since his retirement, into play-by-play mode. Lynn had been part of some pretty good Red Sox–Yankees fights himself back in the '70s, and this melee seemed to take him back.

"If you listen to the tape, it's really funny," says Buckley. "One minute he's telling me about his big day in Detroit, and then he suddenly gets real intense and starts in like, 'Oh boy, A-Rod looks pissed! It looks like they're going to go! They're going to go!'"

By the time everyone on the field had been separated, New York starter Sturtze was bleeding from his left ear, the result of his one-on-three tussle; Rodriguez, Varitek, Kapler, and New York outfielder Kenny Lofton had all been ejected; and the Red Sox had a new infusion of energy to ride out the season.[‡]

"It was one of those brawls where you get to see what kind of people your teammates are," Damon said later. "In our case, we got to see great things—great camaraderie, great togetherness."

[‡] Arroyo was allowed to stay in the game, the justification being that the umpires believed he had not intended to hit Rodriguez.

This first manifest itself in the late stages of that afternoon's game. The Red Sox were down 3–0, up 4–3, down 9–4 (after a six-run Yankee sixth and another ejection, this time Francona), down 9–8 (after getting four back in the bottom of the sixth), and down 10–8 heading into the last of the ninth. Rivera was on to pitch for New York, which with a two-run lead was money in the bank.

Not this time. Garciaparra—who, unbeknownst to most, had been talking money that very morning—led off the frame with a double. He went to third on a deep fly to right by Nixon, and then scored when Millar (4-for-5 on the day) lined a single to center. Bill Mueller was up next, and after working Rivera to a 3-and-1 count, he struck a shot into the Red Sox bullpen to cap the three-hour, 54-minute marathon and an 11–10 Boston win.[§] The entire team greeted Mueller at home plate; and Francona quickly realized he needed to pay extra-close attention to where (and near whom) he was celebrating. In rushing out from the clubhouse (where he had been banished by the umpires), the manager had forgotten to put on his shoes.

Afterward, Francona and Epstein both had a sense of just how important the moment had been.

"It's a huge win for us, and will be bigger if we make it bigger," Francona said. "If we have this catapult us and we do something with it, that's what will really make it big."

Added Epstein: "If we go on to play like this, this will go down as one of the most important victories we had. Today was not about stats or box scores, it was about emotions."

The normally stoic Varitek chided himself for not keeping

[§] It was Mueller's second homer in as many days against New York and the eighth of his career against the Yankees, his most against any team.

his own emotions under control with regards to A-Rod, and in the months and years to come would refuse to autograph any of the countless photos depicting the day's iconic moment—he and Rodriguez, face-to-glove-in-face—that would wind up on the walls of rec rooms and bars across New England.

When Charles Steinberg approached Tek in the clubhouse and told him "You won us the game today," the catcher vehemently denied it. "He thought I meant the fight, but I didn't," explains Steinberg. "I told him, 'That game was postponed until you said your words.'"

In a way, it was if Steinberg had come full circle in his baseball career. He was back in the Orioles clubhouse, being told by Earl Weaver that "you won us the game today" by virtue of his "found stat" on pinch hitter John Lowenstein's batting success against Angels reliever John Montague. The difference was, he was now the one doing the praising.

What did A-Rod think of all this? "I think it's going to take this rivalry to a new level," Rodriguez said. "The intensity is something I've never really seen before."

Although it was only July, it was indeed beginning to feel like the postseason around Fenway Park. The Red Sox won the Sunday night game against New York as well, 9–6, but the true impact of "The Fight" could not be focused on right away because another significant event was looming less than a week away: the July 31 trade deadline.

It turned out that before helping to ensure that the July 24 game could be played, John Henry, Larry Lucchino, and Theo Epstein had quietly met at Fenway that morning with Nomar Garciaparra and agent Arn Tellem to discuss Nomar's expiring contract and what could be done to make the player happier in Boston. But despite a tranquil location for the session (Fenway's family room), there was not much in the way of warmth exchanged between the two sides.[||]

As Lucchino reflects today, the time had come to accept that Garciaparra, the longtime face of the franchise who had once appeared to be on a clear path to Cooperstown and a retired number ceremony at Fenway Park, could not remain a Red Sox.

"We did make another effort to get Nomar signed," says Lucchino. "but when it became clear to us in late July that we were *not* going to get him signed, or that it was going to be extraordinarily difficult to sign him in light of his pending free agency in October, only then—after walking the extra mile, at least in our opinion—did we make a decision that a change had to be made."

Lucchino explains that while ownership still felt Garciaparra had strong value as a player, the key to the decision was a desire to address the team's problem areas before the deadline. In the opinion of Epstein and his baseball operations staff, Boston's biggest needs were better infield defense— Theo deemed this a "fatal flaw," and had numbers that proved Garciaparra's struggles afield since his return had made him a defensive liability—and a reserve outfielder with speed who could start if necessary for oft-injured Trot Nixon.

Other players, most notably slumping pitcher Derek Lowe, were also rumored to be on the trading block, but with every-

---

[||]A few days later, quoted in a *Boston Globe* story, Garciaparra said that the July 24 discussion with Boston management had been about the team, not his own situation. "They asked me what did I think about the team," Garciaparra said, "I said, 'What's the difference between our record now and a year ago? Look at it. One game. What are you worried about? Ride it out.' There was nothing about me."

thing that had happened between ownership and Garciaparra in the 18 months since he first rejected a four-year contract extension, the thought of keeping a clearly angry player with the team one more day than necessary was unappealing to everyone involved.

When Garciaparra went to Francona just three days before the deadline and told him that his Achilles was acting up again, and he thought he would need "considerable" time off down the stretch—maybe even a trip to the 15-day disabled list—it only strengthened the resolve of Epstein and ownership to move him. Yet another red flag was an oblique muscle injury suffered by Pokey Reese, who had filled in so exceptionally at shortstop during Nomar's absence. If Garciaparra was incapable of playing now, who would be able to take his place?

The answer came soon enough. At 4:45 P.M. on July 31, less than three hours before the Red Sox were set to take on the Twins in Minnesota, and after his name was penciled into the starting lineup, Nomar was called into manager Terry Francona's office in the visitor's clubhouse at the Metrodome. Already in uniform, he was put on the phone with Epstein to hear the news that would soon be sending shock waves throughout baseball and New England—even though it had been largely anticipated.

As part of a four-team trade completed mere minutes before the 4 P.M. deadline, Garciaparra was being sent to the Chicago Cubs with minor league prospect Matt Murton in exchange for a pair of Gold Glove winners: shortstop Orlando Cabrera of the Montreal Expos (Nomar's successor) and first baseman Doug Mientkiewicz of the Twins, who merely had to switch uniforms and move his things from one side of the stadium to the other to complete his part of the transaction.

The Cubs had been told about the latest update in Garcia-parra's injury situation—his concern about needing more time off—prior to the trade.

In a separate move announced at the same time, and thus erroneously thought by many then and ever since as part of the "big" trade, the Red Sox acquired veteran Dave Roberts from the Dodgers in exchange for minor leaguer Henri Stanley. Just as the Garciaparra-for-Cabrera-and-Mientkiewicz trade had been made to bring the Red Sox the defensive help Epstein craved, this fulfilled his other wish for an outfielder with speed. Roberts was among the National League leaders with 33 stolen bases, and had been caught only once. He would be counted on in Boston to man right field while Trot Nixon recovered from his latest injury setback, and then provide quickness when needed off the bench.

The details of the Garciaparra trade, which sportswriters and baseball historians agreed was Boston's biggest transaction since selling Babe Ruth to the Yankees in 1920, surprised many fans and experts. They felt that two decent players who had never been All-Stars (or three, if they believed Roberts was part of the swap) was too little compensation for a top-tier performer. The reality, however, was that Nomar was hurt and miserable—and those negotiating with the Red Sox knew it. None of the guys coming to town had ever hit 20 homers or knocked in 100 runs, but Epstein was more concerned with stats like 74—the total number of unearned runs allowed by the Red Sox in their first 102 games, the highest figure in the majors.

"As much as I like the club, I'm responsible for the flaws on the team," declared Epstein, the mastermind behind the deal. Theo had agonized about making it, knowing that in the long history of Red Sox baseball, superstars simply did not get traded—even when they were in obvious decline. But he had stuck to his guns, because, as he put it, "Our defense has not been championship-caliber. In my mind, we're not going to win a championship with this defense. We're a well-rounded club now."

For now, however, it was time for praise. Epstein called the man he had just sent away "one of the greatest Red Sox of all time," while Johnny Damon, a teammate for the past three seasons, offered up, "We just traded away Mr. Boston, a guy that meant so much to the city."

Manny Ramirez said Nomar was the best hitter he had ever seen, and Pedro Martinez gave his usual colorful take: "I'm so used to seeing 'Nomah!' and hearing the people go, 'Nomah!' and No. 5 all over everybody's back. For some reason, I just framed him as a Bostonian, as part of the team. I think a lot of people are going to be sad in Boston."

As for Garciaparra, who had so often closed himself off from the press and teammates in the final, frustrating months of his decade with the Red Sox organization, the words he chose for his parting comments were in part proud, emotional, and a bit defiant.

"If it was in my control, I'd still be wearing a Red Sox uniform. That's the place I know, I love, all those fans, I'll always remember. They can take the shirt off my back, but they can't take away the memories I got. They can't take away the standing ovation that I got when I came back this season and I walked up to the plate. Or the standing ovation I got when I hit the grand slam this year. Or when I hit three home runs on my birthday [in 2002].

"Every time I stepped up to the plate, the fans cheered for me. When I went deep in the hole to make a play, they'll never be able to take away that. What it's meant to me, they all know that every single day I went out there and I was proud to put that uniform on and what it represented."

And with that, Garciaparra took off his gray Red Sox road jersey and pants, put on a white shirt and jeans, and left the clubhouse.

10. RESOLUTION AND RESURGENCE

CHANGE DIDN'T HAPPEN OVERNIGHT, BUT WHEN it came it came quick.

On August 1, 2004, Orlando Cabrera stepped up to the plate for his first at-bat with the Boston Red Sox. The shortstop, formerly of the Montreal Expos, had joined the Sox in Minnesota after the blockbuster trade that sent Nomar Garciaparra to the Cubs, and Cabrera desperately wanted to make a good impression. His teammates would be watching from the dugout to see what the new guy could do, as would the fans back in New England.

The starting pitcher for the Twins was Johan Santana, a crafty lefty on the way to a 20-win season. Cabrera was familiar with him from interleague play, knew Santana had a tough change-up, and was able to hold up his swing when one came in. He guessed a fastball was coming next, and when it did the right-handed batter hit it over the left field wall for a 1–0 lead. The perfect script would have had Boston winning the game by a one-run margin and Cabrera emerging the home run hero, but this being the 2004 Red Sox, things would not be quite that simple.

In the bottom of the eighth, after Pedro Martinez had exited with a 3–2 lead, the Twins had men on second and third with no outs when Justin Morneau hit a deep fly ball to center field. Gabe Kapler made the catch, and even though there was no way he could nab the runner breaking to the plate, he unleashed a long throw that missed the relay man at second base. Cabrera ran over to cut the ball off, but he could not handle it cleanly and was charged with an error as a second run scored. Minnesota won, 4–3, and Cabrera wound up an unfair goat rather than a hero in his debut.

Such was life with the Red Sox during much of May–July 2004. Despite the team's abundance of talent, a rash of injuries along with the tension between Garciaparra and management leading up to the trade had created an atmosphere not conducive to winning. After compiling the best record in the majors during April (15–6), Boston had spent the next 82 games between May 1 and August 1—almost exactly half the 162-game regular season—going a perfectly mediocre 41–41.

There was hope that the trade, along with an electric comeback win over the first-place Yankees in late July, would be the sparks needed to fuel a turnaround. But the Sox had gone just 3–3 since the Yankee game, a contest highlighted by the Jason Varitek–Alex Rodriguez fight, and had now lost twice more since trading Garciaparra. The next two weeks would not prove much better, and on August 15 Boston stood at 64–52—10 and a half games behind New York in the AL East and virtually neck and neck with three teams in the American League Wild Card hunt.

Then, without warning, it happened.

The team that Epstein said was more well rounded after the

Nomar trade began to play like it on a consistent basis. Derek Lowe, who had struggled much of the season to recapture the form that had made him one of baseball's biggest winners in 2002–03, pitched seven gutsy innings on August 16 in an 8–4 victory over Toronto at Fenway that also featured hits from eight of the nine starters and a two-inning save from Keith Foulke (his 20th). In grabbing his fourth win in five decisions, Lowe got 19 of his 21 outs on grounders—his specialty—or strikeouts, a good indication that the improved defense Red Sox general manager Theo Epstein sought in trading Garciaparra for Gold Glovers Cabrera and Doug Mientkiewicz was starting to pay off.

"Sometimes you need a spark," Kevin Millar explains of the trades that saved the 2004 season. "We were just kind of there, just kind of spinning our wheels. It's the same for any sport—any team. When you're in that kind of funk, you need something to get ahead. You saw that with Mike Trout and the Angels [in 2012] and Yasiel Puig and the Dodgers [in 2013]. That year, with us, it was Orlando Cabrera.

"Theo stood up there and made a bold move and you know what? If it didn't work out, he could have been blackballed for life. That was what made Theo so good; he had the ability to make decisions, and he believed at that point that it was time to move Nomar—and Orlando Cabrera was an absolutely wonderful asset to this unit that we were trying to put together, and so were Doug Mientkiewicz and [fellow deadline pickup] Dave Roberts."

It wasn't just the newcomers, however. For much of the year the only consistent hitters on the team had been leadoff man Johnny Damon and sluggers Manny Ramirez and David Ortiz. Now it seemed like everybody else was getting hot at once. Catcher Jason Varitek, at a time in the season when most receivers are beginning to wear down, hit an incredible .444 in August with nine doubles, five homers, 20 RBI, and an OPS of 1.339. Third baseman Bill Mueller, who had struggled through knee problems to a .257 average just one year after capturing the AL batting title, opted for July surgery and returned with a vengeance—hitting .380 in August with numerous clutch hits. Cabrera, the man brought to town for his glove, was contributing a steady stream of doubles to the cause as well.

Then there was Millar, the clubhouse character who in the past two years had helped as much as anyone to create an atmosphere where winning, friendship, and fun could all coexist. He had proven to be an overachiever at the plate with 25 homers and nearly 100 RBI in 2003 before falling back to earth for much of this campaign, and was scuffling along at .269 with very little production when a single impulsive move turned it all around.

"We were in Seattle for a game, watching the Mariners take batting practice," Millar recalls. "Their catcher Miguel Olivo [a .235 hitter] is just raking it, blasting bomb after bomb. He has an open stance, and I've never hit open in my life. So I came back to Fenway for the next series and figure I'm going to hit open like Miguel Olivo. I go deep with three hits, no joke, and then the Yankees come to town and I hit four home runs in a three-game series. It was all because of Miguel Olivo—no hitting coach or nothing else."

Millar pauses and laughs, putting his story into perspective. "In this game, that's what drives me crazy. People don't adjust. When things aren't going right, you've just got to try something crazy, you know? I hit that way the rest of the year, and it absolutely turned my career around."

The hot streak, which raised Millar's average above .300

by mid-August, was indicative of the transformation overcoming the 2004 Red Sox. Free from the tension that hung over the clubhouse during the long months of the Nomar Watch, Boston players were enjoying themselves again.

Broadcaster Uri Berenguer, covering Red Sox games on radio for the Spanish Beísbol Network, noticed the change.

"It was completely different; they were obviously really having fun together," says Berenguer. "It seemed like every day you went in the clubhouse there was something new going on. There had been a couple of road trips before August when you really had to be careful what you said in there. It had been quiet, but now there was music playing again."

Asked for an example of the team's playful clubhouse nature, Berenguer thinks of one immediately.

"I remember this game when Millar had this horrific slide into third base—he landed and it seemed like he left a crater," he recalls with a laugh. "I'm not sure if he was safe or out but it was hilarious. After the game, Pedro had just gotten out of the shower. He was still in his towel, and he grabbed some magazines and put them around the clubhouse as if they were bases. Then he called over, 'Hey Millar! Pay attention—it's like this!' And he started running around making fun of how Millar ran the bases. He even slid.

"That was the kind of chemistry those guys had."

The red lines in front of clubhouse lockers? "They were still there," says Berenguer, "but it sure didn't feel like they were."

For the countless fans who had cheered for Garciaparra during his All-Star run with the Red Sox, and the players and staff who had grown to know and care for him, it was a bittersweet time. There was no denying that the trade had changed the aura around the club, and improved its on-field performance, but it had come at the cost of one of the team's most popular all-time players.

"Johnny Pesky loved Nomar," recalls Pam Ganley Kenn, Red Sox senior director of public affairs. "When Ted Williams died in 2002 and we had the big [celebration] event for him, Johnny was so sad, because he talked about Ted all the time. Nomar was so good with him about it, and that stuck with me.

"It didn't seem to be a good vibe for him [Nomar] here; there was definitely some animosity," Ganley Kenn continues. "But some of the old-school guys up here? They were *not* happy with the trade. I don't remember Bresch [vice president/publications archives Dick Bresciani] being excited about that trade, and I don't remember Larry Cancro [VP/Fenway affairs] being excited either. I think they just saw him . . . Nomar *was* the Red Sox. He was who every little boy wanted to be for that period of time. So that was a shocker; nobody thought it would happen."

Larry Lucchino, who says he worked until the last days before the trade deadline seeking a way to keep Garciaparra in Boston, admits that in the end, having closure to the difficult last stage of Nomar's tenure that started with stalled contract negotiations and extended through the near-trade for Alex Rodriguez and the ongoing Achilles injury was a relief.

"Yes, I think some kind of clarity and resolution of that issue probably helped," Lucchino says. "We'll never know how much Nomar could have helped had he stayed around for the rest of that year; it's impossible to know. But I do think clarity and resolution helped, and a few new players who came in and performed extremely well."

As one of those players, and an athlete who would wind

up playing a major role in one of the greatest moments in sports history, Dave Roberts had an interesting reaction when Theo Epstein called at the trade deadline to tell him he had just become a member of the Boston Red Sox.

Disappointment.

"I was devastated," says Roberts, who was playing for the Dodgers just a couple hours from his San Diego home. "We were in first place; I didn't want to go anywhere. I was at home in Southern California, I was a leader on the team, and we had a great group over there. I hated to leave."

Roberts had been starting in the outfield for the Dodgers, and was among the National League leaders with 33 stolen bases in just 34 tries. His had been a challenging baseball odyssey in which he had to fight to prove himself at every step—from his walk-on days at UCLA to his 28th-round selection by the Tigers to his time as a backup in Cleveland and Los Angeles. He had beaten out by three more heralded, higher-salaried players to win his starting job in L.A., and was playing some of the best baseball of his life.

Now, as he caught a plane for Tampa to catch up to his new teammates, Roberts thought about how he was going to have to prove himself all over again.

"I thought I was going to play a lot, because Trot [Nixon] was hurt," he recalls. "I was going to play right, Johnny [Damon] was going to play center, and Manny [Ramirez] was going to play left. But it turned out to be only for a little while."

Manager Terry Francona talked frankly to Roberts, explaining that Nixon was going to be back sooner than expected and that he would be primarily a role player.

"That's one of the things I appreciated the most about Tito, the way he kind of laid it all out for me honestly from the get-go," says Roberts. "I came to a point where early on I decided that even though I was disappointed, I had to buy in. it wasn't just about me. I was going to do whatever I could to help this team win. Besides, it's hard not to kind of buy into that group. It's a very unselfish group and a great bunch of guys."

Fenway Park was not entirely new to Roberts. He had played there a bit while with the Indians, and had even gone inside the Green Monster to add his signature to the decades of famous and not so famous names lining its dark, dank walls.

"I signed my name, and since my wife was pregnant with our son at the time, I put his initials in there too—CDR for Cole David Roberts. Then I added the date, 9-19-2000, hoping that maybe someday he'll see I was thinking about him while he was in his mom's stomach, and that would be cool. Then maybe he could sign it later."*

Although the Dodgers were in the midst of a pennant race, and played before large crowds at a beautiful ballpark, there was nothing to prepare Roberts for the intensity of Boston baseball. "I learned quickly the magnitude of Red Sox–Yankees," he says. "They had just had the bench-clearing brawl with Tek and A-Rod, so they were still talking about that."

Impressed by the foresight of Epstein and the rest of Boston management to see exactly what pieces were needed to put the team in the best position to win, Roberts felt good being part of the equation. Everybody seemed to know their role, and everything was falling into place.

For anybody who had been watching or playing with the club all season, it was clear that in addition to the terrific offensive tear the Red Sox were on, the other facets of their game were also reaching new levels. The defense, with Cabrera

---

*He did.

and Mientkiewicz on board, was noticeably enhanced; balls were no longer getting through the holes on the left side of the infield nearly as often, which as shown in the Toronto game made a big difference to ground ball pitchers like Lowe and (to some extent) Wakefield. After allowing 74 unearned runs during the first four months of the season, Boston gave up just 20 in the last two months.

In discussing sure-handed shortstops with David Ortiz, Jose Iglesias, and Uri Berenguer during the 2013 season, Pedro Martinez stated that "the best defensive teammate I had in my career was Orlando Cabrera." According to Berenguer, Martinez said that during games when he was behind him in the field, Cabrera would often yell over to the mound and tell him where to pitch the ball to different batters so they would hit it to him at short. In close games, Martinez knew, one or two base hits taken away by gobbled-up grounders could mean the difference between victory and defeat.

So could strong baserunning. Roberts had the green light to steal whenever he wanted, and while he did so very infrequently with Boston because of the high-powered offense, having his speed available in a pinch-running role to get around the bases or to keep the team out of double play possibilities was a huge asset. In early August Boston dropped four one-run games in an eight-day stretch, but later in the month and through September and October the team started doing much better in the close ones.

All of this bode well for the pitching staff, which included five hurlers who started all but five of the season's 162 games.

In addition to Lowe's second-half revival, Curt Schilling continued to show his value as the staff ace with a hot streak as good as anything he had put together alongside Randy Johnson in Arizona. After losing to Tampa Bay on August 9,

Schilling would go undefeated in his last nine starts of the year—compiling an 8–0 record and 2.42 ERA down the stretch to finish as the AL leader in victories and winning percentage at 21–6. Boston actually had a 25–7 record in Schilling's 32 starts, showing that even when he didn't win, he was putting the team in position to do so.

Martinez was clearly no longer this team's ace, even if he didn't want to believe it, but he remained talented enough to be one on most clubs. His 3.90 ERA, while by far the worst of his Boston career (Schilling, by contrast, checked in at 3.26), still placed him ninth in the offensively minded American League. Pedro remained stingy with hits allowed (his 8.005 per nine innings was third in the AL) and he still kept the K Men busy with 227 strikeouts in just 217 innings—including four games of double-digit whiffs in one August stretch of five contests.

Tim Wakefield was another big August performer with a 5–1 record during the month. Overall he would finish 12–10, his seventh season with double-digit victories and a strong comeback campaign after the anguish of letting up Boone's pennant-winning blow the previous October. Having swung between the rotation and bullpen for close to a decade, Wakefield spent his second straight year as almost exclusively a starter—notching just two of his 32 appearances and three of his 188 innings in relief.

By far the most improved starting pitcher for Boston down the stretch was a young hurler who was not even slated to be in the rotation at the beginning of the year. Bronson Arroyo only secured a spot as the number five man due to injuries and ineffectiveness from Byung-Hyun Kim; always equipped with excellent stuff, Arroyo began exhibiting a new level of consistency throughout his starts that translated into victories.

Just 2–7 with a 4.68 ERA after a five-game June losing streak, he went 8–2 the rest of the season with a 3.58 ERA—especially shining away from Fenway Park with a road ERA of 3.06 that placed fifth in the AL (behind, among others, teammate Schilling at 3.00). His final record of 10–9 simply did not do him justice; Boston went 13–4 in his final 17 regular season starts, including 7–0 in September and October.

One of the biggest problems of 2003 for Boston, at least for much of the season, had been the lack of an elite closer to match up late in games against the likes of New York's Mariano Rivera. In Keith Foulke the Red Sox had found that man, as exhibited by his 32 saves and 2.17 ERA over 72 appearances. Although he struggled a bit in mid-season, Foulke finished strong, had 20 appearances in which he pitched more than one inning, and compiled a fantastic road ERA of 1.18. Mike Timlin and Alan Embree had been up and down much of the year in bridging the gap from the starters to Foulke, but both were durable relievers with more than 70 appearances and a history of postseason effectiveness to call on in October.

The end result of all these numbers was one of the hottest stretches by any team in major league history. Starting with the win against Toronto on August 16, Boston went an incredible 20–2 over three weeks to cut New York's lead in the AL East from 10 and a half to just two games. And while they never quite caught the Yankees, by playing .700 baseball for two months—a 42–18 record from August 1 until the end of the regular season—the Sox ran off with what was once a close Wild Card race to reach the postseason for the second straight year.

"For $150 million, this is how we're supposed to play," said Foulke, referring to Boston's payroll (second only to the

Yankees) after nailing down another multi-inning save against the Anaheim Angels on September 8. The victory, Boston's ninth straight, gave them three in a row over an Angels team that many predicted would be facing them in the playoffs. Anaheim still had a chance at the NL West crown, and with outfield great Vladimir Guererro leading the way was also one of the leading Wild Card contenders. Boston's sound beating of them at Fenway Park provided another boost of confidence in a stretch where this feeling was growing on a daily basis.

Nothing gave the Red Sox a greater sense of self-assurance in their ability to make a deep October run, however, than the two men in the middle of their batting order.

Manny Ramirez and David Ortiz formed a historic one-two punch during the 2004 regular season, putting up the types of statistics that brought completely justifiable comparisons to the greatest duo of them all: Babe Ruth and Lou Gehrig. Ramirez (a .308 average, 43 homers, 130 RBI) and Ortiz (.301, 41, 139) were the first American League teammates since Ruth and Gehrig to each bat .300 with 40 homers and 100 RBI in the same season, and the first teammates *ever* to have 40 homers and 40 doubles in the same campaign.

Their appeal went beyond mere numbers. Ortiz's magnetic, gentle giant personality and growing reputation as one of the game's best clutch hitters had made him—with the trade of Nomar Garciaparra—the new face of the franchise. Ramirez, for all of the frustration he caused his manager and fans through unexplained defensive gaffes and mysterious hamstring injuries, was a once-in-a-generation talent who kept things from ever getting boring on Yawkey Way. Garciaparra could never get past his anger and hurt over almost being traded; Manny let his bat do the majority of his squawking.

These were not the only Boston bats making noise, of course. Long-haired Johnny Damon looked like he could walk on water, so it only made sense that he finally enjoyed the type of heavenly season atop the batting order for which management had been waiting. He put up huge power numbers for a leadoff man (.304, 20, 94) while scoring 123 runs, stealing 19 bases, and playing an excellent center field. Catcher Jason Varitek also had a standout year offensively (.296, 18, 73), but it was his take-charge attitude and tireless work with the pitching staff that made him an invaluable presence behind the plate, in the clubhouse, and in A-Rod's face. Millar (.297, 18, 74) had ridden the coattails of Miguel Olivo to another fine year at first base, while second baseman Mark Bellhorn (.264, 17, 82) and third baseman Bill Mueller (.283, 12, 57 in an injury-plagued year) were rock solid.

Another star in the Boston lineup was Fenway Park itself. The Red Sox had one of the best home records in baseball at 55–26 (.679), and fans filled the tiny venue at a record pace—making Boston just the fourth team in MLB history to sell out an entire season while stretching the Fenway sellout streak to 145 regular season games overall. The ongoing efforts to renovate baseball's oldest ballpark continued, with the newest big change being the addition of seats, tables, and food options for hundreds of patrons atop the right field roof. This necessitated removal after more than 30 years of the famous right-field billboard honoring the Jimmy Fund of Dana-Farber Cancer Institute, but the organization's logo found its way to a unique new spot with even better everyday exposure by a heavy-hitting team: the facing of the left field wall.

The festive atmosphere at Fenway remained a big part of its appeal, and Charles Steinberg was always fine-tuning it. Music had been an important part of Steinberg's life since he saw the Beatles as a five-year-old, and he sought ways to get fans at the ballpark more involved through songs. Whereas "Sweet Caroline" by Neil Diamond had been in the rotation of tunes played over the Fenway loudspeakers for several years, Steinberg believed it could become a huge hit if people always knew when it was coming. He began having it played during every game, in the middle of the eighth inning, whether the Red Sox were winning or losing. What transpired was a daily sing-a-long, which, while derided through the years by sports talk radio hosts and cranky columnists as the end of civilization as we know it, has never waned in popularity.

Why the middle of the eighth?

"I like the concept of a second stretch," Steinberg explains. "When you have inspirational music in a ballpark, you prefer generally for it to be on the half inning because you like to lift the crowd as the home team is coming up. If you're going to play mellow songs, you prefer those to be at the end of the full inning when the visitors are coming up. You modulate the energy, so by making 'Sweet Caroline' in the middle of the eighth, after you already had the seventh-inning stretch which lifts you a little bit, now you have in essence an eighth-inning stretch. You've got people singing as you're coming up to bat in the bottom of the eighth."

As Boston continued singing and surging in its efforts to catch the Yankees, the New York *Daily News* took the unusual step late in the summer of assigning a sportswriter to cover the Red Sox like a beat reporter—for all home and away games—through the remainder of the regular season and playoffs. Roger Rubin, who had attended about 50 Boston games for the *Daily News* in a similar capacity the previous summer, was given the honor again.

What made the arrangement so unique for Rubin was that he grew up just a few miles from Fenway Park in Chestnut Hill, Massachusetts, rooting passionately for the Red Sox during the heyday of their 1970s rivalry with the Yankees. Having learned the long-suffering ways of Bosox fans, it was a natural progression for him to start his sportswriting career covering Columbia College football during its epic 44-game losing streak. By the time he graduated he was ready to write about a winner, and the turn-of-the-century Yankees provided the perfect story line.

"I think the Boston Red Sox are New York's third baseball team," says Rubin. "In the same way that people in Boston are interested in what happens with the Yankees, there are a lot of people in New York who are very interested in the Red Sox. Not when they are terrible, but from 2003 to 2007 it was incredible. Boston fans are probably delighted to read about the Yankees when they are a car wreck, the same way the Yankee fans love to read about the Red Sox when they are a train wreck."

While the Sox and Yanks continued on a course that seemed destined to have them collide again in the playoffs, Dave Roberts had something far more important on his mind. His wife, Tricia, was nine months pregnant, and during prenatal testing it had been discovered that their unborn daughter had the gene for cystic fibrosis. Tricia was due to give birth on Sunday, September 19, and Boston had a game scheduled that afternoon at Yankee Stadium. Roberts's goal was to suit up for the contest and then rush back home in time to see the baby born.

"It was a three-game series, starting on a Friday night

[September 17]," explains Roberts. "In the opener, I go in to pinch-run in the top of the ninth, with the Yanks leading 2–1. That's the first time I have a sequence with Mariano Rivera where I got to study him from first base. I knew he was going to hold the ball, and after the catcher goes back behind the plate, Mariano is holding, holding, holding the ball, and then finally throws a pitch. I go on the next pitch and steal second. Then Orlando [Cabrera] gets a base hit to drive me in and tie the game.

"So I got the call right. If I'm on first base, he's going to try and hold the ball. It messes up the base runners' timing. He comes to set, and then you need to go. It's like rhythm. If he holds the ball, but doesn't go into his deliberate set, the base runner gets tense and tight. So that's what a lot of pitchers try and do."

Roberts stored the information for a later date, and Boston wound up winning the game, 3–2, when Johnny Damon singled in another run off Rivera and Keith Foulke shut down New York in the bottom of the ninth. It marked the second time in two months that the Red Sox had gotten to the Yankees' ace reliever, and Boston was now just two and a half games from the top.

They got no closer—for now. New York won handily the next two days, 14–4 and 11–1, and effectively wrapped up the division title. Even more alarmingly, they crushed both Lowe and Pedro Martinez in the process, with Martinez taunted by chants of "Pedro sucks! Pedro sucks!" as he was removed midway through the sixth inning of the finale.

"I'm the most-hated man in New York," Martinez said after the contest, which marked the first time in more than two years he had lost consecutive starts and allowed three home runs in a game. "I wasn't hitting my targets and I made a couple mistakes. Some were good pitches they hit. The others were just my fault. I wasn't expecting anything weird to happen. I was just trying to pitch my game, regain control of my stuff, which I didn't have the previous game [a 5–2 loss to Tampa Bay]. It's coming along, but it's not quite there yet."

Just about the only good news for Boston over this lost weekend in New York came from Dave Roberts, who homered on Saturday and then got home Sunday night in time for the birth of his daughter, Emmy. A few days later, after the Red Sox clinched a Wild Card spot in Tampa (Arroyo getting the win), several of Roberts's teammates surprised him by hiring a chartered plane to take him back to Boston early so that he could be there when Emmy underwent a special test to check for full-blown cystic fibrosis. "That showed me the character of these guys," Roberts says today of the gesture. "It meant a whole lot."

Emmy turned out to be fine, and the 98–64 Sox were headed back to the playoffs and another possible matchup with the Yankees. It was the type of script that begged for a Hollywood ending, and it turned out one was in the works.

11. WINNING AT A FEVER PITCH

Early in the 2004 baseball season, Jessamy Finet and Erin Nanstad were standing in line outside the Cask 'n Flagon Bar across from Fenway Park when a man they had never seen before approached them.

"I knew I'd run into you or Jess eventually," he said to Nanstad. "Here. These are for you. One each."

Nanstad looked down at her palm. In it were two pennies, which she quickly realized were from 1918. As Red Sox season ticket holders whose passion for the team was chronicled in the documentary of the 2003 season entitled *Still, We Believe* (which is how the man recognized them), Finet and Nanstad knew full well the significance of the pennies' production date. Of course, in the spring of 2004, you would be hard-pressed to find anybody in the Greater Boston area, the 351 cities and towns of Massachusetts, or the six states of New England who didn't know it.

Six months later, after a long season of carrying the lucky pennies to games in purses and pockets, the two best friends from East Boston were gearing up with the rest of Red Sox Nation for a final push to make the coins inconsequential.

Like an Army unit doing maneuvers before a great battle, or an orchestra in dress rehearsal prior to opening night, the Red Sox headed out to California for the first game of the 2004 American League Division Series against the Anaheim Angels with bigger dreams on their minds. No Red Sox player or coach would ever admit to taking their opponents in the best-of-five series lightly; even though Boston had swept the Angels in a three-game set at Fenway in early September, scorching Anaheim pitching for double-digit runs in the first two contests, the AL West champs had not gone 92–70 and edged out two very strong divisional opponents by being pushovers.

The Angels had the eventual American League MVP in right fielder Vladimir Guererro, who could hit like Manny Ramirez and run like Johnny Damon. They had another power threat in left fielder Jose Guillen, a strong leadoff man in third baseman Chone Figgins, and experienced veteran pitchers including Bartolo Colon, Jarrod Washburn, and John Lackey. They also had home field advantage—meaning the Sox would need to travel to California a second time if a Game 5 was necessary.

But when asked their feelings heading into the series, Boston players seemed more concerned about improving upon their 2003 ALCS letdown against the Yankees than analyzing a first-round opponent that had won the World Series just two years before. "We expect to win the whole thing or this team definitely is not going to be happy," said Johnny Damon. Manny Ramirez was even more concise: "We have unfinished business."

It was tough to blame the Red Sox for any forward-thinking. After the events of October 2003, and the crazy year that had ensued, how could they *not* be thinking about tossing the Angels aside and getting another crack at the Yankees? Certainly no Red Sox fans had a first-round loss on their mind; if there was indeed a Curse of the Bambino, it would be the ghosts of a certain pinstriped team they would have to worry about, not Danny Glover and his Angels in the Outfield.

One of the luxuries of clinching a playoff spot early was that the Red Sox were able to line up their pitching rotation so that Curt Schilling and Pedro Martinez could start the first two postseason games. The plan worked to perfection.

Schilling, despite nursing an injured tendon in his right ankle (more on that later), won his ninth straight decision dating to the regular season—letting up three runs (two earned) over six and two-thirds innings of Game 1 before giving way to perfect relief help from Alan Embree and Mike Timlin. Boston, meanwhile, jumped on Anaheim starter Washburn for seven runs in the fourth on homers by Ramirez and Millar and a two-run, bases-loaded throwing error by Figgins.

Game 2 was a big test for Martinez, who entered in one of the worst slumps of his career—0–4 with a 7.71 ERA in his last four starts. His struggles had come seemingly out of nowhere, at the end of an excellent season, and there were concerns that some undetermined injury may be the culprit. Pedro quieted them quickly, allowing three runs in seven innings as all of New England exhaled. Colon, however, was even better early on, and took a 3–1 lead into the sixth. Then Varitek hit a two-out, two-run homer to tie the score, and a sacrifice fly by Ramirez gave Boston the lead for good one inning later. Four runs in the ninth off a beleaguered Anaheim bullpen, three scoring on a bases-clearing double by Orlando Cabrera, sealed the deal. "Let's Go, Red Sox!" could be heard throughout the ballpark as the West Coast contingent of the Nation enjoyed the show.

Remembering their own 2–0 ALDS hole against the A's a year before, which they wiped out with three straight wins, the Sox returned to Fenway for Game 3 exhibiting cautious optimism. "When you got a guy hanging over the cliff holding on with one hand, you don't want him to get his other hand up there," said Trot Nixon. "You want to go ahead and stomp on it."

Boston did do some early stomping, taking a 6–1 lead into the seventh inning behind an excellent performance from starter Bronson Arroyo (taking the place of the demoted Derek Lowe). Then Anaheim made its last stand. After three walks and a single plated one run in the seventh, Guerrero—who had been handcuffed all series—hit a two-out grand slam off Mike Timlin to tie the score, 6–6.

There it stayed for three innings, with five relievers including Lowe coming on for Boston, until David Ortiz crushed a two-out, first-pitch fastball from left-hander Washburn over the Green Monster for an 8–6, 10th-inning clincher. Washburn, the Game 1 starter, had been brought in to face Ortiz in place of Anaheim's formidable closer Francisco Rodriguez, who manager Mike Scioscia felt was tiring after 38 pitches and nearly three innings.

"He [Washburn] just made a mistake," said Ortiz after his first of what would become a regular habit of postseason walkoffs. "He gave me a slider that was up. Kind of high. I was looking for a pitch in the strike zone. They were pitching me good the whole series. They were trying to make sure to give me a pitch away. I was just trying to lock myself in and see a pitch that I could hit."

The celebration at a darkening Fenway was reminiscent of the previous year's festivities, when Trot Nixon homered to beat Oakland in Game 3 of the ALDS—the major difference, of course, being that Big Papi's bash had clinched the *series* rather than just one game. The crowd lingered as "Dirty Water" blared, the players came back out and sprayed folks in the lower boxes with champagne, and Red Sox fans everywhere began channeling their energy to help the Yankees beat the Twins in the other divisional round.

In the losers' clubhouse, meanwhile, Angel Darin Erstad offered a prediction: "These boys are winning the World Series. That's the deepest team I've ever seen. They have every piece of the puzzle. I don't see anybody beating them."

By the next night, after New York overcame a 5–1, eighth-inning deficit on the road to beat the Twins, 6–5, in 11, Boston knew who was going to try. The Yankees' four-game win over Minnesota set up the rematch to end all rematches, the baseball equivalent of Athens vs. Sparta, USA vs. USSR, Rocky vs. Apollo, or any other epic matchup real or imagined.

The 2004 American League Championship Series opened at Yankee Stadium on October 12, with pitchers Mike Mussina and Curt Schilling on the hill. The Red Sox felt confident about their chances for the game and series, because in Schilling they had the most dominant postseason pitcher of his time—a guy who took to the mound that night with a lifetime mark of 6–1 and a 1.74 ERA in 12 career playoff starts, nine of them won by his team.

Schilling, always confident in his ability, stated in the pre-game press conference much the same thing he had told Theo

Epstein at his Thanksgiving table 11 months before. "I want to be part of a team that does something that has not been done in almost a century. I'm not sure I can think of any scenario more enjoyable than making fifty-five thousand people from New York shut up."

Then came the tendon felt 'round the world.

Although Schilling and Terry Francona had both downplayed the pitcher's ankle injury during the ALDS, going so far as to say that it would be no problem at all, this was clearly not the case. The Yankees scored twice in the first and four times in the third, as Schilling, laboring in obvious pain, had trouble pushing off and landing on his right leg. He was gone by the fourth inning, while Mussina, in contrast, set down the first 18 Red Sox in order and entered the seventh with a perfect game and an 8–0 lead.

Although Boston showed grit in rallying late to narrow the gap to 8–7, and even brought the tying run to the plate in the ninth, New York's eventual 10–7 victory was a double blow. Not only were the Red Sox down in the series, they were also down their best pitcher—possibly for the rest of the year.

The official diagnosis for Schilling's injury was a torn tendon sheath in his ankle. Each time he threw a pitch, the unsecured tendon was flapping over his ankle bone and causing him sharp pain. The next day, before Game 2 of the series got under way, the Red Sox announced that Schilling would need surgery on his ankle and would miss his next scheduled start.

Then, when it seemed things could not get worse, they did. The Game 2 matchup featured Jon Lieber against Pedro Martinez. Lieber had pitched well against the Red Sox during the regular season, while Pedro, in trying to rebound from his Game 7 meltdown of 2003, had continued to struggle against the Yanks. In the last series of the year between the teams, on September 24, Martinez had blown a late 4–3 lead in a game eerily reminiscent of the previous year's nightmare. After the game, clearly frustrated in his inability to put away his nemesis, Pedro had told reporters in an emotional interview that "It was all me. I wanted to bury myself on the mound. . . . What can I say? I just tip my hat and call the Yankees my daddy."

Now, next to "Yankees Suck!" and "19-18!," a new chant in the schoolyard ranting portion of this rivalry was about to be unveiled:

"Who's Your DAD-DY?! Who's Your DAD-DY?!"

As soon as he stepped on the mound, Pedro heard it from the 55,000 folks Schilling had failed to shut up in Game 1. Six innings later, when John Olerud touched him for a two-run homer and the winning runs in a 3–1 New York victory, Martinez heard it even louder. Although he pitched well, Lieber was better, and now Boston was down 2–0 in the series.

Just a few days before, Boston players and fans had felt it stronger than ever: *This was the year.* Now, barring a major turnaround, it was going to be yet another long winter of replaying lost opportunities.

As his teammates were licking their wounds and flying to Boston for Game 3, one Red Sox player took it upon himself to personally try and keep their spirits up. Dave Roberts had accepted the fact he would not be getting much playing time in the postseason, so he concentrated on making sure those who were out there knew he believed in them.

"Mark Bellhorn and Johnny Damon were two guys in particular who were really struggling in the ALCS," says Roberts. (Through two games, Bellhorn was 1-for-8 and Damon

0-for-8 with five strikeouts.) "I tried to be a teammate, psychologist, and friend, pumping them up, telling them to be positive. They were getting booed, and I kept telling them to keep their heads high."

There is an interesting history of rainouts and big playoff games when it comes to the Red Sox. In 1975, several days of rainouts in the World Series allowed Boston manager Darrell Johnson to pitch his rested ace Luis Tiant in the must win Game 6 against the Cincinnati Reds, won on Carlton Fisk's home run (Boston lost Game 7.). In the 1986 World Series, after Boston's heartbreaking loss in Game 6, rain gave Sox manager John McNamara an extra day of rest for red-hot lefty Bruce Hurst, whom he started in place of Oil Can Boyd in Game 7. (The Sox lost, although Hurst pitched well.)

Now it was raining again, and Game 3 in Boston, originally scheduled for Friday, October 15, was canceled. Fans who had come in for the game were told their tickets would be honored on Saturday, as each game was getting pushed back one day.

This was not what William "Ted" Spencer wanted to hear. The vice president and chief curator of the Baseball Hall of Fame had driven more than four hours from Cooperstown, New York, with his two sons and son-in-law to see the game, and it had looked like the rain was going to hold off until they got to Route 128, at which point it started monsooning.

Spencer had waited nearly 20 years to see his beloved Red Sox back in the World Series. A Quincy, Massachusetts, native who was named after the great Ted Williams (his dad, a cop and ardent admirer of Williams, added the Ted when he noticed young William held his rattle in his left hand), he grew up going to about 10 games a year at Fenway, sometimes with his own father but most often with Father Daley and the other altar boys from St. Anne's in Wollaston. He further honed his love for the game as a batboy for the Quincy town team that his dad managed, and playing himself for the Quincy Boys Club.

His career had taken him away from the Boston area—first to Philadelphia, then to Cooperstown—but he maintained his love for the Sox and enjoyed getting the chance to secure artifacts and mount exhibits devoted to Boston players and Fenway Park. The toughest part of his job, he liked to joke, was having to walk around the museum every day looking at displays devoted to the myriad accomplishments of the New York Yankees.

Each year Hall of Fame president Jeff Idelson (another Red Sox fan, from Newton, Massachusetts) and PR director Brad Warren spent their October going into locker rooms after the clinching games of the ALCS, NLCS, and World Series, asking players for gloves, cleats, or other items that they could bring back to Spencer and his staff for use in mounting exhibits. The previous fall, one of the items they returned with was the bat Aaron Boone used to hit his ALCS-winning home run off Tim Wakefield, and placing this in the 2003 postseason display wreaked havoc on Spencer's emotions. More than anything else, he hoped that when it came time to create the '04 playoff exhibit, he could fill it with items highlighting a Boston championship run.

Although the Friday rainout meant Spencer and his family would miss Game 3—they needed to be back in Cooperstown on Saturday—it was good news for the Red Sox. With each game now pushed back a day, Game 5 starters Pedro Martinez and Mike Mussina would get an extra day of rest. This also increased the likelihood that Schilling, who was working with the team's medical staff on various possible solutions for his ankle issue, might be able to make another appearance.

It was the first break of any kind the Sox had gotten in the series, but it wouldn't mean a thing if they couldn't win at least one of the next two contests.

Game 3 at Fenway Park started on an upbeat note with an appearance by the Cowsills, a family singing group from Newport, Rhode Island, that recorded several hits in the 1960s and was the basis for television's *Partridge Family*. The group sang the National Anthem as well as their 1968 classic, "Hair," which had been played at Fenway all summer as the musical accompaniment to a video showing all the wild hairdos on the Red Sox team—from Johnny Damon's shoulder-length Jesus/Caveman look to the cornrows of Bronson Arroyo.

It was another nice touch from Steinberg, but by the fourth inning the song the chilly Fenway crowd could have used most was "Help!"

At first it appeared to be shaping up to be a good old-fashioned Fenway slugfest. The Yankees took a 3–0 lead in the top of the first, the Red Sox went up 4–3 in the second, the Yanks went back ahead 6–4 in the third, and then the Sox tied it at 6–6 in their half of the third. By this point both starters—Kevin Brown for New York and Bronson Arroyo for Boston—were gone.

Unfortunately for the Red Sox, that's where the seesaw stopped going both ways. The Yankees tacked on three quick runs in the fourth, and with the Boston bullpen getting torched, Tim Wakefield got up from the dugout bench and approached Terry Francona. Wakefield was slated to start Game 4, but the way this game was going Boston wouldn't have the relievers necessary to line up for the next several contests.*

"A bunch of us were sitting together in the dugout, and I think it was [backup catcher Doug] Mirabelli who said, 'We should do something about this. We can't waste Timlin, Embree, and everyone in the pen,'" recalls Wakefield. "So I say, 'Maybe I should go talk to Tito about it?' and they all say yeah. So I go up to Tito and say I can pitch, and he says, 'Well, go ask D-Lowe if he'll pitch tomorrow.'"

So Wakefield went down the other end of the dugout again and asked Derek Lowe—who had been removed from the rotation due to a late-season slump—if he wanted the Game 4 start. Lowe, who had been itching to pitch in the series anyway, said sure.

Wakefield quickly hurried down to the bullpen and started warming up. At first fans who knew he was scheduled to start the next day were confused, but after he came in and the game moved on, they realized what was happening. Wake, the ultimate warrior, the guy who had been left off postseason rosters to save other players, had gone back and forth from the rotation to the bullpen when asked, and even served as a closer for a time, was "taking one for the team."

The final score was 19–8. The Yankees had 22 hits, including five by Hideki Matsui, four each by Gary Sheffield and Bernie Williams, and three by Alex Rodriguez. Matsui also had two of the team's four home runs and two of its eight doubles. By the late innings, as each New York player's

---

*Although Schilling had only pitched three innings in the first game, Francona had pitched five relievers one inning each, thus not putting too much burden on any of them for use later in the series.

series batting average was posted on the center field Jumbo-Tron, fans could be seen shaking their heads in frustration. They sounded like softball averages.

Despite the beating, to which he contributed five hits and five runs over three and a third innings, Wakefield got a standing ovation from the smattering of fans still seated behind the Red Sox dugout when he left the mound after his third inning of work. "Yeah, that felt kind of weird with us getting killed, but it was greatly appreciated," he remembers. "We just wanted to get this game over with and start thinking about the next one."[†]

In his postgame press conference, Francona announced that Lowe would be starting Game 4, and expressed his gratitude for Wakefield's gesture. "When we were in the third inning and we're three or four pitchers in, it was getting ugly. Because Wake did what he did, we were able to stay away from Timlin and Foulke. They can throw multiple innings tomorrow and give us a chance to win. We got into a position we didn't want to get in. Wake really, really picked us up. And he would have stayed out there and pitched more. He's a professional and he—when we win tomorrow, we'll have Wake to thank for that."

Although most Boston fans were hanging their heads as they left the ballpark, one elderly gentleman was actually excited—former Red Sox second baseman and coach Bobby Doerr. "I ran into him on the ramp near the elevators, and he said, 'You know they are going to come back and win this thing,'" recalls the *Herald's* Steve Buckley. "I said I wasn't so sure, and he said, 'No, I'm serious. Did you see how they played the game tonight, how they used Wakefield? They

---

[†] The author was one of those standing and applauding.

played this game tonight like they want to stay in the series. They didn't give up. Everything they did tonight was to win this series—and they are *going to win it!*'"

Another person doing his best to keep the faith was vendor Rob "Peanuts" Barry. The former pitcher at Dedham High School and Northeastern University had worked at Fenway for more than 20 years, and was known for the incredible accuracy with which he could toss bags of peanuts across several sections of seats and into the hands of a waiting patron. On a dare he had once thrown a bag of nuts from the fence along the first base side of Fenway all the way across the diamond to the third base side *during a game,* so he knew something about believing in miracles.

"A friend of mine told me to meet her over at the old Baseball Tavern after Game 3," Barry recalls. "We sat down at a little table and everybody was dazed. I decided that I was going to convince my friend Leo, another vendor, that we were going to come back and win. So I go over to him, look him in the eye, and say, 'Tomorrow Derek Lowe pitches a gem! Then you have Pedro going—nuff said! Then you have Schilling going, and he has the heart of a lion!' We all went from being totally bummed out to everybody going hysterical and yelling this over and over together.

"And then it actually started happening!"

The next day, as columnists and radio talk shows across the country were declaring the series over, the Red Sox began trickling in to the clubhouse for Game 4. Somebody had found an article in which Gary Sheffield had trashed the Sox, and put it on everybody's chair by his locker. Then Kevin Millar showed up, and started telling anybody in the room who would listen that "They better not let us win tonight."

Later, in an on-field interview with Dan Shaughnessy of

The Boston Globe prior to the game, Millar responded to some ribbing from the columnist by saying, "Let me tell you— don't let us win today. We've got Petey [Pedro Martinez] tomorrow . . . then we've got Schill in Game 6 . . . and in Game 7 anything can happen. *This is it! Don't let the Sox win this game!*"

Millar's confidence flew directly in the face of this fact: no major league team had ever come back from a 3–0 deficit to win a playoff series. In fact, only two teams in any of the four major North American professional sports (baseball, basketball, football, and hockey) had done it, and they were both hockey clubs—the 1942 Toronto Maple Leafs (versus the Detroit Red Wings) and the 1975 New York Islanders (versus the Pittsburgh Penguins).

"Everybody expected us to lose, so we had *nothing* to lose," explains Dave Roberts. "The genius of Kevin Millar, Johnny Damon, and all those crazy personalities on the team was that they had an understanding of what we were up against, what had happened in 2003, and knew that we shouldn't take ourselves too seriously. If you take things too seriously, you succumb to the pressure."

Keith Foulke had a similarly healthy outlook.

"We kind of made a deal with ourselves to just go out there and play as hard as we can," Foulke says. "Go out and do your job, have fun, and if things work out, we're going to win. Then we're going to come back and do it tomorrow, and the next day, and the next day."

Across Red Sox Nation, fans tried one more time to keep the faith. In Natick, Massachusetts, Herb and Janet Crehan had started a tradition many years before in which they hung a Red Sox flag by the front door as long as the Sox were alive in the playoffs. After Game 3, which they had endured watching on TV at a wedding reception filled with Yankee fans, Janet had said, "Those bums, they aren't going to win anything. I'm taking the flag down."

Not so fast.

"I pick my spots, and usually I just say 'yes dear, yes dear,'" says Herb Crehan. "But on this particular occasion I said, '*Do not touch that flag*. I'm going to the game tomorrow night, they're going to win, and that flag is going to stay up until they are eliminated.' She gave me a strange look—and then backed off."

Back in Cooperstown, Ted Spencer was not so confident. In fact, the events of Game 3 had been so hard for him to take that he decided he would skip watching Game 4 altogether rather than chance seeing the Yankees celebrating on the Fenway grass. His first grandchild had been born in Boston that March, and there was video footage of Grandpa Ted holding him and saying, "Liam, the Red Sox will win it all in your lifetime." Now he wasn't so sure.

Although Derek Lowe entered Game 4 with a 2–3 record and a 9.08 ERA against the Yankees during 2004, all logic and prior statistics were about to start getting thrown out the window. Lowe didn't quite pitch the gem Rob Barry predicted, but he certainly held his own. After he allowed a two-run homer to A-Rod in the third inning, the Red Sox went ahead 3–2 in the fifth on RBI singles by Orlando Cabrera and (with two men scoring) David Ortiz off New York starter Orlando Hernandez. An inning later, after allowing a one-out triple to Matsui, Lowe left with the lead—but Mike Timlin failed to hold the fort as Bernie Williams and Tony Clark gave New York the lead with RBI singles.

The score remained 4–3 heading into the bottom of the ninth inning, with Yankee ace reliever Mariano Rivera on the mound. Although the Red Sox had beaten Rivera twice during the regular season—on a homer by Bill Mueller in July's fight game and a single by Johnny Damon in September—there was no reason to think the most dominant closer in history would crack now. Rivera had already saved two games in this series, including one in which he didn't even arrive at the ballpark until mid-contest after returning from a family funeral in Panama.

In the press box high above home plate, reporters like Steve Buckley of the *Boston Herald*, Ken Powtak of the Associated Press, and Roger Rubin of the New York *Daily News* all stole glances at their computer screens, thinking about the postmortems on the Red Sox season they were about to write. And just a short distance away from them, in a private suite occupied by members of the Red Sox executive staff, Larry Lucchino took out a yellow legal pad and started doing his own writing.

"I started drafting a few postgame remarks," he recalls, "regarding our determination not to let this happen to us again, and that we were determined to redouble our efforts and to redouble our commitment financially and otherwise, because we were getting tired of finishing number two to these guys." George Mitrovich—a friend and former speechwriter for Bobby Kennedy—stood by with a laptop ready to help further craft Lucchino's words into the ultimate "Wait until next year" address.

All through the playoffs, Dave Roberts had thought about a conversation he had had with Terry Francona shortly after joining the team. Trot Nixon had come back, Roberts was no longer starting, but Tito had told him "I just want you to know that you're as important as anybody, and there is going to be a situation where we need you. Be ready."

So far, with the exception of one pinch-running appearance in the ALDS when he did not advance a base, Roberts had spent the playoffs playing his other role as a cheerleader and confidant to his teammates, keeping their spirits up through tough at-bats and tough games. On this night, however, he could sense that he was going to be needed for something more. The situation Francona spoke of was coming.

In the fifth inning Roberts went to the clubhouse and started getting loose. He already knew the windups and tendencies of every pitcher in the Yankee bullpen, and had gone over them on video with team video coordinator Billy Broadbent. By the seventh inning, he was back in the dugout, and when the ninth loomed with Boston still trailing by one run, he knew his time was *now*.

"I'm at the end of the dugout, holding my helmet, getting my juices flowing, just watching the situation play out," Roberts recalls.

Kevin Millar led off the inning—and walked.

"Kevin always put together at-bats, and he had a great at-bat against Mariano," says Roberts. "Once that 'Ball Four' was called, I looked out at Tito at the end of the dugout, and he just kind of nodded his head and winked at me. He summoned me right there with the wink, and I went out to first."

Roberts went in to pinch-run for Millar, as Bill Mueller stepped to the plate. Yankee first baseman Tony Clark tapped Millar on the leg as a greeting, and coaches Dale Sveum (at third) and Lynn Jones (at first) signaled to let Roberts know that the plan was for Mueller to bunt him over. But Roberts didn't want Mueller to give himself up—the wink from Francona meant the manager wanted him to steal second. He got this message across to the coaches, and they removed the bunt sign.

Rivera threw over to first three times to keep Roberts close to the bag—almost nabbing him on the third one. Then, when he saw the pitcher finally go to his complete set and start his delivery, Roberts took off for second—sliding in safe just under Derek Jeter's sweeping tag on a near-perfect throw from catcher Jorge Posada.

A few moments later, Mueller singled up the middle and Roberts came around third and slid in with the tying run. The game was knotted at 4–4, and the Red Sox were alive.

Four excruciating innings later, the Dynamic Dominican Duo came through as they had all year. Ramirez led off with a single off Paul Quantrill—one of several former Red Sox on the Yankees' ALCS roster—and David Ortiz pounded a 2-and-1 fastball into the Yankee bullpen for a two-run homer and a 6–4 win. It was 1:22 A.M.

Fenway Park exploded, just as it had nine days earlier when Ortiz sent the Angels packing with a similar blast. The entire team ran out to greet Big Papi at home plate, and the looks on their faces made it appear they were celebrating another series-clinching shot rather than just one win. That air of confidence—and the ability it gave the Red Sox to play smart and well instead of scared—would need to sustain them through three more games.

Above home plate, the reporters went to work again on new leads. Larry Lucchino had long since put aside his yellow pad.

Game 5, which started as the sun still shone at Fenway at 5 P.M., pitted the well-rested Martinez against Mussina. The K Men were out in full force for Pedro atop the Green Monster, knowing that this might be the last game at Fenway Park in a Red Sox uniform for the pending free agent. The fans got an infusion of good karma when Jordan Leandre—a four-year-old cancer patient at Dana-Farber Cancer Institute's Jimmy Fund Clinic—sang the National Anthem, and this carried over into the early part of the game.

The Red Sox got to Mussina for three hits (one an RBI single by Mr. Everything Ortiz), two walks (one with the bases loaded), and two runs in the first inning, but missed a chance to perhaps break the game open when Mueller struck out with the bases loaded.

New York got one back against Pedro on a leadoff homer by Bernie Williams in the second, and after that both pitchers settled into a groove. By the sixth inning it was still 2–1 Red Sox, but after loading the bases with two outs, the Yanks surged ahead on a three-run double down the right field line by Derek Jeter—yet another case where Pedro couldn't quite put away the Yankees. The 4–2 lead lasted into the bottom of the eighth, when Ortiz came up once again.

By this point the country had taken notice of Big Papi and his clutch-hitting abilities, but there came a point—perhaps this was it—when he passed into another level of greatness reserved for a select few performers. Ortiz smashed a home run off Tom Gordon to start the eighth, into the Monster Seats and just below a huge billboard urging Sox fans to "Keep the Faith."

Then, before the crowd could die down, Millar had worked another clutch walk, Roberts went in to pinch-run, and Trot Nixon got him to third on a hit-and-run single. Once again Rivera came on to shut the door, and once again he couldn't—as Jason Varitek hit a sacrifice fly to score Roberts and tie the game, 4–4.

In Cooperstown, Ted Spencer was a nervous wreck. He had given in to his emotions and decided to watch Game 5, but the anxiety was getting to be too much. Jumping up from the living room couch, and without a word for his wife, Patty, he grabbed his jacket and his last cigar and headed outside for a walk.

"I figured I'd smoke the goddamn thing, walk a little, get back in half an hour, and the whole thing would be over," he recalls. "I live on Main Street, a block and a half from the Hall of Fame. It's 10, 10:30, a dark, misty night, and nobody else is outside. I'm walking along, and here comes another lone figure from the other direction.

"It's dark out, and I can't tell who it is, but when he passes me he starts to laugh. I turn around, and it's my son, Matthew, who lives a few blocks from me. He couldn't take it anymore, either, so he also went for a walk."

Spencer did what came naturally—and asked his son a question.

"What was the score when you left?"

"Four–two."

"Oh," he updated Matthew excitedly, "they got two runs and tied it up."

They laughed some more and kept walking. Spencer finished his cigar, and then they both went back to his house for an update.

The game was *not* over, not by a long shot. It wound up going 14 innings, passing the previous night's contest to become the longest postseason game in history, and the drama kept coming.

In the Yankee ninth, with Ruben Sierra on first and two outs, Tony Clark slammed a ball off Keith Foulke down into the right field corner, good for extra bases and what looked to be a 5–4 lead. But right as the ball was nearing the short fence by Pesky's Pole, it hopped up and into the stands for a ground rule double—meaning Sierra had to stop at third. It was as if Johnny Pesky himself reached out to grab the ball and alter history. Miguel Cairo came up, needing just a single for a two-run New York advantage, but Foulke got him to pop up to first.

As the action extended into extra innings for the second straight night, New York continued to miss chances to pull ahead. The Yanks left six men on base between the ninth and 13th innings, *five* of them in scoring position, but the Sox didn't break. Showing the confidence he had in Wakefield, Francona inserted him into the game in the 12th, and Wake's knuckleball was dancing better than ever. The problem was that the catcher who normally handles Wakefield, Doug Mirabelli, was not in the game. Francona did not want to take Varitek's superior bat out of the lineup in a must-win situation, so he would have to deal with the knuckler as best he could.

Soon Varitek was diving and leaping like a cat, doing anything he could to keep the wildly sinking pitches from getting by him. It was as if he was back in his parents' backyard, throwing balls off the wall of the house to hone his reaction skills.

In the top of the 13th, three balls *did* get by Tek, allowing runners to move up to second and third base with two outs. It appeared as if Wakefield may suffer the horrible fate of being the last-game loser *again*, this time for pitching *too well*. Just one more ball bouncing off Varitek's glove would give New York the lead, and fans had to wonder when Francona might send Mirabelli in to relieve the flustered receiver.

But Sierra swung and missed on a 3–2 pitch, Tek squeezed it tight, and the score remained tied. The catcher and pitcher both sprinted to the dugout, Wakefield pumping his fists and yelling with enthusiasm.

Still alive.

It remained tied when the Sox came up in the bottom of the 14th against Esteban Loaiza. Bellhorn struck out, Damon walked, Cabrera struck out, and Ramirez walked, bringing Ortiz up with two outs and two on. The fans stood as one, waving signs like "One More Time Papi," as broadcasters speculated if he could indeed deliver in the clutch *one more time.*

Loaiza had good stuff, and went ahead 1-and-2, but Ortiz saved himself by barely fouling off several pitches—and then crushing a huge drive to right field that hooked just foul as Papi shook his head.

Finally, on the 10th pitch of the at-bat, Ortiz lined the ball to center field—not very hard, but well placed. Damon was off like a flash from second, and Bernie Williams didn't even bother to throw toward the plate as Johnny sprinted across it and into the embrace of on-deck batter Doug Mientkiewicz. The Sox had staved off elimination again, and the victory with three shutout innings in relief went to Wakefield— the man whose selfless act two days before had helped make all this possible.

Ted Spencer had gone to bed after the 13th, feeling that there was no way this one was going to end well, and now his phone rang. It was his son, yelling about Ortiz's game-winning hit, and Spencer made himself a promise right then and there:

I'm going to watch everything from now on. It may kill me, but they deserve it. I'll sacrifice myself for the good of the team.

Up in Toronto, brothers Peter and Bobby Farrelly were thrilled to see Ortiz deliver yet again, but also a bit nervous.

Huge Red Sox fans who grew up in Rhode Island, the Farrellys had risen to fame after moving to Hollywood and writing and directing such blockbuster films as *Dumb and Dumber* and *There's Something About Mary*. In the spring of 2004 they had been sent the script for a movie called *Fever Pitch*, written by Babaloo Mandel and Lowell Ganz, about an obsessed Red Sox fan who has to choose between the team and the girl he loves.

"It was the first time I read a script that I felt was perfect, and I didn't want to rewrite," recalls Peter Farrelly, who played high school baseball and was a Carl Yastrzemski fanatic as a kid growing up in the 1960s and '70s. "We lived and died with the Sox, so we knew it was something we had to do."

The cast included Jimmy Fallon as the overzealous Red Sox fan, Lenny Clarke as the beloved uncle who bequeaths him terrific season tickets, and Drew Barrymore as the workaholic, baseball-phobic girlfriend. Although much of the filming took place in Toronto, the directors and their production team—led by producer Kris "Mudd" Meyer, a former security guard at Fenway—spent several weeks in Boston shooting in and around Fenway.

It was one of the best times of their lives. Friends and family seemed to come out of the woodwork, stopping by the trailers on a nightly basis to party with the Farrellys, Meyer, and the crew. The Red Sox offered their full cooperation, even allowing the brothers to film with players including Johnny Damon, Jason Varitek, and Trot Nixon. For the scenes where Fallon is seated at the ballpark talking with his fellow fans, they recruited local Boston actors, including Jessamy Finet and Erin Nanstad—the ladies with the lucky 1918 pennies—to add to the authenticity. Finet was one of the film's highlights as the wisecracking blonde who gave Drew Barrymore hell for not knowing about the Curse of the Bambino.

"Everybody was great, from Terry Francona to the players

to the fans," says Peter Farrelly. "We shot a few times right after games, including the big scene when Drew jumps down from out of the stands, right beside Johnny Damon, and then runs across the field to Jimmy's seats. We wanted the stands to be full for filming, so I walked out to home plate during the seventh-inning stretch, got on the microphone, and said, 'We're filming a movie for 10 minutes after the game. If you can just stay that long, you'll be in the movie.' Almost everyone stayed."

Now, however, the brothers had a problem.

"When we started filming, the original script was that the Red Sox don't win but Jimmy gets the girl," explains Peter Farrelly. "They lose to the Yankees, but he's grown as a guy and he's learned to have a relationship with someone other than the Red Sox. His life is better, and so is hers.

"But then when we were shooting in Toronto, things started changing," he continues. "All along, we were thinking, What if they *win*? Babaloo and Lowell wrote an alternate ending when the Red Sox made the playoffs. But then when we started to come back against the Yankees, that's when we really started thinking, we're going to have to get back to Fenway and start reshooting some of this stuff."

In trying to rewrite the ending to their season, the Red Sox had staved off elimination twice in their own home. Now they would have to do it twice more in the scene of their greatest nightmares: Yankee Stadium. To keep up spirits back on Yawkey Way, Pam Ganley Kenn recalls, the Red Sox public relations department blasted "Tessie" throughout the offices every day. "From the time I got to work in the morning until I went home," she says, "someone would be playing it."

There would be no "Tessie" played in the Bronx on October 19, but the script for Game 6 hit all the right notes.

Curt Schilling, the man brought to Boston for this very moment—to beat the Yankees in October as he had done with Arizona—was on the mound, but he wasn't at anywhere near his physical best. The flapping tendon in his right ankle, which had made it impossible for him to pitch effectively in Game 1, was now being held in place by a sheath made from attaching the skin around the tendon to the tissue beneath it. To make sure the 20-minute procedure went off correctly, Red Sox team physician Dr. William Morgan had practiced on a cadaver before performing the actual surgery on Schilling in a back room at Fenway Park.

Apparently practice made perfect. Although blood could be seen staining his sock as it seeped out of the sutured area throughout his seven-inning appearance, Schilling was brilliant—letting up just four hits and one run to lead Boston to a 4–2 win over Lieber and the stunned Yankees. "I've never been involved in anything like that," Schilling said after the game, and for once the big guy seemed at a loss for words.

In addition to Schilling's heroic effort, two key plays—both necessitating calls overturned by umpires—played a major factor in the outcome of what would forever be known as the "Bloody Sock Game."

In the fourth inning, struggling Mark Bellhorn hit a fly ball to deep left field that was initially ruled a double, but later correctly changed to a three-run homer when it was determined it hit a fan's hand before bouncing back onto the field. Then, in the eighth, with Bronson Arroyo on in relief, Alex Rodriguez hit a squibber back toward first—and slapped it out of Arroyo's hand when the pitcher ran over to try and tag him near first base. A-Rod was called out for interference, helping kill a late New York rally, and doctored images of him holding a purse over his slapping wrist have lived in online infamy ever since.[‡]

Not quite every Red Sox fan on hand was able to stay for the finish. "There were six of us at Game 6," says Kevin McCarthy of the K Men. "We learned to not go to Yankee Stadium in red face paint, but we were there for Curt Schilling. Around the fourth or fifth inning my brother stood up with his K card, and there were these two huge drunks. One of them punched my brother in the head, ripped the K card, and threw it over the balcony. Then my son grabbed the guy and started punching him. The cops came over, I told them what happened, and they threw all four of us out. We did the perp walk with the two drunks."

One year and three days after falling at Yankee Stadium in Game 7 of the 2003 ALCS, the Red Sox were back to try again. Derek Lowe, who had been deemed unfit for service in the Boston rotation to start the postseason, was now being charged on two days' rest with winning one of the biggest games in team history—and certainly the biggest in the century-long rivalry between these two proud franchises.

The suspense, at least a large portion of it, was ended early. David Ortiz hit a two-run home run off Kevin Brown in the first inning, and Johnny Damon did his teammate one better—crushing *two* homers, a grand slam in the second to make it 6–0 and a two-run shot in the fourth, both off Javier Vasquez. It was a case of very good timing for Damon, who

---

[‡] After this and their July matchup, when Arroyo hit A-Rod to start the melee at Fenway, it's a safe bet these old high school rivals did not exchange Christmas cards.

had come into the game hitting .103 for the series but will be remembered for his Game 7 blasts, not his six-game slump.

This offensive jackpot was more than enough for Lowe, who allowed just one hit—an RBI single to Jeter—through six innings. Yankee fans got to enjoy a few more "Who's Your Daddy?" chants against Pedro when he inexplicably entered the game in the seventh and let up two quick runs, but by this point it was already 8–1. Martinez and the rest of the Sox had some margin for error.

"I was down in the media room, in the bowels of Yankee Stadium, when they brought Pedro in," says the *Herald*'s Steve Buckley. "When they touched him up a little bit, for a few anxious moments my institutional knowledge of the history of the franchise had me thinking, 'Could this be happening *again*?'"

It wasn't. The only thing happening on this night was something that had not happened in the history of professional baseball.

Up in the visitor's broadcast booth, Joe Castiglione of Red Sox flagship station WEEI 850 AM knew he was about to make the biggest call of his 22 years doing Red Sox baseball. He had thought hard about what he wanted to say.

"I wanted to get across that this was the most important win in Red Sox history," says Castiglione. "I couldn't explain why, but it *was*, because the Yankees always won the game that decided the championship. Until now."

The last out, as so many of the outs did in this series, came after midnight—at 12:01 A.M., to be precise. Alan Embree induced Ruben Sierra to hit a grounder to Pokey Reese, a forgotten hero of the early season when he filled in so brilliantly for Nomar Garciaparra at shortstop. Reese threw it over to first base and Doug Mientkiewicz, who will also always be connected with Nomar as one of the defensive whizzes picked up in the dramatic deadline trade that turned Boston's season around.

Castiglione made the call:

Ground ball to second base . . . Pokey Reese has it . . . he throws to first—and the Red Sox have won the American League pennant! Move over, Babe, the Red Sox are American League champions!

Keith Foulke, who had pitched brilliantly in Games 4, 5, and 6 but was not needed in this one, ran in from the bullpen and found Francona in the melee at the mound. "Damn you, Tito, that should have been me in the game at the end!" Foulke recalls saying to his manager with a smile. "I've always wanted to be the one to get that last out!"

He would get his chance.

Red Sox fans had been distraught at the thought of the Yankees celebrating a championship on Fenway grass. Now it was the Red Sox doing the hugging on the Yankee Stadium lawn, and Frank Sinatra was keeping quiet. People who had braved ridicule by going to Yankee Stadium in Boston jackets and caps danced in their seats, their joy no longer something to hide.

"For a few seconds, I was like, 'Oh my God,'" recalls Steve Buckley. "I had seen things happen so many times to the Red Sox. I covered the '86 World Series, and so many of the other games. Now they had finally come out on top."

Even George Steinbrenner, who a year before had hurled insults at the defeated Boston team as their bus pulled out of the Yankee Stadium parking lot bound for the airport, told Stadium workers to keep the lights on so the Boston fans could celebrate a little longer.

Darth Vader had a heart after all.

In the postgame press conference, David Ortiz was asked if he could explain how the team maintained its confidence even when it trailed 3–0 in the series.

"One day I was driving from my house [to Fenway Park] on a work-out day and I saw a big sign on the street that said 'Keep the faith,'" Ortiz explained. "And I saw it was a photo of Manny, it had the big smile. I just parked in front of the photo and I just sat down for a minute and just thought about it, you know, we've been through the whole year. Then I went to the field and I just expressed myself to my team-mates about what the Boston nation has been waiting for us and what they expect from us. So it doesn't matter if we are down 3–0.

"We just have got to keep the faith."

It is hard to imagine how winning a World Series could be anticlimactic for a team, especially a team that had not won one in 86 years. But that was absolutely the case for the 2004 Red Sox. They had completed the greatest turnaround in sports history and had exorcised the demons of their past all in one week, and nothing they did against the National League champion St. Louis Cardinals was going to top it.

Of course if they *lost* to the Cardinals, well, that might be another story. If they fell short again in the World Series, as they had in 1946, 1967, 1975, and 1986—always in seven games—wouldn't Yankee fans still be able to taunt them about 1918? People still remembered the '67 Impossible Dream Red Sox fondly, as well as the '75 team led by rookie phenoms Fred Lynn and Jim Rice. But those teams hadn't gone all the way, so the Red Sox were still thought of as the franchise that couldn't win the big one.

In the end, there would be no need to worry about such possibilities. The 2004 World Series was one of the most one-sided in history.

The Red Sox won four straight games and never trailed for a single inning. St. Louis had a 105–57 record during the regular season, the best in baseball, and had a Hall of Fame manager in Tony LaRussa. They had two 40-homer sluggers in Albert Pujols and Jim Edmonds, a deep starting pitching staff with four 15-game winners, and a strong bullpen anchored by closer Jason Isringhausen and his 47 saves. Three Cardinals—center fielder Edmonds, catcher Mike Matheny, and third baseman Scott Rolen (who also hit 34 homers)—won Gold Gloves for their fielding brilliance.

Against the Red Sox, this group looked like the 1962 Mets.

There were two times in four games that the Cardinals had an opportunity to make the 100th World Series a real contest. In Game 1 at Fenway Park, the Red Sox took a 4–0 lead in the first inning thanks to *another* David Ortiz home run, off Woody Williams, and by the end of the third inning had a 7–2 advantage. Then St. Louis battled from way back, much as Boston had done in the ALCS opener at Yankee Stadium. They chased Boston starter Tim Wakefield with three fourth-inning runs, and in the sixth tied the game, 7–7, with two more against Bronson Arroyo.

Boston went back ahead, 9–7, in the seventh on RBI singles by Ortiz and Manny Ramirez, but the Cards struck *again* in the eighth, getting two runs on a pair of errors by Ramirez in left field. They had men on first and second with only one out in a 9–9 game, and the heart of their order coming up in Pujols, Rolen, and Edmonds. But just as Curt Schilling was brought to Boston to beat the Yankees, Keith Foulke now did what *he* had been acquired to do. After intentionally walking Pujols to load the bases, he got Rolen to pop out to third and struck out Edmonds.

In the bottom of the eighth, after an error by usually sure-handed shortstop Edgar Renteria, Mark Bellhorn stepped in—batting under .200 in the postseason, but with home runs in two straight games—and made it three in a row with a two-run blast off Julian Tavarez and the Pesky Pole in right. Foulke set St. Louis down in the ninth, and Boston had dodged a big bullet with an 11–9 win.

When Curt Schilling woke up at seven on the morning of Game 2, he told reporters after the game, he couldn't walk or even move. "I honest to God didn't think I was going to take the ball today," he said. "I didn't think I *could.*"

He did, and what he did with it further sealed his legend.

Jason Varitek, perhaps fueled by one of his regular visits to Trutony's Deli in Newton before heading into the ballpark, hit a 400-foot triple to deep center in the first inning to give Boston a 2–0 lead. Schilling made the advantage stand up, throwing six innings of four-hit baseball and allowing just one unearned run. The Sox showed patience at the plate, drawing six walks to go with eight hits, and won, 6–2, to take a 2–0 lead in the Series heading to Missouri for Game 3.

St. Louis was a much friendlier environment for Boston fans than New York. Folks could wear their Red Sox hats and shirts and jackets and not worry about being ridiculed or challenged to a fight. Lynne Smith, known back home as "The Fenway Hat Lady" because she literally *wore* the ball-park—or a miniature model of it, complete with Green Monster and lights—on her head, was asked numerous times by fans at Busch Stadium to take photos with them, and was happy to oblige.

The third inning of Game 3 marked the second and last opportunity the Cardinals had to make this a competitive series, and once again they couldn't take advantage. Starter Pedro Martinez, making what would turn out to be his last appearance in a Red Sox uniform, got early support on a Manny Ramirez home run in the first inning, and had a 1–0 lead into the bottom of the third. Then St. Louis showed some life. Pitcher Jeff Suppan (yet another former Red Sox faced by Boston in the postseason) managed an infield single, and Edgar Renteria hit a ball to right field that Trot Nixon misplayed into a double.

With men on second and third, and nobody out, the Cardinals had a chance to do some major damage against Martinez, who had already endured some tough moments in the playoffs. When Larry Walker hit a ground ball to second base, Boston's strategy was to concede the run and get the sure out at first base. Bellhorn, playing deep at second for this reason, threw to first to get Walker.

But Suppan, seeming confused, stopped midway to home plate—and then tried to go back to third. David Ortiz, playing first base because of the lack of a designated hitter in the National League ballpark, spotted Suppan in no-man's-land and gunned the ball across to third baseman Bill Mueller, who tagged Suppan to complete the unusual double play. Pujols grounded out, and the game—and effectively, the series—was over. Martinez wound up pitching seven shutout innings, and Boston won, 4–1.

The morning of Game 4, *Fever Pitch* directors Peter and Bobby Farrelly made a decision. They were already planning to go back to Boston to film a new ending for their movie if the Red Sox won the World Series, but they knew a *perfect* ending would include having the stars of the film and team all celebrating at the end. The Farrellys specialized in comedies, but they wanted this to be *real*.

They chartered a plane for St. Louis, and made sure their production team, film crew, and stars Jimmy Fallon and Drew Barrymore all got to Busch Stadium. Appealing to Major League Baseball for on-field access, they were given the okay based on their previous access at Fenway—provided they did not interfere with the player celebration in any way. Their stage was now set for a perfect ending; they just needed the Red Sox to hold up their end.

Derek Lowe, like Martinez a free agent who was unsure if he would be with Boston in 2005, got the start in Game 4. This gave him the unique possibility of winning the deciding game of all three playoff rounds after being demoted from the starting rotation before the postseason. A victory would be the ultimate way of both proving his full worth to the coaching staff and setting himself up for a big payday.

Johnny Damon helped Lowe on his way by homering in the first inning, Boston's fourth straight game scoring in the opening frame. Trot Nixon added a two-run double in the third, one of his three doubles on the night, and the 3–0 lead stood up. Lowe wound up going seven three-hit innings (the exact line turned in by Martinez the day before), and Arroyo, Embree, and Foulke held St. Louis at bay the rest of the contest.

Back in Boston, fans watched or listened to the final innings in living rooms, bars, bedrooms, and anywhere else they could. Parents kept their kids up or woke them for the ninth inning, among them Ken and Shelley Leandre. Their son, Jordan, was the four-year-old cancer survivor who had delighted the crowd with his National Anthem rendition before Game 5 of the ALCS.

"I felt like Jordan had been a good-luck charm," says Ken Leandre. "He used to sit in front of the TV and point at the screen and say he was 'throwing out magic' and the next thing you know, Manny or Ortiz would hit a home run. We loved that he had something he loved and could have a good feeling about instead of the hospitals and needles."

The good-luck charm within the Red Sox team itself was Johnny Pesky, the shortstop-manager-coach-legend who had been employed by the Boston organization for most of his 65-plus years in baseball. The Sox made sure Johnny got to St. Louis for Game 4, which he watched from the stands with Charles Steinberg and Pam Ganley Kenn, who helped him with his public appearances and looked at him like a grandfather. When the game moved into the late innings with the Red Sox ahead, the trio got up to make their way down to the visitor's clubhouse.

Then, as they were leaving their section, fans began politely clapping for Pesky as they would a war hero. It meant a tremendous amount to him, because in a way he was an old warrior here. After all, it was in this city in 1946 where he had been accused of "holding the ball" and costing the Sox a World Series title. He now felt all was being forgiven.

By the ninth inning, Pesky was in a small room off the main visitor's clubhouse watching the last moments of the game unfold on a video monitor. The Farrelly brothers, meanwhile, were arranging for Jimmy Fallon and Drew Barrymore to get onto the field after the final out so they could get their perfect ending.

And Keith Foulke, who in 11 games and 14 innings pitched during the postseason allowed just seven hits and one run, was getting the chance he had joked with Francona about back in Yankee Stadium.

After Pujols singled to lead off the ninth, Foulke retired Rolen and Edmonds. Edgar Renteria stepped in and took the first pitch for ball one. Up in the booth, Joe Castiglione got ready to make his call:

Swing and a ground ball, stabbed by Foulke. He has it, he underhands to first . . . and the Boston Red Sox are the World Champions! For the first time in eighty-six years, the Red Sox have won baseball's world championship! Can you believe it?

On the field, Jason Varitek leaped into Foulke's arms for a hug. In the clubhouse, Johnny Pesky stood up, raised his arms in triumph, and hugged Pam Ganley Kenn. "If I was 50 years younger, I'd have probably been jumping up and down like a crazy man," he said later. When the players made their way into the clubhouse, moments later, Schilling, Millar, and others embraced Pesky as well.

Jeff Idelson, president of the Hall of Fame, was also in the clubhouse—seeking artifacts that fans could enjoy for years to come at Cooperstown. His wish list was to get something from Curt Schilling, Manny Ramirez—named MVP of the World Series with a .412 average—Orlando Cabrera, David Ortiz, and Derek Lowe.

"There's a tempo to it, because you want to let people celebrate," Idelson explains. "It's about understanding people and getting them at the right moment. You don't want to say something like, 'Hey, take that champagne out of your hand and go get this for me.'"

Idelson already knew Curt Schilling from when he had visited the museum with his kids, so he went up and asked if he could have the cleats that he had inscribed with "KALS" to raise awareness about amyotrophic lateral sclerosis (ALS), or Lou Gehrig's disease. Schilling said sure.

"Then he said, 'Do you want the sock too'—meaning the

bloody sock," recalls Idelson. "I said sure, we'd love the sock. He didn't have it there, so his in-laws drove it up to the museum a few weeks later."

Next Idelson got a hat from Martinez, and a bat from Ramirez. He asked Cabrera for his glove, and got that too—along with a hug. "Cabrera's whole family was there," recalls Idelson. "He couldn't believe I was asking him for his glove, and he was so proud. He said it was one of the great moments of his life."

It would be a fun winter in Cooperstown for curator Ted Spencer.

As players and their families celebrated all around them, the Farrellys managed to film the final scene of *Fever Pitch*—a lovers' embrace by Fallon and Barrymore right down on the field as Red Sox players celebrated behind them. Peter Farrelly also scooped up some dirt to save, and got photos of his son Bob with the World Series trophy by the pitcher's mound.

A few hours later, Jessamy Finet and Erin Nanstad were walking back to where they had parked their car at a downtown St. Louis hotel. On a whim, the two East Boston girls had decided to fly to Chicago, rent a car, and drive to St. Louis for Game 4. They didn't have tickets, but managed to get some in the second-to-last row of the upper deck. They also brought their lucky pennies.

Now, with no extra money left for lodging, they planned to sleep in their rental car before heading back to O'Hare Airport the next morning.

Suddenly, they heard a scream from behind them. "JESSAMY! ERIN! What are *YOU* doing here?" It was Drew Barrymore, Finet's on-screen nemesis. The girls had no idea that the cast and crew from *Fever Pitch* had been at the game, and didn't notice them filming the on-field embrace. But it turned out that they had parked their rental car at the same hotel where the filmmakers were staying, and the Farrellys insisted that Finet and Nanstad party with them and spend the night.

It sure beat sleeping in the car.

A short while later, the girls were sipping champagne, courtesy of Red Sox traveling secretary Jack McCormick, when Jimmy Fallon called them over. "I know you girls are big fans," he said, and put something from his pocket into their glasses.

It was dirt from the mound. They drank it. It tasted gritty but good.

Now *that's* a perfect ending.

12. AFTER THE MIRACLE

WHEN THE RED SOX LANDED AT DAWN ON THE morning after winning the World Series, they were greeted at Logan Airport not by huge mobs of screaming fans—most folks were sleeping in after nearly a month of late nights— but by several dozen state troopers, firefighters, and Massport workers. The honor of carrying the 30-pound World Series trophy off the plane went to Ellis Burks, the veteran from the "old" Red Sox who had come back to give an infusion of class and experience to the 2004 crew, even though he only played in a handful of games due to his two knee surgeries.

"When we were on the plane, Curt Schilling, Pedro Martinez, and Tim Wakefield had suggested that I carry the trophy off," Burks recalls. "I was completely surprised and shocked that they would want me to do it, but it also meant a lot to me."

The decision was a subtle way of saying that this title wasn't just about the '04 Red Sox, but also about all the past Boston teams—including those that Burks played on in 1988 and 1990—that couldn't quite make it all the way. A few days later, when the city turned out 3.2 million strong for a three-mile "Rolling Rally" through downtown streets and into the Charles River, among the homemade signs that fans held up to the players waving from duck boats were many mentioning heroes of the past along with Big Papi, Manny, and Pedro.

When the team came out with its 2005 media guide the next spring, the cover inscription beneath a photo of the championship celebration read:

"This championship isn't just about these 25 guys. This is for every fan who has ever been to Fenway Park. This is for Johnny Pesky, Bobby Doerr, Dom DiMaggio, and Ted. This is for Yaz and Lonborg, Tiant and Fisk, Evans and Rice. This championship is for everyone who came so close and for everyone who cared so much."

The 2004 season changed everything. The moment the last out of the World Series was recorded, the Red Sox went from cursed losers to the greatest comeback story in baseball history. The entire team was named *Sports Illustrated*'s "Sportsmen of the Year," and players like Johnny Damon and David Ortiz became heroes of the late-night television circuit and bestselling authors. When Tim Wakefield visited Dana-Farber Cancer Institute around Christmas with the World Series trophy, the adult patients were more excited than the kids, because they appreciated just how long it had taken to reach that day.

Bill Buckner bristled when reporters asked him how it felt to "be forgiven" after 2004, because he didn't think he had anything to apologize for. He was right, but by finally getting the 86-year-old monkey off their backs, the Red Sox could focus on building the best team they could for the present and future rather than having to spend so much time trying to outlive the past.

"It altered the history of the team on a dime," says Richard Johnson, curator of the Sports Museum in Boston. "There are people of a certain age who say, 'Oh yeah, I think of the Red Sox the same way now as I did 10 years ago.' Really? It's impossible! You can't. Ask people in a country that hasn't won a World Cup, or won their only World Cup at a certain point. There are teams that are expected to lose, and the question about the Red Sox for years was how far-fetched would the scenario be? Okay, we've had the ball go through Buckner's legs—can we have a more bizarre occurrence? Sure, a dog could run on the field and trip a Red Sox player who is about to score the winning run in the seventh game of the World Series.

"There are any number of things that I guess you could imagine happening, but the things that we *did* experience and that we *did* witness were bizarre and hurtful enough. The only thing I don't buy are the people who say, 'Ohhh, I feel so sorry for myself for having rooted for this team all these years.' Are you kidding? You could be a Cubs fan. You could be a Cleveland Indians fan."

The Red Sox did plenty of celebrating over the course of the six months after October 2004. The World Series trophy made a visit to all 351 cities and towns in Massachusetts, all of New England, to Florida for spring training, to California and the Dominican and even New York City. Perhaps its most powerful stop was at Walter Reed Army Medical Center in Washington, D.C., where players got to meet heroes of a different sort—recovering Operations Enduring and Iraqi Freedom service members.

Everybody expected Dr. Charles Steinberg and crew to

put together an amazing show for Opening Day, but they still outdid themselves. As the theme from *2001: A Space Odyssey* was played by members of the Boston Pops and Boston Symphony Orchestra, a banner for each of the first five Red Sox World Series titles was unfurled on the Green Monster wall—1903 . . . 1912 . . . 1915 . . . 1916 . . . 1918—and then, just as the music was reaching a crescendo, a huge banner reading "WORLD SERIES CHAMPIONS 2004" fluttered down, covering them all and the entire length of the wall as the crowd gasped and then cheered wildly.

United States service members back from fighting in Iraq and Afghanistan carried in the World Series rings from beneath the banner, and after Boston native James Taylor sang "America the Beautiful," each member of the 2004 team was called up individually to receive his ring. Even '04 players now on different teams including Derek Lowe (who had left as a free agent) and Dave Roberts (granted a trade to the Padres so he could play more regularly) made the trip, a gesture which absurdly drew criticism from some national media but was entirely appropriate.

"I started the season on the disabled list, so I missed the first two weeks of the season; that made it easier," says Dave Roberts—who, naturally, received one of the day's largest ovations. "There was still controversy. I remember people saying, 'You're a Padre now, you shouldn't go.' John Kruk on *SportsCenter* said, 'I can't believe he went.' Obviously I wasn't playing, and if I don't go, I'm making this whole situation about me. This moment, and ultimately getting the ring, is bigger than just me."

The 2004 World Series banner was raised up the centerfield flagpole by Johnny Pesky and Carl Yastrzemski, two of the legends who would no longer have to answer for championships lost, and a total of 28 former players like Jim Lonborg and Luis Tiant were invited on the field to join in the celebration. Making the day all the sweeter was the opponent—the New York Yankees—who comported themselves like gentlemen and stood atop their dugout steps during the entire ceremony.

A bit later, when the New York team was introduced as part of the traditional Opening Day festivities, players like A-Rod and Jeter and Mussina received boos, as is par for the course at Fenway. Mariano Rivera, however, got a huge ovation—not for his class or talent, which he has in abundance, but as thanks for blowing Game 4 of the ALCS so the Red Sox could start their comeback. Rivera realized this unscripted mass ribbing, and his huge grin and wave was one of the day's most endearing moments.

Then the Red Sox got back to work. There may have been expectations by some fans that the team would rest on its laurels and do a season-long victory tour, but the 2005 Red Sox won 95 games and tied for the AL East title (although the Yankees officially won by virtue of their 10–9 edge in head-to-head play). They didn't get fat and happy.

"If you don't win for 86 years, there is a sense of futility—in the Red Sox case, futility dashed with a little bit of pathos or romance about it all, and a little bad luck, curses, etc.," says Red Sox president Larry Lucchino. "All of that is going to change once a historic record like that is changed or broken. So a change was inevitable. It didn't diminish our fire, though. We had a saying after '04—'Any group of schlemiels can win once.'"

The Red Sox won more than once. They returned to the playoffs in 2005 and in 2007 won their second World Series in four years with another four-game sweep—this time over the Colorado Rockies. For seven years starting in '05 they averaged 92 wins a year, and built one of baseball's best farm systems—developing outstanding players like Dustin Pedroia and Jon Lester and Jonathan Papelbon and Jacoby Ellsbury. They sold out a record 820 straight games (including 26 playoff contests) at Fenway between May 2003 and April 2013, and continued to upgrade the ballpark to the point where on its 100th birthday in 2012 it was placed on the National Register of Historic Places. This guarantees it will be spared the wrecking ball for decades to come, fulfilling the promise John Henry, Tom Werner, and Larry Lucchino made when they purchased the club in 2002.

Then, just when it seemed that it was all coming to an end—after the 2011 team had an epic September collapse amidst the "beer and chicken" controversy, manager Terry Francona and general manager Theo Epstein left under a cloud of controversy, and an angry, unlikable 2012 team bottomed out at 69–93 under insufferable manager Bobby Valentine—they performed a miracle of another kind.

With a new manager in John Farrell, and a largely new roster lacking in superstars (save for David Ortiz, the remaining 2004 holdover), they gathered up a city reeling from the Boston Marathon tragedy and carried it all the way to another improbable World Series title. Players who had been journeymen in prior years exceeded all expectations, while stars who had slumped or suffered from injuries in 2012—most notably pitchers Lester and John Lackey, and outfielder Ellsbury—came back strong. And after bombings at the marathon resulted in four deaths and hundreds of serious injuries, the Red Sox made Bostonians smile again with a wild ride through the playoffs and a wild trademark: beards that made them look like a bunch of bat-swinging lumberjacks.

Charles Steinberg sees what makes the 2004 and 2013 clubs unique in their own right—and what makes them similar.

"The 2004 season was of unparalleled meaning to previous generations," he explains. "It was the 'finally,' the 'at last,' the 'now I can die in peace.' It was for so many players and fathers and grandmothers. You did it the hardest way possible. After the seven-game ALCS punctuated by Aaron Boone's shot into the night in 2003, you have a strong team in 2004 but then go down 3–0 and 19–8. So you did it the myopic way. You taught a whole generation of children about not giving up. You connected to the past as well as the future.

"Now you have 2013, and you not only won the World Series, but you did it the hard way once again—coming off your worst season in years, when expectations could not have been lower. So there were three story lines: worst to first, three World Series in 10 years—which only four franchises have done—and the third story line, which was the most dramatic—how this club of happy, hairy passionists connected with their city when the city needed a boost the most. We have been in a societal culture where the phony cool is to be emotionally aloof and cold, and here was the most beautiful reality from Big Papi and his openheartedness right through the hairs on the chins of a slew of ballplayers who were proud to love baseball, proud to love Boston, and proud to love each other."

So what is the final legacy of the 2004 Red Sox? They were an outstanding team, to be sure, but there are clubs like the 1975 Cincinnati Reds and 1927 Yankees with more Hall of Famers. The '04 Sox played .500 baseball for half the season, and didn't even win their own division. If there was no Wild Card, they would not have been in the playoffs, let alone the World Series. They were not a dynasty, for even though Boston won again in 2007, it was with a largely different team. The 1972–74 Oakland A's and 1996–2000 Yankees were dynasties, not the 2004 Red Sox.

So how should they be remembered?

"Great baseball teams, to me, are teams you know by the personalities woven into their fabric as much as anything in wins and losses or statistics," says Richard Johnson. "If somebody asked me who led the '04 team in home runs and RBIs, I would guess it was probably Manny, but I wouldn't know how many. Why? Because the predominant emotion—the predominant reaction to that team—was their ubuntu, or spirit. They had it—of course they had it.

"It was a team where everybody contributed something. It wasn't a typical Red Sox team from history, where if one of the stars doesn't come through, they lose. This was a team where everybody found a way to pick it up and do something, and they genuinely seemed to enjoy each other's company. This wasn't 25 cabs for 25 players. Everybody was riding the bus, and Francona was wise enough to know when to let things alone and when to step in. He realized this was a group of men."

Miracle Men.

RESOURCES

Books
Steve Buckley, *Red Sox: Where Have You Gone?*
Johnny Damon, *Idiot*
Terry Francona and Dan Shaughnessy, *Francona*
Tony Massarotti, *Dynasty*
Tony Massarotti and John Harper, *A Tale of Two Cities*
Seth Mnookin, *Feeding the Monster*
David Ortiz and Tony Massarotti, *Big Papi*
Dan Shaughnessy, *Reversing the Curse*
Glenn Stout and Richard Johnson, *Red Sox Century*
Mike Vaccaro, *Emperors and Idiots*
Tim Wakefield and Tony Massarotti, *Knuckler*

Other Resources
ASAP Sports transcripts
Associated Press articles, 1990–2013
Baseball-reference.com
Boston Globe articles, 1990–2013
Boston Herald articles, 1990–2013

Faith Rewarded: The Historic Season of the 2004 Boston Red Sox
(DVD)
Fever Pitch (film)
Four Days in October, ESPN *30 for 30* (film)
New York *Daily News* articles, 2000–2013
New York Times articles, 1990–2013
Redsox.com
Red Sox Magazine, 2000–2013
Red Sox media guides, 2000–2013
Red Sox yearbook, 2005 edition
SABR.org

INDEX